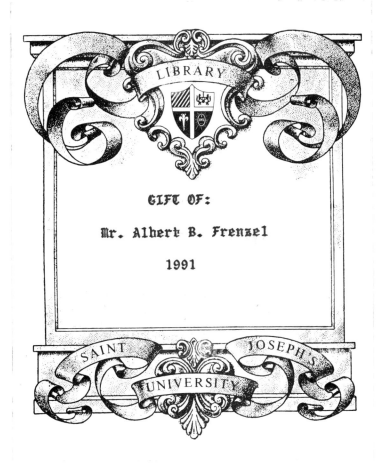

THE DISCOVERY OF THE
Bismarck

THE DISCOVERY OF THE
Bismarck

by Robert D. Ballard

with Rick Archbold
Introduction by Ludovic Kennedy

*Illustrations of the Bismarck wreck
by Ken Marschall
Technical and historical consultation by
William H. Garzke, Jr. and Robert O. Dulin, Jr.*

A WARNER/MADISON PRESS BOOK

Design and compilation © 1990 Madison Publishing Inc.
Text © 1990 Odyssey Corporation

First published in the United States of America by
Warner Books Inc.
666 Fifth Avenue, New York, New York 10103

A Time Warner Inc. Company

Library of Congress Cataloging in Publication Data

Ballard, Robert D.
    The discovery of the *Bismarck* / by Robert D. Ballard:
    introduction by Ludovic Kennedy

p. 232 cm.

ISBN 0-446-51386-5
1. Bismarck (Battleship) 2. World War, 1939–1945—Naval
operations—Antiquities. 3. North Atlantic Ocean. I. Title.
VA515, B5B35 1990
940.54′5943-do20
90-31343 CIP

BOMC offers recordings and compact discs, cassettes and
records. For more information and catalog write to BOMR,
Camp Hill, PA 17012.

(Half-title page) *The* **Bismarck** *and her sister ship*
Prinz Eugen *silhouetted on the horizon in May of 1941.*

(Title page) *The* **Bismarck** *preparing to depart on her
maiden voyage.*

(Opposite) *Robert Ballard and his son Todd at work on
deck during the 1988 expedition to find the* **Bismarck.**

**Produced by
Madison Press Books
40 Madison Avenue
Toronto, Ontario
Canada M5R 2S1**

Printed in Italy

To the memory of my son Todd Alan Ballard,
and to all those young men — both in war and peace —
who have died before their time

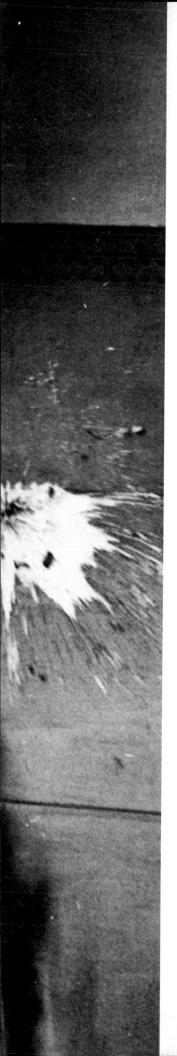

Contents

Hitler, Goebbels and other Nazi notables
look on as Bismarck's granddaughter
christens the Third Reich's newest
battleship on February 14, 1939.

Introduction

by Ludovic Kennedy

One afternoon in the summer of 1989, I was listening half-heartedly to the news on the car radio when I heard something which made me at once turn up the volume and take my foot off the pedal. Dr. Robert Ballard, the announcer said, the man who had discovered the *Titanic*, had now found and photographed the German battleship *Bismarck*. The *Bismarck*? Sunk in 1941 with the loss of all but a hundred survivors! And in a flash my mind went back forty-eight years to the most exciting five days of my life.

For me it started on the evening of May 23, 1941, when, as a Royal Naval Reserve Sub-Lieutenant, I was officer of the watch on the bridge of the fleet destroyer *Tartar*. At the time we were escorting the old battleship *Rodney* westwards from the Clyde across the Atlantic. It was, I recall, a routine sort of watch, my main duty being to check on our bearing and distance from *Rodney* and alter course and speed as she did.

Around 9 P.M. the buzzer from the wireless office sounded, and the signalman of the watch, name of Pearson, put his hand in the voicepipe and began hauling up the signal box. This was the time of day when the Admiralty sent out a U-boat Disposition Report, and we expected it to be that.

It was prefixed MOST IMMEDIATE which the U-boat Disposition Report never was and came from the cruiser *Norfolk* on patrol off Iceland.

1 BS 1 CR 66.40N 28.22W
Co 220 Sp 30

"Pearson," I said, "Does this mean what I think it means?"

"Yes, sir. One enemy battleship, one enemy cruiser, my position sixty-six forty North, twenty-eight twenty two West, Course 220, speed 30 knots."

Thus did we learn of the break-out into the Atlantic of the giant *Bismarck* and her consort *Prinz Eugen*, bent on severing the convoy lifeline that was keeping Britain supplied from North America with food and fuel and weapons.

If this news was a shock, worse was to come when my servant called me in the morning.

"Heard the news, sir?"

"No." (He knew there was no way I could have heard it.)

"*Hood*'s gone. And *Prince of Wales* damaged."

The British commander in chief, Admiral Tovey had sent our most famous battle cruiser and newest battleship to intercept the German squadron as it raced southwards along the Greenland coast. And this was the result! *Hood*, the most-loved ship in the Navy, the epitome of Britain and her Empire, sent to the bottom with the loss of all but three of her 1,400 men, and *Prince of Wales* with more than half her guns out of action, having to disengage because of damage. If this was what *Bismarck* could do to two comparable warships in twenty minutes, what couldn't she do against the convoys from America?

In the middle of the following night the *Bismarck* gave her pursuers the slip, and for the next two days *Rodney*, our sister ship *Mashona*, and ourselves bucketed about the ocean in the vilest weather in search of her: there were few occasions when I came off watch that I didn't find my cabin a shambles, with books, wireless and photograph frames strewn about the deck.

The *Bismarck* was eventually found again, then crippled by a lucky torpedo hit on her rudders. On the eve of her final battle we went to action stations and remained there all night while the *Tartar* rolled and yawed and the wind shrieked in the halyards and we were all drenched in spray. What would the morning bring? Would Admiral Tovey who had now joined us in his flagship *King George V* order us to attack with torpedoes while the battleships engaged with their guns? I rather hoped so, for it would give me the chance to use my movie camera, the only one in the fleet.

Sadly we were too low in fuel for such a high-speed venture to be considered. But we stayed to watch the final battle; first *Bismarck*, the ship which for the last four days had been in the very marrow of our lives, emerging from a distant rain squall, black, massive, beautiful, the most marvelous-looking warship that I or any of us had ever seen; then *Rodney* and *King George V* deploying for attack and at ever-decreasing ranges pumping shell after shell into her until, an hour later, the pride of Hitler's navy had been reduced to a shambling, burning wreck. It was not a pretty sight, but the job had to be done. Towards the end we saw for the first time the enemy in person; puppet-like figures running aft along the upper deck and jumping into the sea. Then, like a great waterlogged whale, the *Bismarck* turned over and sank.

So great an impression did these events make on my mind that in time I wrote a documentary film and book about them. During my research I discovered that a number of survivors were sure the *Bismarck's* crew scuttled the ship before they left her. Not only did survivors Gerhard Junack and Werner Lust tell me this, but it is also recorded in the official and hitherto unpublished Admiralty report of the interrogation of the *Bismarck's* survivors. This speaks of "...a considerable body of evidence to support the view that the inevitable end of *Bismarck* was hastened by the explosion of especially prepared scuttling charges ... which had been fired, some at the sea water inlets and discharges, others in the turbine rooms, boiler rooms and auxiliary machinery rooms. All watertight doors and flooding valves were left open and the ship sank ten minutes after the charges were fired."

It is worth emphasizing this, for some British patriots, wanting to preserve the myth that the Navy's guns and torpedoes sank the *Bismarck* unaided, continue to discount all reports of scuttling. That she would have foundered eventually, there can be little doubt; but the scuttling ensured that it was sooner rather than later.

Like all who took part, friend or foe, in that extraordinary operation, I never imagined that the *Bismarck* would ever be heard of again; and it speaks volumes for the courage, perseverance and skills of Dr. Ballard and his team that, despite appalling weather and many setbacks they succeeded in locating her, six hundred miles west of Brest and three miles down.

The finding of the wreck brings the whole story back to life. When I study the graphic pictures of her resting so squarely and upright on the sea floor, I see her as little different from the pictures of her commissioning; still proud and graceful, half at peace yet half still menacing, a ghostly monument to the craft of her builders, the eternal tomb of two thousand German sailors.

After May 1941, *Bismarck* was a creature of the past. Now, rediscovered, she is of the present and the future, a ship like the *Constitution* and the *Victory* and the *Mary Rose*, frozen in time yet, unlike them, beyond human visitation. For another astonishing contribution to his museum of the sea, Dr. Robert Ballard deserves our grateful thanks.

Ludovic Kennedy

Ludovic Kennedy, pictured opposite in naval uniform in 1941, is the author of *Pursuit: The Sinking of the Bismarck.*

CHAPTER ONE

Prologue

July 18, 1988—
Eastern Atlantic Ocean

Inside the control room of the *Starella* the low-intensity red lights gave an almost ghastly cast to the faces of the five men who stared like zombies at a wall of computer screens and control panels. Occasionally the navigator called out our position, or the sonar operator noted a target that was beyond the range of *Argo*'s video cameras; otherwise there was only the soothing sound of a flute concerto playing on the stereo, and the background noise of the ventilator fans. Except for the incessant rising and falling motion of the ship we could as easily have been in a space capsule orbiting the moon. But this was not a scene from a science-fiction movie. It was simply the afternoon of the seventh day of our search for the wreck of the World War II German battleship, the *Bismarck*.

I lean forward to take a closer look at an image from the ocean bottom aboard the research vessel *Starella* during our 1988 search for the *Bismarck*.

"Debris coming up on the forward camera," called out my nineteen-year-old son, Todd, who was at the *Argo* controls. This was Todd's third expedition with me, and he was becoming a real pro at "flying" our remotely controlled underwater camera vehicle.

Half-heartedly I glanced up at the bank of television screens. The black-and-white video images showed the landscape passing by *Argo* as it inched along the ocean floor three miles below us. Gradually the unmistakable shape of a loop of wire lying on top of the soft bottom mud swam into view. We had been seeing small pieces of debris such as this for days.

"Could be part of the rigging for the main mast," commented Hagen Schempf, as cheerfully as he could. Hagen, the data logger on this watch, was the only German national on board.

"Could be part of the rigging for anything," I replied glumly.

In desperation I reached for a book sitting close by and began leafing

through its pages, looking for a picture of the *Bismarck* that showed the mainmast with its battle standard flying proudly. When I found one, I stared at it long and hard—but there was no way of knowing if what we had just seen came from the *Bismarck* or not. I took a swig from my Coke. If anyone was a candidate for zombie status at this point in our expedition, it was I. I was tired and discouraged, and more than a little frustrated.

What had happened to the wreck of the *Bismarck*, the most powerful battleship of Hitler's navy? All the eyewitnesses believed she had sunk in one piece. Had the ship exploded after she sank? Or had she imploded from the deep ocean pressure and been crushed and twisted into a billion pieces? Were the fragments of wreckage we had been finding all that was left of such a mighty machine of war? The possibility didn't bear thinking on, yet it was becoming inescapable. This was the area where the ship had gone down. These bits of wire,

Hagen Schempf and I stare at the video screens, looking for some clue that would link the debris we are seeing with the *Bismarck*.

metal, gears, wooden planking we were seeing on our video monitors *must* be from the *Bismarck*.

I glanced down again at the book in my hand. A young German officer looked back at me, saluting confidently. This was Burkard Baron von Müllenheim-Rechberg, the highest-ranking officer to survive the sinking, and his book, *Battleship Bismarck*, was an account of the ship's first and final mission. It was required reading for anyone interested in the subject, and on this expedition it had become a sort of Bible through which we hunted again and again for inspiration.

If I hadn't met the baron I might not even be here, I mused. That meeting had taken place less than a year ago at the Frankfurt International Book Fair where I was promoting the German edition of my book about the discovery of the *Titanic*. During a long morning at the display booth of my publisher, Ullstein, I had picked up a copy of the baron's story. Although my German is rudimentary, I was able to grasp enough of the text to be enthralled.

Later, at a lunch hosted by Ullstein, I was seated next to a distinguished gentleman in his late seventies, with an erect posture and bald pate. He greeted me politely in excellent though accented English. This was the baron himself. He was very correct—a bit standoffish, I thought, but perhaps this was due to the fact that he was European, and from an older generation. We chatted politely for a while, then I broached the subject that had been growing in my mind since I had first picked up his book.

"It might be interesting to go and look for the *Bismarck*," I suggested.

I don't remember exactly what he replied, but his response was cool. I think maybe he was still sizing me up. I pressed on, anyway.

"Who would be the best source for determining where the ship is?"

"Well," he replied rather stiffly, "you must ask the British. They were chasing us. They were the ones trying to sink us."

For the rest of the meal we talked of other things. But I couldn't get the *Bismarck* off my mind. In the days and weeks that followed, my determination to go and look for the lost titan grew. The story had taken place in the spring of 1941, the year before I was born. Those were the dark days of the war for the British, when only Great Britain and the Empire stood against Hitler. The German navy had threatened Britain's maritime lifeline, the convoys that ferried supplies across the Atlantic and kept her from starving into surrender. The *Bismarck*'s first mission had lasted only eight days; like the *Titanic*, her first voyage was her last.

But what of the sensitivities involved? I had assumed the baron's coolness was due to shyness or native reserve. But just as possibly it was a reluctance to reopen old wounds. On the other hand, he had written a book about his experiences, so surely he couldn't object . . . . Still, the *Bismarck*'s final hours must have been a nightmare to live through, and I knew from experience that finding the ship might be hard on the survivors.

The *Titanic* had sunk an awfully long time ago—more than seventy-five years—and only those survivors who were very young children at the time are still alive. Even so, our finding the lost liner was an emotional experience for them. How much more difficult would it be for men now in their sixties and seventies who had experienced the horror of battle at sea and lost close friends when the ship was sent to the bottom?

And what would the world think? Would I be accused of glorifying a Nazi warship—and by extension the Nazi regime? Still, it would be a remarkable experience to look again on this feared war machine, to discover how well or poorly she had survived the relentless British artillery barrage during her final battle. Just the simple act of finding her would illuminate one more artifact in the vast museum of the deep ocean, whose historical displays are only now within our technological reach. And it would be an opportunity to relive a riveting, pivotal moment in the history of World War II, one that may have significantly affected the course of that conflict.

But now, as I came back to the present and the frustrating reality of our inconclusive search, I wondered what I had gotten myself into. The *Bismarck* had eluded the entire British Home Fleet for days in 1941. For a week we had been systematically searching the area around the positions the British warships had recorded in their logbooks, and all we had to show for our efforts were some puzzling pieces of unidentifiable wreckage. Would the *Bismarck* escape her pursuers once again?

Lieutenant-Commander Burkard von Müllenheim-Rechberg at the time he served on the *Bismarck* and (bottom) as he looks today.

Freiwillig zur
KRIEGSMARINE

EINSATZ
DER DEUTSCHEN KRIEGSMARINE

CHAPTER TWO

The Pride of the Reich

*Hamburg, Germany—
August 24, 1940*

(Left) Recruiting posters for the German navy prominently featured the Nazi battle ensign that was hoisted up the *Bismarck*'s mast on its commissioning day.

Captain Lindemann reviews his men (top) and returns a salute (above) followed by Commander Oels and Lieutenant Commander von Müllenheim-Rechberg.

The sky was gray and a chill east wind blew across the River Elbe, threatening to lift the service caps from the heads of the young German sailors standing at attention along the upper deck of the *Bismarck*. In northern Europe autumn comes early. On the quarterdeck (the stern portion of the upper deck) the members of the fleet band tried to keep their hands and their instruments warm; they wanted their first notes to be true ones as the newest battleship in the fleet was officially commissioned into the Kriegsmarine, the German navy. The battle ensign had already been piped on board and attached to the halyard of the stern mast. Two signalmen held the rope tight and waited for the order to hoist.

Captain Ernst Lindemann addressed his crew from a raised platform on the quarterdeck, but many of his two thousand men heard only snatches of the speech as the wind played tricks with his words. The officers who stood close to the captain fared better. One of these was Lieutenant-Commander Burkard von Müllenheim-Rechberg, a thirty-year-old career navy officer from an aristocratic Alsatian family with a long military tradition. He listened approvingly as Lindemann quoted Prince Otto von Bismarck, who had united Germany in the nineteenth century and turned it into a great European power: "Policy is not made with speeches, shooting festivals, or songs, it is made only by blood and iron." It was due to words such as these and actions to match them that Bismarck became known as the Iron Chancellor. Now an iron ship bore his name.

Lindemann gave the order, the blood-red battle ensign shot up the mast and was whipped out by the stiff breeze. In the flag's upper lefthand corner was a black iron cross. In the center, enclosed in a white circle, was a bold Nazi swastika. Like the navy that flew it, the ensign was an uneasy compromise between tradition and political reality. Under Grand-Admiral Erich Raeder, the Kriegsmarine had retained the traditional naval salute except for official occasions such as this one, had refused to dismiss its Jewish officers and had forbidden all officers to get involved in politics. But it was nonetheless Hitler's navy and, like it or not, that navy was now at war with England. As the ensign flapped proudly in the wind, the fleet band struck up a stirring rendition of "Deutschland, Deutschland, über alles," the national anthem.

Apart from a few representatives of Hamburg's Blohm and Voss shipyard, which had built the *Bismarck* and where the massive and not-quite-finished ship lay moored, no civilians were present at this ceremony and

Thousands give the Nazi salute as the giant hull of the *Bismarck* slides down the slipway (below left and right) on Valentine's Day, 1939.

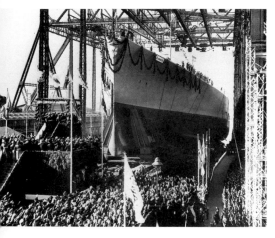

A shield bearing the Bismarck family coat-of-arms decorated the prow of the *Bismarck* at her launching. The same oak-leaf motif decorates the crest (below) worn today by *Bismarck* survivors.

no reporters covered it. Every effort was being made to keep the *Bismarck*'s state of readiness secret from the British.

How different it had been a year and a half earlier on February 14, 1939, before the war had begun. Then a huge crowd had watched as Frau Dorothea von Loewenfeld, granddaughter of Bismarck himself, had christened the ship. They had heard the Führer give an uncharacteristically short but nonetheless stirring speech—only fifteen minutes. The event had been trumpeted in Nazi newsreels and on the front pages of German newspapers and had been noted with self-satisfied superiority by the *Times* of London: "There is perhaps some significance in the name given to the first of Germany's new great battleships. She and her consort [*Tirpitz*], which is to be launched shortly, are built under the provisions of the Anglo-German Naval Agreement which prescribes a limit to German naval tonnage of thirty-five percent of British tonnage. That limit, as far as battleships are concerned, would hardly be reached if Germany's present battle fleet, built and building, were to be doubled. It may be thought symbolic therefore that the new ship should be named after the Chancellor who always set his face against naval rivalry with Great Britain."

By the time of the *Bismarck*'s commissioning in August 1940, no one in Britain was downplaying the German naval threat, least of all Prime Minister Winston Churchill. The war at sea was going from bad to worse for the British. German submarines were playing havoc with under-protected Atlantic shipping while the British Admiralty remained preoccupied with the very real possibility of a Nazi invasion. Meanwhile all eyes were on the skies as the Battle of Britain raged, diverting attention from the devastating loss of merchant ships that was rapidly threatening Britain's ability to survive. Rationing, introduced in January 1940, was becoming more severe. Merchant ships were being lost at two to three times the rate they could be replaced. In August alone, 268,000 tons were sunk by U-boats, which could now operate from occupied France's Atlantic ports, 450 miles closer to Britain's vital sea lanes.

Churchill had begun the war as First Lord of the Admiralty—the same post he had held in World War I. He was well versed in naval strategy, and he took a hands-on approach in naval matters. And he was worried about the threat posed by the new German ships. As well as the *Bismarck* and her sister ship, *Tirpitz*, both nearing completion, there were the battle cruisers *Scharnhorst* and *Gneisenau*, which had taken part in the successful German invasion of Norway in April. Finally there was the heavy cruiser *Prinz Eugen*, nearing completion in the Germania shipyards at Kiel. The prospect of a naval force made up of even one of these state-of-the-art battleships, combined with one or two battle cruisers and possibly a heavy cruiser or two as well did not sit lightly with the British prime minister.

While Churchill rallied the British people with his rhetoric, and the Battle of Britain wore on, the men of the *Bismarck* prepared for the ship's first sea trials. The crew were mostly raw recruits in their late teens and early twenties, fresh from eight weeks of basic training where they had learned to fire a rifle and sleep standing up. They were volunteers, not conscripts—proud Germans caught up in the great tide of war. They came from every corner of the Third Reich, from farms and mines and factories, from villages and towns and cities. Many of them had never set foot on a ship docked in harbor, let alone felt the stomach-turning heave and fall of stormy seas far from land. Most were ignorant of the distinguished history of the German navy, had never heard of the 1916 Battle of Jutland, when the Kaiser's fleet sank more ships than the British.

The *Bismarck*'s technical and gunnery crews had begun arriving in April while workmen were still clambering over the superstructure, hammering and welding from dawn to dusk. Work was still going on when the bulk of the crew arrived in August. Until their quarters were ready they lived on nearby dormitory ships, but training began immediately. Practically everyone who saw her was impressed with the *Bismarck*'s size, her beauty and the power of her armament. Of those crew members who survived, many remembered thinking that their new ship was unsinkable, "floating life insurance," the safest place to spend the war. It was almost impossible to imagine the destruction of such an armor-plated goliath.

Twenty-year-old Hans Zimmermann first saw the *Bismarck* at twilight, "a great, gray colossus" silhouetted against the sky. He thought how impressed his father—a steelworker who had served in the World War I German navy—would have been by this marvelous ship; then he congratulated himself on his good fortune at being assigned as a stoker to such a powerful vessel at the very beginning of his time in the Kriegsmarine. Heinrich Kuhnt, a machinist's mate who worked with the big turbines, looked on his new ship as a technological marvel and was sure he would be safer here than on the light cruiser *Karlsruhe*, on which he had

(Below) Six of the *Bismarck*'s crew pose proudly in their new uniforms. Otto Höntzsch stands at the far right.

(Below) Stoker Hans Zimmermann in his Kriegsmarine uniform.

been serving during the invasion of Norway. Disabled by a British submarine, the *Karlsruhe* had had to be abandoned and sunk. Otto Höntzsch, an antiaircraft gunner, was astonished by the ship's gigantic size. Nineteen-year-old Franz Halke, who was being trained as part of the staff that operated the computers for the big guns, was also impressed. He had joined the navy because he liked the smart uniform and thought it might help him attract the girls he was too shy to talk to. But when he explored the ship's seemingly endless catacombs he must have wondered if he had really come so far from the coal mines in which his father toiled.

In the cracks between the strict routines of military life the young crew found time to make friends, tell dirty jokes, write letters to parents or girlfriends, or complain about overstrict superiors. They talked about how the war was going, wondered if it would all be over before they put to sea, which everyone expected would be early the following year, 1941. On every front the Reich seemed unstoppable. France had fallen in June, then Norway; it seemed that Britain would be next. Soon, they speculated, all western Europe would be part of the new German empire.

Before sailing on the *Bismarck*, Franz Halke (above) was photographed in full-dress uniform as was his friend Heinz Jucknat (right). Alois Haber- ditz (below) also visited the photographer's studio with his girlfriend during his Christmas leave in Hamburg.

Franz Halke had already made friends with two others assigned to the after computer room, Heinz Jucknat and Adolf (Adi) Eich. During off-duty hours, when they weren't on shore leave, they played poker or blackjack and drank beer in the ship's canteen, passing around a big two-liter mug (the next-to-last drinker always had to pay for the round). Sometimes there was music. Adi played the guitar and usually several accordions joined in.

The three comrades were often joined by Alois Haberditz, a high-spirited Austrian who belonged to the antiaircraft crew. He was a talented mime and mimic who had their chain-smoking captain's ramrod posture and stiff walk down to a turn. He also did good impressions of Commander Hans Oels, the ship's executive officer, for whom rules and regulations were everything.

The men may have occasionally made fun of their captain with his slicked-back blond hair, but he was nonetheless a very popular figure. Almost everyone agreed he was the perfect commanding officer—strict yet human. Many referred to him as "our father," and few hesitated to go to him with their personal problems. Others told stories of jumping to attention when he walked by, only to be greeted with a kind word. Years later, survivors would speak warmly of this man they had barely come to know.

At the age of forty-five, Kapitän zur See Ernst Lindemann was on the rising crest of a career that had already exceeded expectations. Because of his frail constitution, few had thought he would make it through the first year of cadet training. But his slender frame concealed an iron will and a

sharp mind that put him at the top of his class. He had seen active duty in World War I, become an expert in naval gunnery, and was noted for his self-discipline and hard work. His remarkable human qualities added to this professional record made him a natural to command Germany's newest and most powerful warship.

The *Bismarck* was a dream come true for a career naval officer. She was fast and sleek, with an elegant silhouette and a jaunty flared bow. More than one-sixth of a mile long (820 feet, 4 inches), 118 feet wide at the widest point along the waterline, and with a displacement of 44,734 tons (48,626 when fully loaded), she well exceeded the 35,000-ton limit laid down in the Anglo-German Naval Treaty under whose terms she was supposedly built. Her eight 15-inch (380-mm) guns in four twin turrets were the biggest ever mounted on a German warship and made her more than a match for the firepower of any single battleship or battle cruiser in the entire British fleet.

Defense is at least as important as offense on a battleship, and the *Bismarck* was no exception to this rule. In fact, 44 percent of the ship's total weight consisted of various thicknesses of armor. Not surprisingly, among the most heavily armored areas were the four big gun turrets, A, B, C, and D working from forward to aft and known as turrets Anton, Bruno, Caesar and Dora. Here the armor ranged in thickness from 5 to 14 inches. Elsewhere the thickness of the protection depended on the importance of the area being protected. The conning tower and communications tube leading between it and the armored decks were almost as heavily protected as the big turrets. The vital innards—including the three sets of geared turbines, the twelve high-pressure boilers and the ammunition

(Above) The *Bismarck* is outfitted at the wharf of the Blohm & Voss shipyard in the summer of 1940.

The captain of the *Bismarck*, Ernst Lindemann.

The *Bismarck* on her trials in November, 1940.

magazines—were located within the heavily armored citadel which occupied roughly 50 percent of the belowdecks space and was protected by an armored deck above, armored transverse bulkheads fore and aft, and the armored belt on the sides of the hull. The welded double hull was designed so that the outer layer would receive and disperse the impact of a torpedo hit, minimizing damage. Finally, belowdecks the ship was divided into twenty-two watertight compartments that could be sealed off if a shell or torpedo caused a leak. Unlike the similar compartments on the *Titanic*, these were truly watertight. In short, the design of the *Bismarck* aimed to realize the dream of Germany's Admiral Tirpitz, who had described the ideal battleship as "an unsinkable gun platform."

THE *BISMARCK* IS MADE READY

The *Bismarck* was like a small floating town that could be self-sufficient during several months at sea. In September of 1940 as her sailing date neared, the ship was filled with stores—from flags and flour to potatoes and light bulbs—to serve a company of over 2,000 men.

(Top) Making and repairing shoes in the cobbler's shop.

(Above) Food is prepared in one of the galleys. From here cooked food was ladled into pots and then carried to the mess decks.

(Above right) Sailors touch up the camouflage on the ship's side. The false bow wave, designed to confuse enemy range finders, is clearly visible.

(Left) Supply vans unload provisions at the wharf in Hamburg.

(Below left) Meat is hoisted up from one of the ship's cold storage areas. These could accommodate 300 sides of beef and 500 dressed pigs.

(Right) During sea trials crewmen practice evacuating a wounded seaman.

There is no room on a warship for luxury, and the *Bismarck*'s appointments were spartan: every inch of space was functional. As in the Royal Navy, the men slept and ate in the same quarters, stowing their hammocks by day. The *Bismarck* was a floating military encampment, where cooks, barbers, tailors and shoemakers fed and clothed the ship's company while the engineers and technicians kept the ship in top working order. All efforts were aimed toward a single paramount purpose: to make the battleship the most efficient naval gun platform in the world. Soon the new recruits and the more seasoned sailors were starting to mesh into a complex, well-oiled war machine.

On September 15, 1940, three weeks after commissioning, the nearly

Departing from Hamburg down the River Elbe with the aid of a tug on September 15, 1940.

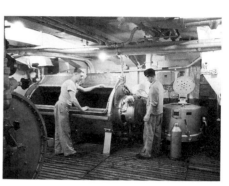

(Top) The steam press in the ship's laundry.

(Middle) The anti-aircraft guns on the port side are made ready for action.

(Above) The tailor shop. In battle, a tailor, a cook or a cobbler would go to assigned battle stations like everyone else.

finished battleship departed Hamburg for the eastern Baltic, out of range of British air attacks. In order to reach these protected waters she had to pass through the Kiel Canal. This shallow passage across the base of the Jutland Peninsula had presented a challenge to the *Bismarck*'s designers. Because of it, the ship could not exceed a draft of 33 feet. This meant the ship was broader in the beam than British battleships of equivalent size. As it turned out, the *Bismarck*'s breadth was an advantage in combat: it made her steadier in rough seas and provided extra stability when the big guns were firing. But it took a considerable feat of seamanship to pass through the narrow canal without damaging the ship.

For the next two months the *Bismarck* was based at the port of Goten-hafen (now Gdynia) in occupied Poland, a few miles west of Danzig

(Gdansk). Most of the time however, she was at sea, testing her shipboard systems and working up to full speed as she cruised in the Gulf of Danzig. Even at full power the huge ship surged forward smoothly, with only the slightest bow wave. Lindemann was particularly delighted when Walter Lehmann, his chief engineer, reported that top speed proved to be 30.8 knots, slightly better than the design speed of 30 knots. This would make the *Bismarck* very difficult to catch if she ever broke out into the Atlantic.

At last it was time to test the artillery—the moment the crews of the four big turrets had been waiting for. The heavy shells were lifted by mechanical hoists from the magazines situated below each turret on the middle platform deck, then rammed into place. Over the ship's telephone came the order to fire from Commander Adalbert Schneider, the ship's first gunnery

The *Bismarck*'s big guns fired their first salvo during her trials in November, 1940. The slight recoil that occurred when the large turrets such as Caesar and Dora (above) were in use, confirmed that the ship was an ideal gun platform.

officer. The gun crews wore earplugs, but the sound was still deafening when the big guns boomed, then the ship rocked gently with the recoil. High in the foretop observation post the spotters watched for the distant splashes indicating the fall of shot.

The tests went superbly. In only one area did the new battleship perform poorly: she was unable to maintain a straight course without her rudders, and could only steer with extreme difficulty when relying solely on her propellers. So if her rudders were damaged in battle, she would become a much easier target. Much has been made of this "fatal flaw" by various writers, but rudders are a weak point in all warships, and the chances of them being hit are very small.

In early December ship and crew returned via the Kiel Canal to Hamburg, where the workers of Blohm and Voss were to apply the finishing touches, including the completion of the secondary battery directors. Meanwhile, most of the crew were released on Christmas leave, the last time they would see friends and relatives before the *Bismarck* headed out on its first mission. Lieutenant-Commander von Müllenheim-Rechberg spent two weeks of his leave skiing in the Bavarian mountains. Alois Haberditz spent Christmas in Hamburg with his girlfriend and her family. His other friends went home, Adolf Eich to Düsseldorf and Franz Halke to the nearby town of Bochum. Heinz Jucknat went all the way to Eben-rode in East Prussia, rich farm country where he had trained as a government milk inspector. His mother prepared the usual Christmas feast: roast goose stuffed with apples, red cabbage and mashed potatoes washed down with many glasses of his father's homemade red currant wine.

Stoker Hans Zimmermann was one of the unlucky ones assigned to the skeleton crew that remained on board ship over the holidays. He was not even given leave to go ashore Christmas Day, although he had been invited home by one of the Blohm and Voss dockworkers with whom he had become friendly. Finally, just before the new year, he received a few days leave and five Reichsmarks. When he returned to his home town, he ran into an old school chum named Hermann Emmerich, who informed

A German Type VII U-boat similar to Herbert Wohlfarth's *U-556* which "adopted" the *Bismarck*. The adoption certificate (below) declared "before Neptune, the ruler of the oceans" that the *U-556* would stand beside the *Bismarck* "whatever may befall her on water, under water, on land or in the air."

him that he, too, was on the *Bismarck*. The ship was so big that Hans had never heard Emmerich's name or even seen him on board.

In late January 1941, the ship was ready to go, but a sunken ore carrier now blocked the canal. So the *Bismarck* waited and the crew fretted. Occasionally the monotony was broken by a night air raid. Alarm bells rang and the antiaircraft crews rushed to their positions. But none of the bombs dropped near the ship, and no hits on enemy aircraft were noted.

In February, one amusing incident broke the boredom of the delay. This was the *Bismarck*'s adoption by *U-556*, herself undergoing final fitting out nearby. The U-boat's commander, Herbert Wohlfarth, hatched a scheme to persuade Captain Lindemann to let the *Bismarck*'s band play at his boat's commissioning. In Germany and Britain it was common for towns to adopt ships and regiments, so Wohlfarth, whose nickname was Parsifal, decided to adopt the *Bismarck*. Using his skills as a cartoonist and his well-developed sense of humor, he prepared an antique-looking adoption certificate, promising to protect the *Bismarck* against all dangers. The document was illustrated with two drawings: one was of the knight Parsifal, his right hand holding a sword and his left thumb warding off torpedoes aimed at the *Bismarck*; the other showed Wohlfarth's tiny sub towing the mammoth battleship. Lindemann laughed heartily when

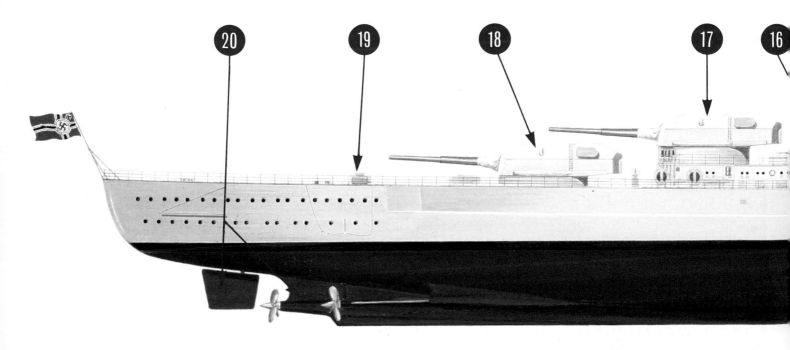

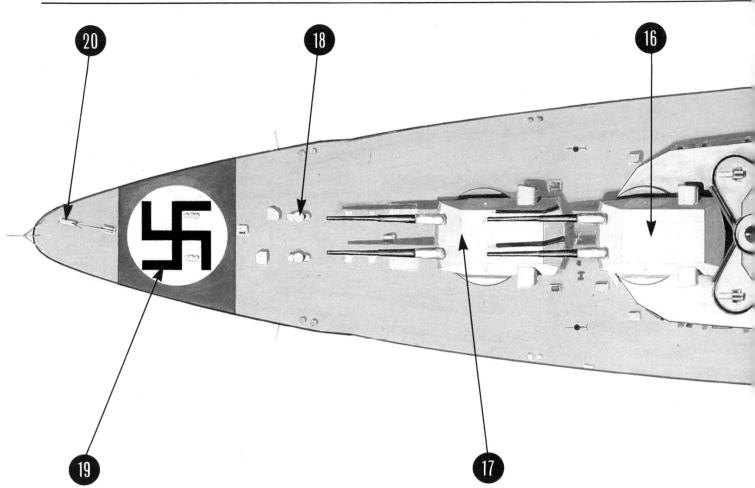

THE *BISMARCK*: An Overhead View

1. Bow anchor & anchor wells.
2. Swastika for aircraft identification.
3. Bow anchor capstans.
4. Forward breakwater.
5. Turret Anton (15-inch guns).
6. Turret Bruno.
7. Second breakwater.
8. 37-mm antiaircraft guns.
9. Secondary armament, 150-mm gun turrets.
10. 105-mm antiaircraft guns.
11. Secondary fire (gunnery) control range finder.
12. Port side crane (for planes & launches).
13. Catapult extended.
14. Captain's & admiral's launches on hangar roof.
15. Aft fire (gunnery) control station.
16. Turret Caesar.
17. Turret Dora.
18. Capstans for stern anchors.
19. Stern swastika.
20. Stern anchor chain.

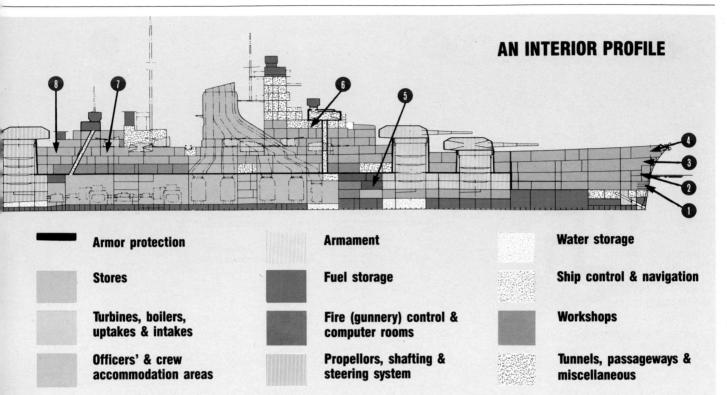

AN INTERIOR PROFILE

■ **Armor protection**

Stores

Turbines, boilers, uptakes & intakes

Officers' & crew accommodation areas

Armament

Fuel storage

Fire (gunnery) control & computer rooms

Propellors, shafting & steering system

Water storage

Ship control & navigation

Workshops

Tunnels, passageways & miscellaneous

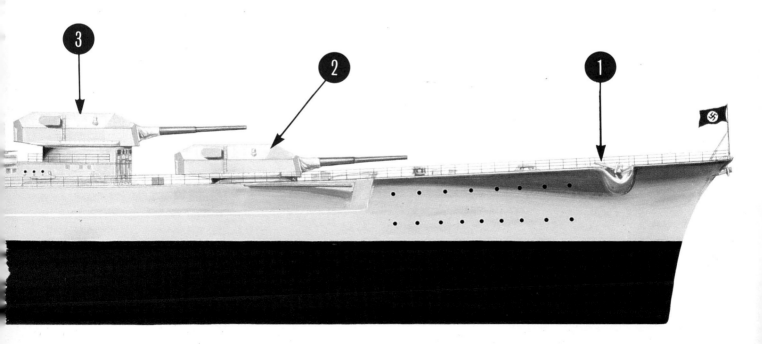

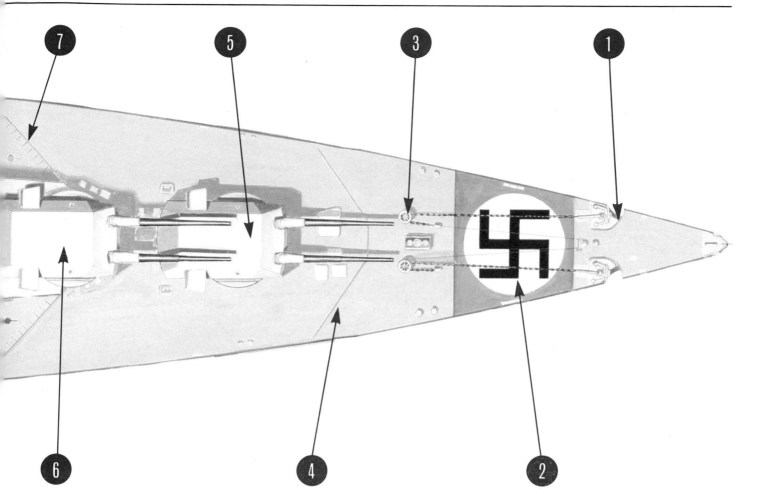

(Above) A pilot perches above the cockpit of his Arado 196 reconnaissance plane as it is hoisted back on board after a test flight. (Below) The ship's crane is swung out as the Arado is brought back on board.

Wohlfarth presented the certificate to him and readily agreed to provide the ship's band. Neither man could know how close the cartoons would come to depicting reality.

In early March the canal was finally cleared, and the *Bismarck* returned to the Gulf of Danzig for more sea trials and battle practice. Again her great guns boomed out over the empty water. Again the four Arado-196 floatplanes were launched from the catapult amidships and buzzed overhead, reporting the fall of shot from the long-range guns. During battle practice, everything was done to simulate the actual conditions of a naval engagement. As soon as the alarm was sounded, men rushed to their battle stations along prearranged pathways—bad luck to anyone who moved too slowly or happened to be in the way. As planes towing targets zoomed in, the antiaircraft batteries put up a firestorm of flak. When the imaginary enemy came in sight, invariably it was named after the famous British battle cruiser *Hood*, the epitome of British sea power. Parts of the German ship were assumed hit and damaged, men wounded and out of action. Time and again the imaginary *Hood* was sunk. As the days passed and drill followed drill, the men of the *Bismarck* came to hate that name with a passion.

During these final exercises the *Bismarck* was joined by the brand-new heavy cruiser *Prinz Eugen*, which was to provide escort on her first foray into the Atlantic. Once there, the two ships were to link up with the battle cruiser *Gneisenau*, still in the harbor of Brest, and prey on British shipping. (*Scharnhorst* would not be ready before July due to repairs required to her boilers.) So the *Bismarck* and the equally new *Prinz Eugen* practiced maneuvers together while Captain Lindemann awaited his final orders. If all went according to plan, the mission would commence during the last week of April. On April 6, *Gneisenau* was put out of commission by a torpedo hit during a British air raid, reducing the raiding force to two. Then on April 23, the *Prinz Eugen* fell victim to a magnetic mine, which damaged her propellor shafts and ruptured the bulkheads in some of her fuel tanks, and had to go into drydock for repairs until May 2. As a result, the departure was delayed until the latter half of May.

Captain Lindemann was impatient for the *Bismarck*'s first mission, but he was also apprehensive about the officer under whom he would serve. Even though the task force now consisted of only two ships, the Naval High Command had elected to place the Fleet commander, Gunther Lütjens, in charge. Lütjens and his staff of sixty-five would sail on board the *Bismarck*, and Lindemann would have to defer to his authority.

Captain Lindemann and Admiral Lütjens could not have been more different, except in their devotion to their jobs. At age fifty-one, Lütjens was tall, thin, aristocratic and austere. He kept his own counsel. Many found him a cold fish; others said he was simply shy, that the reserved manner concealed a delightful wit. Whatever the truth, he seldom showed emotion and almost never laughed. And while he was a fine tactical commander, he lacked the human qualities that can inspire a crew and maintain morale in difficult circumstances. Lindemann was, of course, far too professional to let his dissatisfaction show, but no doubt he would have preferred a less dour superior.

Lindemann probably consoled himself with the knowledge that Lütjens had already proven himself in the war at sea. He had led the highly successful commerce-raiding expedition earlier that year when the *Scharnhorst* and *Gneisenau* had broken out into the Atlantic through the Denmark Strait and spent two months sinking merchant ships and eluding all British attempts to entrap them. By the time the two ships escaped to Brest on March 22, they had sunk thirty ships, captured three others and distracted numerous British warships in an attempt to find them. There was every reason to expect that the powerful *Bismarck*, more than a match for any single British capital ship, could outdo these exploits.

At the beginning of May, with the *Bismarck*'s first mission only days away and rumors flying through the crew, excitement was raised with the news that Adolf Hitler planned to visit the ship on May 5. The decks were scrubbed, uniforms were pressed, and the ship's barbers worked overtime to make sure every last man was presentable for the Führer. Franz Halke, trained as a barber before the war, was pressed into service to help handle the overload.

The short trip from Gotenhafen out to where the *Bismarck* lay at anchor apparently had not agreed with the Führer. He looked pale as he stepped on board accompanied by Field-Marshal Wilhelm Keitel, chief of the general staff. "On land I am a hero, but at sea I am a coward," Hitler had once told Admiral Erich Raeder. He did not understand naval strategy and he was not close to the naval establishment. But he loved the idea of battleships, and had proudly shown Raeder sketchbooks filled with his

Fleet commander Admiral Gunther Lütjens in a pose that captures his forbidding presence.

own designs for maritime monsters, some with 32-inch guns (these would have required a ship larger than could be built by any German shipyard).

Notable by his absence from Hitler's entourage was Admiral Raeder himself. The reason for this absence is not clear, but most writers attribute it to political savvy. He knew the Führer was nervous about risking German ships in the Atlantic, fearful of the embarrassment he would suffer if any were sunk by the British. Raeder had not informed his commander in chief that the *Bismarck* was scheduled to depart on May 18. And he had told Lütjens to plead innocence of his sailing date if asked.

Admiral Lütjens greets Hitler with a naval salute while staff officers behind him give the Nazi salute.

The ship's company was mustered proudly on deck as the supreme leader of the Reich inspected the ranks. Antiaircraft gunner Alois Haberditz stood stiffly at attention as Hitler, Keitel, Lindemann and Lütjens walked down the ranks. Trying to stare straight ahead, Haberditz caught a glimpse of the Führer's gaze. Nearly fifty years later he still remembered that moment when Hitler's cold eyes looked right through him.

After the troop inspection, Hitler toured the ship. He seemed attentive and interested but said almost nothing. In the after gunnery computer room, Sub-Lieutenant Friedrich Cardinal explained how information from the fire control station—speed, course, wind direction, relative position of enemy ship, time elapse between firing and shell splash—were fed into the machines and the calculations sent swiftly back to the gunnery officers so they could correct their aim in the heat of battle. This brush with the Führer was a big moment for Heinz Jucknat and his buddies Adolf Eich and Franz Halke, who sat stiffly in front of their instruments as Cardinal expounded and Hitler and Keitel listened. At one point Hitler leaned forward to peer more closely at the direction-finding computer, placing his right hand on Eich's shoulder and his left hand on Jucknat's. Neither of them breathed. When the official party had left, Heinz and his friends joked about the experience, but they were deeply proud their section had been singled out for such attention.

Fourth gunnery officer von Müllenheim-Rechberg was among those invited to lunch in the wardroom. The food was vegetarian, Hitler's preference, and he ate in silence. Müllenheim-Rechberg was too far away from the head of the table to hear all of Hitler's rambling post-lunch oration, but it ranged over a variety of topics, including the oppressed German minority in Romania and the unlikelihood the United States would enter the war.

At this point, Captain Lindemann, who like his colleagues had been listening in polite silence to Hitler's ramblings, spoke up. He for one was not prepared to dismiss the chance that the United States would come to Britain's aid. It had happened in World War I at a time when the U.S. was at least as isolationist as now. There was a nervous silence around the table as the assembled officers waited for the Führer's reply. Commander Oels, the *Bismarck*'s first officer, turned red with embarrassment at this affront. Then Lütjens stood up and made a closing speech about the progress of the war at sea.

Four hours after boarding the *Bismarck*, Hitler and his party left. Now Lütjens and Lindemann could get on with final preparations for their mission, code-named Rheinübung, Exercise Rhine. Their orders were to steam through the Danish Islands and enter the Norwegian Sea through the passage between Jutland and the southern coasts of Sweden and Norway. They were then to proceed northward along the Norwegian coast and into the North Sea, breaking out through the Iceland-Faroes passage without being detected by the enemy. Already oil tankers and resupply ships were steaming to prearranged positions in the Atlantic and the Arctic so the task force would be able to refuel and reprovision during three months at sea.

If the breakout were successful, great harm was possible, as the success of recent commerce-raiding indicated. And, unlike previous raiders, the *Bismarck* and *Prinz Eugen* had permission to attack escorted convoys. While the *Bismarck* engaged the escorts, *Prinz Eugen* would attack the merchant ships. With the *Bismarck* leading a campaign of maritime guerrilla warfare, no British merchant ship was safe. Potentially, large parts of the British Home Fleet would be diverted in an effort to find her and *Prinz Eugen*, an almost impossible task in the days before long-range radar and satellite surveillance.

On May 17 the *Bismarck* pulled away from the wharf at Gotenhafen. On board were 2,206 men, including the admiral's staff, members of the German Luftwaffe to fly the Arado aircraft, merchant marine officers to man any captured ships, and several war correspondents who would record the *Bismarck*'s exploits and describe them in patriotic prose for domestic consumption. Soon afterward she anchored within sight of the Polish port to take on her final supplies and to load up with fuel. All the next day provisions were loaded and bunker oil flowed into the ship. At one point a fuel hose ruptured and by the time the problem was corrected and the spilled fuel cleaned up, it was too late to continue. And so on the eve of her first operational mission, the battleship was 200 tons short of fuel. With a storage capacity of 8,000 tons, this shortfall seemed at the time a tiny detail of no consequence.

The British Admiralty was not ignorant of the threat posed by the *Bismarck*, but Churchill continued to believe that she would not put to sea until the *Tirpitz* was also ready. Nonetheless, British intelligence had been following the battleship's progress from shipyard to sea trials with intense interest. They knew she was ready for action. But the ocean was huge and although they had noted increased German reconnaissance flights over Iceland's Denmark Strait, suggesting the *Bismark* might take that route into the Atlantic, they still had no real idea where she intended to go, or when.

The elegant flared lines of the *Bismarck*'s prow are displayed in this photograph of her awaiting action in the north Atlantic.

HITLER COMES ON BOARD

The visit of the Führer on May 5, 1941, was a big event in the short life of the *Bismarck*. For many of the men on board, this was the first time they had seen the German leader up close.

(Left) Hitler returns the salute of the ship's company. Admiral Lütjens (center) and his staff officers stand beside him.

(Above right) During his tour of the ship, Hitler pauses in front of the open aircraft hangar, flanked by Lütjens (left) and Lindemann (right).

(Above) Hitler reviews the ship's company mustered along the port side.

(Right) On the quarterdeck the Führer stands in front of turret Dora, which points astern.

The Convoy Lifeline

After the fall of France, Britain and her Empire stood alone against Germany. Only the ships that brought food and material, particularly from North America, prevented her quick surrender. German U-boats and surface raiders preyed upon these convoys of ships in an effort to sever this lifeline. That is why the breakout of the Bismarck *into the Atlantic shipping lanes was a cause of such great concern to the British Admiralty.*

(Right) In the harbor of St. John's, Newfoundland, a convoy forms up for the dangerous passage across the Atlantic.

(Below) Early in the war, a patrol of British warships searches for surface raiders in the North Sea. This kind of concentration of force was not effective at protecting merchant shipping.

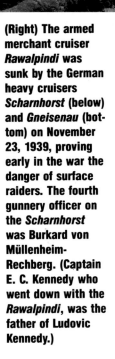

(Right) The armed merchant cruiser *Rawalpindi* was sunk by the German heavy cruisers *Scharnhorst* (below) and *Gneisenau* (bottom) on November 23, 1939, proving early in the war the danger of surface raiders. The fourth gunnery officer on the *Scharnhorst* was Burkard von Müllenheim-Rechberg. (Captain E. C. Kennedy who went down with the *Rawalpindi*, was the father of Ludovic Kennedy.)

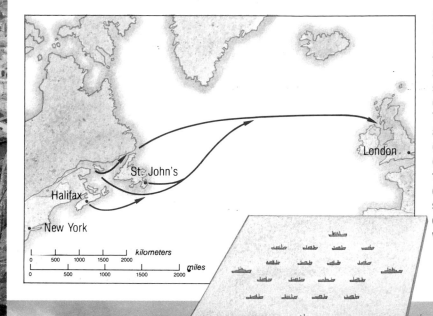

(Left) A map showing the approximate route of convoys from Canada to Scotland. The inset shows a typical convoy formation. The merchant ships are in rows and an escort ship is on each side. In practice it was often difficult to keep the ships together, especially in bad weather.

(Above) Destroyers on convoy duty in the North Atlantic.

CHAPTER THREE

Our Hunt Begins (1988)

La Coruna, Spain—July 9, 1988

Our 1988 *Bismarck* expedition couldn't have begun more badly. As our ship left the port of La Coruna wrapped in a dense morning fog, many of the crew were still violently ill from some bad clams we had eaten the night before. (My nineteen-year-old son, Todd—on board as a member of the technical team—was one of the sickest.) Matters deteriorated as the morning wore on. In the Bay of Biscay the fog was replaced by high winds and heavy seas. If you weren't green already, you soon would be. In such circumstances a deep-ocean search is unpleasant, extremely difficult and very dangerous. Adding to my concerns was our ship, the aging *Starella*, from Hull, England, which had proved barely adequate in the gentler conditions of the Mediterranean. I wondered whether this converted freezer trawler, not designed for towing at the low speeds my equipment required, was up to the job.

A lot was riding on my shoulders. I had assured my backers that finding the *Bismarck* would be a breeze

(Above) I look out from the deck of the *Starella* (right) as we depart in July of 1988.

compared to the hunt for the *Titanic*. Now my reputation was on the line, along with future attempts to look for sunken wrecks. As a Woods Hole scientist I have the freedom to pursue the projects that interest me—if I can find the money. But now that I head up the Center for Marine Exploration and have a big staff on my payroll, raising money is a continual concern. Woods Hole gives me a home and the credibility that goes with belonging to a well-known scientific institution, but it doesn't pay me. It took me many years to put together the first *Titanic* expedition. Over time I've developed good relationships with the National Geographic Society and the U.S. Navy, both of whom support different aspects of my work.

A transponder is launched from the stern of the *Starella*.

As far as the navy was concerned, the official reason for the second *Titanic* expedition, when we explored the wreck, was to test our JASON prototype, JASON Junior. After *Titanic*, however, other funders appeared. One of the main backers for the *Bismarck* expedition was the Quest Group, a company formed by Don Koll and Marco Vitulli, two West Coast businessmen interested in promoting undersea exploration. National Geographic and Turner Broadcasting had also put up money.

But explorers are supposed to find things. During the Mediterranean phase of this year's cruise we had indeed found something—a small concentration of amphoras off the western tip of Sicily that just might turn out to belong to a Roman shipwreck. But at this point the evidence was inconclusive. We would only know for sure when we returned next year. Finding the *Bismarck* would make this year's cruise an unqualified success.

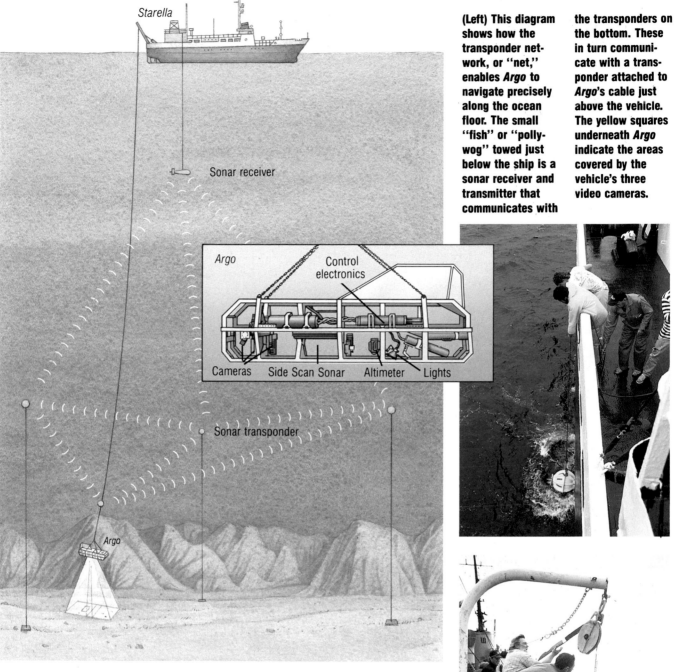

Starella

Sonar receiver

Argo

Control electronics

Cameras   Side Scan Sonar   Altimeter   Lights

Sonar transponder

Argo

(Left) This diagram shows how the transponder network, or "net," enables Argo to navigate precisely along the ocean floor. The small "fish" or "polly-wog" towed just below the ship is a sonar receiver and transmitter that communicates with the transponders on the bottom. These in turn communicate with a transponder attached to Argo's cable just above the vehicle. The yellow squares underneath Argo indicate the areas covered by the vehicle's three video cameras.

(Top) A transponder disappears below the surface.

(Above) The polly-wog is lowered from its crane.

The weather stayed bad and many people stayed sick as we steamed out toward the area where the *Bismarck* went down, roughly 600 miles west of Brest, France, in the middle of empty ocean where the bottom is three miles deep. It remained nasty when we reached the site on the morning of July 11 and began to launch our first of three transponders. These acoustic beacons form an underwater network or "net" that allows us to navigate with pinpoint precision along the ocean floor. The transponders communicate with the ship by means of a receiver dubbed the pollywog, which is towed just astern. The information received is instantly processed by the navigational computer, and the result—our position inside the net—appears on the computer screen at the navigator's station in the control van.

The first transponder landed on nice flat bottom—an abyssal plain in ocean geology jargon—but the second and third landed on the side of a mountain. Underwater mountains would interfere with the transponder signals and hamper both an acoustic and a visual search strategy. An acoustic search uses *Argo*'s side-looking sonars to scan a wide swath of the ocean floor for any major chunks of wreckage or seriously disturbed bottom. But in rough terrain, even something as big as the *Bismarck* can easily be lost in the sonar "shadow" cast by an underwater hill.

During a visual search, *Argo* is towed close enough to the ocean floor for its video cameras to see even the smallest piece of man-made debris (many deep-water wrecks leave a trail of debris a mile or more long). Because the vehicle is so close to the bottom, sudden changes in topography can prove to be too much for *Argo*'s pilot—the flyer—to handle. And if *Argo* were to crash, the damage could be serious. Worse, the cable could break and *Argo* would be lost.

Frank Smith (left) gestures over his winch controls.

The mountain might not have bothered me so much if it weren't for Frank Smith and his sick winch. The hydraulic winch is probably the single most important piece of equipment on the ship—it's the beast of burden that reels in or pays out *Argo*'s long coaxial cable. If it failed while the vehicle was at the bottom, we'd be left trailing our two-ton sled on three miles of rope with no way to haul it in. We'd have to cut the cable and leave half a million dollars' worth of technology on the ocean floor. So I listened carefully to what Frank had to say.

Frank was a burly Texan who handled the orneriest winch as if it were a docile workhorse. He's a warm-hearted, hard-working guy, but he is also something of a doom-and-gloomer. "I'm worried about the winch, Bob," he kept telling me. "It could go at any moment." In this case, I had to admit his pessimism was justified. My deck crew chief, Tom Dettweiler, a normally unflappable veteran of the *Titanic* expedition who had worked with Jacques Cousteau, also warned me about the winch. We'd already had one breakdown; the next one could happen any time. The less work for that winch the better—and hilly bottom meant working the winch to death as the flyer changed altitudes to suit the terrain. If there was any way to stay away from that mountain, I was going to try.

Tom and Frank were also worried about the *Starella*'s ancient A-frame. Without this hoisting mechanism that sits at the stern of the ship, we would have no way of launching or recovering *Argo*. During the Mediterranean portion of the cruise one of the seals on the A-frame's hydraulic lift mechanism had broken, causing it to start leaking oil. The hydraulics had kept working until we could make it into port and conduct repairs. But the problem would likely recur.

With all these things pressing in on me, I studied my map of the search area and weighed my options. Four British ships on the scene during the *Bismarck*'s final battle in May 1941 had recorded three different sinking positions. The distance between these points was as much as six miles—quite a discrepancy. But this could be attributed to the fact that the

navigators were as preoccupied with the battle as everyone else and that the terrible weather for the previous twenty-four hours had made it almost impossible to get a good star fix. So the positions were based on dead reckoning, estimated latitude and longitude calculated using the ship's course and its speed since the last celestial fix combined with estimates of wind and current. To arrive at the area within which we believed the wreck would be found, I had allowed for a margin of error of two miles outside all three points. When I drew a rectangle that enclosed all the sinking positions with two miles to spare, it gave me an area of almost 200 square miles.

Only one of the three sinking positions was to the west of the mountain, over a flat area marked on our benthic charts as the Porcupine Abyssal Plain. This position had been plotted by the navigator aboard the HMS *Rodney*, one of the two battleships to engage the *Bismarck*. And it had been confirmed by a destroyer that had observed the battle. However, the ship that had been closest to the *Bismarck* when she sank, the *Dorsetshire*, had estimated a position well east and slightly to the north of the *Rodney*'s position. The other battleship in the final fight, the flagship *King George V*, compounded the confusion by recording a position well to the south of *Dorsetshire*'s.

So much for my assumption that the British Admiralty would be able

(Above) To the left of Frank Smith at the winch controls can be seen the take-up drum for *Argo*'s 20,000-foot (6,060-meter) cable.

(Below) Preparing to lower *Argo* at night over the stern of the *Starella*.

to guide me straight to the sinking site.

Given the state of my equipment, I had to like the *Rodney*'s fix, which was also considered the official sinking position. Not only was it corroborated by another ship, but it would allow me to begin my search over flat mud bottom. If nothing turned up in this area, I might risk going after that dangerous-looking mountain.

Shortly after midnight on July 12, excitement was high as our underwater robot vehicle *Argo* swung precariously from the A-frame preparatory to launch. It was a nightmarish scene, this night-lowering in bad weather, and very risky—a fact I was even more aware of than usual, because my son Todd had insisted on taking part. Garish floodlights illu-

(Above) Todd and I lend a hand as *Argo* is prepared to go into the water.

(Right) Tom Dettweiler directs the launch.

minated the deck crew clad in yellow slickers as they clung to the lines attached to *Argo*'s frame to prevent it from swinging wildly. One mistake and *Argo* would become a 2-ton wrecking ball that could kill a man in an instant. Slowly the A-frame creaked aft until *Argo* was suspended out over the stern. Tom gave the signal and the sled was lowered gently into the Atlantic swells. As it did so, both seals blew on the hydraulic lifts and oil began to leak. I heard Tom, who'd spent hours repairing those seals, curse colorfully. The A-frame was still functional, but it was clearly a time bomb that could go off at any moment. My anxiety about our equipment went up another notch, but at least the launch was over and everybody was still in one piece.

This was Todd's third expedition with me, and he'd already become one of my best *Argo* flyers, with a sure hand on the joystick control. I wasn't so sure of his handle on his own life, however. He had been a wild teenager, and that streak was still very much in evidence as he prepared to set off for his first year of college. Maybe if I had been home more he would have had an easier time. If I have one regret about having chosen the life of an undersea explorer, it's the cost to my family. For the past twenty years I have been away so much that sometimes my two sons seemed like strangers. Todd was much less of a stranger now, after the time we'd spent together recently. Last summer, after a navy expedition he had joined, we had traveled together in Europe. I looked forward to the time I would be spending with him in the next couple of weeks.

Two-and-a-half hours after the launch, our aquatic sled with its video cameras and sonars and still cameras had descended to the bottom. Now the search could begin. Since we were working over a flat plain, I had elected a sonar search strategy. So we deployed *Argo* at sonar height— roughly 50 meters (140 feet) above the bottom. This meant we could survey a swath roughly 1 kilometer (2,800 feet) wide with each pass. And with no mountains or ridges in the way, anything as big as the hull of the *Bismarck* would come in loud and clear.

Now the familiar rhythms of a mid-ocean search took over as we towed *Argo* at the painstaking speed of one knot across the ocean floor. My team was divided into three watches. Each watch was on duty for four hours, off for eight. So if you stood the noon to 4 P.M. watch, you also got the graveyard shift, midnight to 4 A.M.

(Below left) Before the first launch three members of our team used a block and tackle to pull *Argo* out of its garage on the fantail.

The new watch generally arrives ten or fifteen minutes before the end of the shift. Each newcomer is briefed by the person at the position he's responsible for, and then takes over.

A watch usually begins with some banter and backchat. Perhaps there's a debate about what music to play over the van stereo. But the talk slowly ebbs away as the minutes tick slowly by, and each person concentrates on the job at hand. The flyer keeps one hand on the joystick, one eye on the altitude readings and one on the sonar print-out. Meanwhile, the navigator guides the ship, relaying course changes to the bridge and watching the computer plot that indicates where exactly we are inside our transponder net. The *Argo* engineer monitors all the vehicle's systems and, when we are at visual altitude, runs the cameras. The data logger records everything the sonar "hears" or the cameras "see." Meanwhile the watch leader keeps an eye on everything and makes tactical decisions: Should we go and take a closer look at that tantalizing sonar target, or keep on course?

(Above) *Argo* goes into the water.

The control van reminds me of a space capsule. Once you're inside you might as well be orbiting the moon, so detached are you from the world outside. The red lights, which keep pupils from dilating so video images look clearer, gives the scene a somewhat ghostly quality. The long narrow space is crammed full of technological gadgetry: keyboards, computer screens, television monitors, data recorders, sonar readouts. Come to think of it, being on a tiny ship in the middle of the ocean has much in common with being in outer space. By day there are no points of reference. By night there are only the moon and the stars.

During a sonar search the routine becomes ever more numbing unless something interesting takes shape on the sonar print-out. You don't even get to stare at black-and-white television images of mud, as happens when *Argo*'s three black-and-white video cameras are at viewing altitude. Then, at least, a fish may swim by to relieve the tedium. Or a glacial

(Below) Watch leader Sam Nichols checks our position on the navigational chart.

(Above) Captain John Nichols (no relation) at the ship's wheel.

erratic—a boulder deposited by a melting iceberg—may loom into view.

Many people prefer the eight-to-twelve watch, which allows them to preserve the routine of dry land most closely—asleep at night and awake during the day. But the younger members of the team often gravitate to the graveyard shift. After midnight there are fewer spectators hanging around, and the conversation can flow freely. Also, this shift is often the one when things happen. Babies always seem to be born in the wee hours of the morning, and ships seem to get found. It was during the graveyard shift that we found the *Titanic*. That was one of the reasons why I put Todd on the twelve-to-four watch. I wanted him to be in on the kill. I also knew he wouldn't mind being up in the middle of the night.

Also on Todd's watch was Hagen Schempf, a twenty-seven-year-old graduate student in engineering from MIT completing his Ph.D. on robotics while working for me at Woods Hole. He was helping design the robot arm for JASON that would be tested in the Mediterranean when we investigated the possible Roman shipwreck we had just found off Sicily. Hagen was also German born, the only German national involved in our expedition.

As we began our 1988 search that July morning, my first priority was to check out the western slope of the mountain. If the wreck had landed anywhere along the incline, it would probably have slid down and ended up on the plain. So by searching along the base of this geologic feature I would, in effect, be searching the whole slope. I plotted my first "line" on the navigational chart, a transit from north to south along the edge of the incline.

The long run from north to south only told me that the mountain would indeed be trouble. On sonar it looked very steep. After this close-up encounter, I decided to stay in the flatlands, working my way west in a series of north/south passes less than a kilometer apart so that the sonar swaths would overlap. This is the technique known as "mowing the lawn" that oceanographers use when they are looking for a wreck. There was no way I could miss anything as big as the *Bismarck*—unless it were buried in the bottom sediment or had been blown to smithereens.

It was already mid-afternoon when we began to angle northwest away from the mountain toward a position where we could begin our second transit from north to south, but now a sporadic technical problem began to haunt us: the vehicle was crabbing. At this slow speed, underwater currents combined with the surface motion of the *Starella* were sometimes causing *Argo* to swing widely. There was no danger to the vehicle, but the swinging meant our sonars were covering an erratic swath—sometimes the right-looking sonar was actually looking left, and vice-versa. This irregular motion wouldn't have been all that serious in a visual search, since the down-looking cameras don't care about the vehicle's orientation, but it really hampered an acoustic search. When *Argo* was crabbing, large targets might get missed entirely. However, I had no choice but to continue and hope the problem would go away.

Darkness had closed in when we turned south to begin this line. *Argo*, oblivious to the passage of days, inched forward through regions of eternal night and unthinkable pressure. The sonar record remained blank, its depth indicator steady, indicating a bottom undisturbed by the wreckage of war. For the moment the crabbing problem seemed to have abated.

Later that night a nasty storm passed through, making life even more unpleasant and the underwater course of *Argo* even more erratic. The *Starella*'s crew rigged safety lines on deck so that people wouldn't slip or be washed overboard. Getting to and from the van became an adventure, a little like climbing a wet mountain that keeps moving under your feet. For those who had never been to sea before, it was a real baptism, but nothing like being aboard one of those World War II destroyers, I thought, which were built for speed, not stability. In heavy seas a destroyer's bow often completely disappeared beneath a big wave. Sometimes it would heel so far over, that it seemed sure to capsize. It couldn't have been fun

(Below) The sonar operator examines a sonar print-out. During an acoustic search, as was used in 1988, *Argo* is deployed at an altitude of roughly 50 meters above the bottom. This means its sonars can survey a swath approximately one kilometer wide (assuming the bottom is flat), and will pick up any significant piece of wreckage within that area.

being aboard one of the destroyers that chased the *Bismarck* in weather even worse than this. Perhaps our storm was an omen. If it was, I hoped it meant we were getting close.

Through the night and the storm we moved southward. Those who could, slept, but many lay awake listening to the loud drone of the *Starella*'s engines that were working overtime to keep us on some semblance of our course. The whole vessel shook with the engines' vibrations, shuddered each time we crashed into a big wave. We had been searching for barely twenty-four hours, but it was already beginning to seem like an eternity.

On any sea expedition, the expectation and excitement quickly subside as routine takes over. Sonar searches are especially boring. Sonar can pick up small pieces of debris and relatively small changes in bottom topography, but it is often difficult to tell the difference between geology and something man-made. Very small pieces of man-made material, especially if they are lying flat and present no real profile for the sound wave to bounce off, can get lost in the "noise," the inherent margin of error in any sonar system. Soon you begin to wonder if the machine is working—all that paper coming at you looking like a photograph of a snowstorm, an acoustic whiteout. You begin to yearn for a look at mud, at anything.

(Left) Bill Lange adjusts *Argo*'s cameras while the vehicle travels slowly along the ocean floor three miles below. During a visual search *Argo* is flown a few meters above the bottom so that its cameras can spot tiny pieces of man-made debris. If the debris is part of a larger debris field (a trail of man-made material a mile or more in length left by a ship as it sinks to the bottom) it usually leads us to the wreck.

Between watches people sought to escape the tedium. Everyone had brought a stack of books. Some began to eat too much or drink too much beer. On this trip you could almost always find a group in the mess—the ship's dining room—playing cribbage, part of an ongoing tournament inspired by Frank Smith. When Frank wasn't minding the winch he was often engrossed in a game or teaching a neophyte how to play. Across the corridor, in the ship's lounge, one or two people were usually using the VCR, watching *Ghostbusters* for the umpteenth time. And there was almost always someone down below in the ship's science lab. This was where we kept the off-line computers and where the film crew stored its camera equipment, but it was also home to a small arcade of video games. Video golf was big in 1988. So was *Wheel of Fortune*. Todd and his buddies sat there by the hour when they were off duty.

When the weather was fine, people not on watch would sometimes gather on the bow for a game of poker.

Almost everyone had seen the videotape of *Sink the Bismarck!* Now many members of the team sat reading the baron's book, *Battleship Bismarck*, or Ludovic Kennedy's *Pursuit*—a fascinating recreation of the events of May 1941 from both the British and the German sides. People began to identify with various characters in the story, to imagine what it must have been like on board one of those spartan, crowded warships. The *Starella's* mostly British crew were particularly keen about our quest—the *Bismarck* story was part of their cultural heritage. A number had served in the Royal Navy and could recite famous sea battles—the Armada, Copenhagen, Cape St. Vincent, Trafalgar. The *Bismarck* was one of them.

I wondered how the hunt for the *Bismarck* was affecting Hagen Schempf, data logger on the twelve-to-four shift. He had been keen to come on this cruise, but had given me no indication that he saw our quest as something personally significant. It was mainly a chance for him to go to sea on his first research expedition. He had fit into our team with ease, getting along with almost everyone, always ready with a laugh or wisecrack. In some ways he seemed older than his twenty-seven years; in other ways he was almost boyish, more like Todd.

Although born in Germany, Hagen had spent little of his life in his homeland. But he had been fascinated with ships and the sea from the time he was a youngster. As a boy he had even built a model of the *Bismarck*, but he did not remember the details of the story. Like many Germans of his generation, he was aware of the events of World War II, but did not dwell on them. The *Bismarck* was just a famous ship that had been sunk in the war and on which a lot of people had died. It was history. On the trip out Hagen and I had talked about the story—he had devoured the baron's book—but if it had touched him in some way, he did not show it.

By the time daylight returned we were on our next line, less than a kilometer to the west. As we moved north the storm gradually abated, but still the ship rolled and heaved in the swells, making it difficult to tow *Argo* in a straight line. And despite the calmer surface conditions, the vehicle again began to crab badly. Who knew what our sonars were missing?

Finally I had had enough. At 8:30 A.M. I ordered a course change to the east, back toward the mountain. This would be an experimental run to find out if the swinging motion could be curtailed. At 10:30, as we neared the slope, I ordered another turn, this time back to the west. So much for my bright idea—the course alteration had made little difference.

About an hour after noon, as I was thinking of heading to the mess to see if any lunch was left, Todd's excited voice suddenly interrupted the quiet.

"We're getting something on sonar!"

I looked over at the sonar trace and, sure enough, shadows were beginning to form, interrupting the endless flow of flat bottom sediment.

"Sonar target 150 meters to port," reported Hagen.

I walked over to look at the dark-brown image that was being burned onto the paper.

"That's it! That's got to be it! That's got to be the ship."

Todd was a lot more confident than I was. This wasn't big enough to be a ship. But it did indicate a depression of some sort, in the bottom.

Todd looks on as the *Starella*'s chief engineer, John Brown, works at the navigation controls.

"Sorry, Todd, but that looks like geology to me," I responded. "Maybe we'll come back and take a look at it later. Right now I want to start another line."

A few minutes later the sonar trace was back to its monotonous regularity. I'd seen a million sonar targets more impressive than the one we'd just encountered. I wasn't about to get excited now. Still, this was the first sign of anything on the bottom and that, at least, was encouraging.

By the time we had completed our next line to the west, I was beginning to grow restless. I was ready for something to happen. So far I hadn't even seen the bottom. That sonar target began to get bigger in my mind, to seem more interesting. I started toying with the idea of taking a visual run over the area. If nothing else, it would be a change of pace. At least then we might see something: a slow-moving sea cucumber, perhaps a crab scuttling across our view, or even a Coke can thrown overboard from a passing freighter. After all, this had been a busy shipping lane for many centuries. There was bound to be *something* to look at down there.

As sunset approached I ordered the navigator to set a course toward the target we'd spotted just after noon. We turned north. Hours passed, more empty bottom was surveyed by sonar.

As midnight approached Todd's watch straggled into the van, all except Todd. It was five minutes to twelve and there was still no sign of my son. Late again. As Hagen gamely set off to rouse him from his bunk, I cursed under my breath. A few minutes later Hagen returned with a disheveled, tousle-haired Todd in tow. I glared at my son but said nothing as he took his place in the flyer's chair.

Todd was about to turn twenty that summer of 1988, but he was still trying to prove himself and not sure how, still figuring out how to be the son of the man who'd found the *Titanic*—and it wasn't easy. Already he had been late for his watch a couple of times. I had put him on Hagen's team, hoping that he would be a steadying influence. But my son was showing no signs of imitating the older man. At least Hagen took it all in good humor. I'm sure he found Todd's sloppiness annoying, but instead

of getting angry he would rib him mercilessly. And Todd was spunky; he gave as good as he got. Hagen seemed to like Todd and a bond did seem to be forming.

The watch settled in, and soon the van was quiet except for the soft music playing on the stereo as each person concentrated on his task. I stared at the navigational chart on which I had penciled our course. We were still steaming north, directly toward the sonar target. We had already covered the area well, I told myself. Nothing the size of the *Bismarck* could be there, at least sitting on top of the mud, but who knew what was buried under it?

"Sonar target 135 meters to starboard," Hagen reported.

"Alter course to o-eight-five," I responded. It was time to drop down and look at some scenery.

"Todd, go down to 6.5 meters."

"Roger that," replied Todd.

"Nice and easy now." I didn't really have to say anything. Todd knew what he was doing.

Obediently he pushed gently forward on the joystick, automatically causing the winch on *Starella*'s deck to reel out cable. When flying *Argo,* Todd's daredevil streak disappeared completely. Once at his post, he was all business—the most conservative of my flyers, the least likely to take chances. Now he lowered *Argo* slowly, then leveled off right at 6.5 meters (20 feet) above the ocean floor. This was high enough to miss hitting anything except a cliff or the hull of a ship, but close enough for *Argo*'s cameras to get a clear look at the bottom. And *Argo*'s forward-looking sonar would provide ample warning of a big obstacle.

Argo's cameras now showed us the images of flat featureless mud we knew so well. Few people realize that most of the planet is mud. Anyone who thinks undersea exploration is a glamorous profession should spend a few days locked in a stuffy shipping container on a heaving ship in the middle of the gray Atlantic staring at mile after mile of soft gray sediment.

Minutes ticked by. Then the seabed began to discolor—a sure sign of disturbance. And whatever had done the disturbing, it was almost cer-

Hagen Schempf watches as I lay out a new search line on the navigation chart.

tainly not geological.

I stared at the indistinct image coming into the view of *Argo*'s forward-looking camera.

"Switch to down-looking," I ordered. "Okay, zoom in."

The *Argo* engineer's fingers played over the keyboard, instantly sending an electronic message along the coaxial cable to *Argo*'s on-board computer. In a split second the television image I was watching changed from a distant view to a close-up.

"It definitely looks man-made," I muttered.

"I told you this was the ship," Todd said excitedly.

Hagen and I smiled at each other. Todd had already found the ship twice on this cruise, and we had been searching not quite two days. It had become something of a running joke.

"If it is, at least you didn't sleep through it," Hagen cracked.

The tiny piece of debris—if indeed it was debris—was impossible to identify, but it wasn't a natural part of the sea bottom. It looked like a piece of twisted ribbon.

Argo crawled forward. All eyes were riveted to the television monitors, waiting for the next clue. The bottom was now seriously disturbed. Then another ribbony piece of debris slowly came into focus. Then another.

"That looks like it could be metal," Hagen commented.

"Absolutely. But where on the ship did it come from?" I responded.

I tried to fit these tiny images to the great ship we were searching for. Maybe they were fragments of some sort of light armament. In my mind I relived the harrowing last battle of the *Bismarck*, the merciless British shelling, the fires raging on the deck. Could the blasted bits we were seeing be a result of that conflagration? The *Bismarck*—if this was part of the lost battleship—was being coy. The debris we were looking at was nondescript, unidentifiable.

"Dad, the cable has jumped the traction unit!" Todd shouted.

"All stop!" I yelled automatically. Any problem with *Argo*'s cable could mean disaster.

As the *Starella* slowed to a standstill, the motion of the swells became more noticeable.

I ran out of the van and back to the fantail, where Frank Smith was surveying the situation. The traction unit is a large multi-grooved wheel on the winch that keeps the cable from slipping. Sometimes, when the ship drops down quickly off a big swell, the cable can go slack and actually jump out of the grooves. This is what had just happened.

Fortunately, the deck crew had seen situations like this before. Quickly they rigged Chinese fingers to the cable to take up the tension. Once this was done, the weight was no longer on the traction unit, and *Argo* would maintain its current altitude while the deck team worked on the traction unit without danger. In no time they had checked the cable for damage, found none and placed it back in its grooves. An hour after the alarm, everything was back to normal.

For the next few hours we crisscrossed the target area. We found more debris, some of it tantalizingly suggestive, but nothing conclusive. Each time we encountered an interesting object I ordered the *Argo* engineer to

Inside the van the atmosphere was tense when *Argo*'s cable jumped the traction unit.

Todd hoses down the cable on the traction unit with a rust-inhibiting preservative.

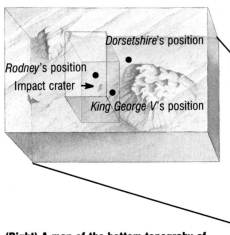

(Right) A map of the bottom topograhy of the Northeastern Atlantic with an inset showing a blow-up of the *Bismarck* search area. The highlighted rectangle (above) represents the area we searched in 1988. The massive volcanic complex on the right—it reminds me of a giant molar—was the mountainous area we wanted to stay away from.

shoot a still with the Electronic Still Camera (ESC). This recent addition to *Argo*'s equipment gave us high-resolution black-and-white pictures far superior to the muddy video images we were watching. (The color still camera was also shooting away, but its film wouldn't be developed until we were back on shore.) Just before 5 A.M. we spotted what looked like a series of gears on a shaft. Could that be part of some kind of gun-turning mechanism? Hagen had stayed on after his watch ended. Now he and I pored over our books about the *Bismarck*, but could match it to nothing.

There was now no question in my mind that the area we were investigating was an impact crater. At the very least this debris was associated with something that had fallen from the surface and hit with enough force to disturb the bottom and leave quite a bit of evidence.

My brain clicked into overdrive, racing over the possibilities. As I saw it, the *Bismarck* wreck site and surrounding area should consist of three separate elements: the main wreck itself; heavy pieces that fell off at the surface; and debris blasted off during the course of the battle.

Unlike the *Titanic*, which except for the iceberg wound was undamaged before she sank, the German battleship had endured a battle almost an hour and a half long. British shells had torn apart the super-structure of the ship as she continued to steam northwest. Some of this material must have fallen overboard. If this was what we were looking at—pieces blown off during the shelling—then we were likely still southeast of the main wreck, since as far as we know the ship kept moving slowly until about half an hour before she sank. Our best guess was that the distance between the first debris from the battle and the sinking position could be as much as 9 miles (14 kilometers).

Or perhaps the impact crater had been caused by a heavy part of the ship that had fallen when the ship turned turtle before she sank. The *Titanic* boiler we discovered in 1985 had fallen straight down after the ship broke apart at the surface. And it would have taken something heavier than a boiler to make this mark in the sediment. Perhaps the small fragments we had found so far had broken off as this heavy piece fell, or when it hit.

Given the size of the crater and the absence of big pieces of wreckage, it didn't seem possible that this was where the main wreck had hit. The crater was too small—bigger than a football field, but not by much. The *Bismarck* was 820 feet (250 meters) long. And our sonar search had already told us that nothing big enough to be the *Bismarck* was nearby.

Yet this crater had to be associated with the battleship in some way. It lay only 1,860 yards (1,700 meters) from the *Rodney*'s estimated position of the sinking. No other ships were known to have gone down near here. Only the *Bismarck* sank during the battle and she failed to score even a single hit on the British attackers. Any debris from the battle would have to be the *Bismarck*'s. Surely it was just a question of scouring the area until the wreck turned up.

By 8 A.M. we had seen enough of the crater. I decided to operate on the hypothesis that it had been caused by heavy debris shot off during the battle. If so, the main wreck should be as much as nine miles to the northwest. On this assumption, we extended our transponder net and began searching to the north.

Over the next several days I tested out this hypothesis and every other one I could think of. We looked northwest, we looked north, we looked south, we looked farther west. We looked east yet again. But the only scent we found was a short plume of debris leading north from the impact crater, getting lighter as we went north. (At least this told me that the main debris field, when we found it, should be on a north/south axis, since underwater currents are usually consistent over a wide area.)

Finally, having exhausted all other possibilities except the mountainous area to the east, I returned to investigate the impact crater more thoroughly. In days of searching a section of sea floor roughly 30 miles (48 kilometers) square, it was the only area of debris I'd discovered. Now, as we looped back and forth, saturating our visual coverage, we found more and more suggestive evidence. Were these rings something to do with optical range finders for the *Bismarck*'s guns? Were the loops of wire—or rope—parts of the *Bismarck*'s rigging? Where on the deck did that section of piping come from? Hagen and I spent hours trying to match these objects to the battleship. We tired ourselves out, and we ended up with

(Top) We puzzle over the meaning of the impact crater we have found.

(Above) Searching the British Admiralty charts recording the *Bismarck*'s final battle, I try to calculate where the earliest debris from the battle should be.

nothing conclusive. We'd found lots of wood, and we knew the *Bismarck* had a wooden deck—but that was the closest we could come.

I struggled to fit the evidence before us to what I knew of the *Bismarck* and other shipwrecks. Not every ship finds its way to the bottom in wonderful condition, I reminded myself. In my career I've seen ships and submarines that literally disappeared into the bottom mud. Was it possible that the *Bismarck* had landed here and somehow been completely buried?

Gradually, I began to construct a theory consistent with the clues we had found.

Suppose, I suggested to my skeptical colleagues, that the ship sank like a bullet—the nose of the bow first—and plunged into the mud at high speed, perhaps losing bits and pieces of superstructure on the way. What remained would be an impact crater and a scattering of debris, nothing more. Hagen made elaborate calculations and estimated that for the "bullet" to leave a crater this size the ship could have reached a descent speed of 25 knots and hit at a 20 degree angle. It was possible. So I espoused this

With a plastic model I demonstrate the theory that the *Bismarck* hit the bottom like a bullet and buried itself in the mud.

theory for the documentary film cameras. By the time I'd finished, I had almost convinced myself. "I'm certain this is the *Bismarck*," I said for posterity. But was it really? Only when we got home and developed all the color slides from *Argo*'s still cameras, would we know for sure.

For a few more days we combed the area, searching for the missing key. We reconfigured *Argo*'s cameras to give us a side view with more sense of three dimensions, but despite the improved images, the wreckage remained anonymous.

There was no point looking elsewhere now, just in case we were wrong. Oil was continuing to leak from the A-frame. The winch had held up so far during lowerings of one hundred hours or more when it was required to do only the minimum of work. I knew my equipment couldn't handle a mountain. I had said the *Bismarck* would be a piece of cake. If this was all that remained of the mighty battleship, it was not proving to be a very tasty piece.

Aboard the *Starella*, the grumbles of discontent were audible. Subcommittees of experts had come to the conclusion that Ballard was deluding himself. There was no way this was the *Bismarck*. I kept up a confident front. In the absence of proof to the contrary, this had to be the ship.

Todd, of course, backed me all the way. He had been on the watch that found the first debris. He was convinced we had discovered all that remained of the once-proud battleship.

Throughout our 1988 *Bismarck* expedition it seemed as though the gods were toying with me. As we recovered *Argo* for the last time, they

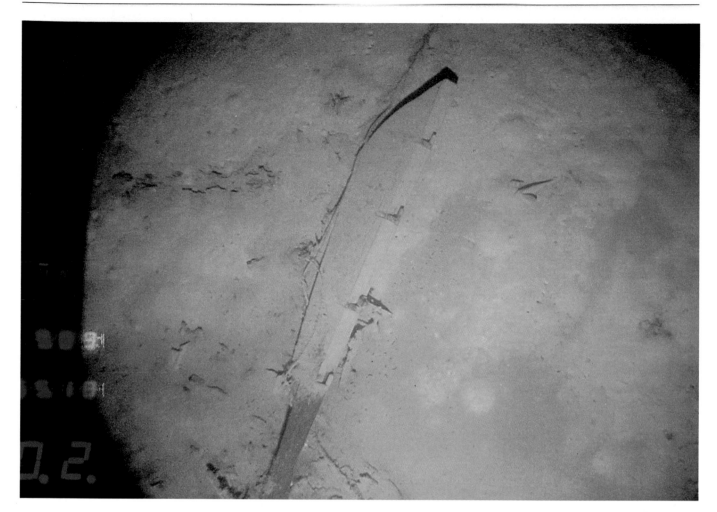

delivered a double insult. Ten meters from the surface, the winch failed. Tom Dettweiler and his men improvised with block and tackle and managed to bring the vehicle the rest of the way to the surface. As our underwater explorer's tailfin broke into view, Tom leaned over the rail to latch a line onto the frame. As he did so one of his ribs snapped, a rib he'd injured earlier in the year during a routine recovery. Tom left the site in pain, and the rest of us departed in a cloud of uncertainty.

On July 21, one week after we had discovered the impact crater and the first shards of debris, we headed for home. Seldom in my career have I experienced such a hollow feeling. Even if we had discovered the *Bismarck*, what did we have to show for it? I hoped that when we developed our hundreds of color slides, they would provide the missing piece of the puzzle.

A few days later I sat alone in my office at Woods Hole. The lights were off and the curtains were drawn as I looked at slides from *Argo*'s color still camera. The color was great, the images were crisp and clear. Click: another piece of nondescript wreckage. Click: a twisted ribbon of metal, gold in color—could that be copper? Click: a piece of wooden decking. Click: a beautifully preserved wooden rudder.

A rudder! Damn!

I felt like someone had driven a stake into my heart. That rudder must have belonged to a nineteenth-century sailing ship. The impact

The sight of this teak rudder ended any possibility that the wreck we found in 1988 was the *Bismarck*. The four mounting pins that attached it to its housing are clearly visible.

crater, the debris that I'd tried to force-fit to the *Bismarck* story suddenly leapt into focus. Of course. A sailing ship would be just the right size for that crater. And all the evidence we had found now made sense. Other slides showed clear chunks of the ship's wooden hull. Those rings I'd turned into optical range finders were step rings from a wooden mast. The mast itself had rotted away. The strips of metal were copper flashing, probably lining for the hull. One slide gave me a clear look at what seemed to be a bilge pump.

I glanced over at the huge map of the world's oceans that lines one of the walls of my office. Somewhere in that vast hiding place the wreck of the *Bismarck* still lay.

(Below) What remains of the rings that held the sail to the wooden mast.

(Right and below far right) The wooden hull of the wrecked schooner emerges from the bottom mud.

A four-masted *Inca* class sailing schooner from the early part of this century, similar to the ship we found.

About the time I was sitting staring dumbly at that wooden rudder, Hagen Schempf was in southern Germany, paying a call on the Baron von Müllenheim-Rechberg, the highest-ranking surviving officer of the *Bismarck*. Hagen carried a sheaf of black-and-white pictures taken by *Argo's* Electronic Still Camera—crisp digital images we thought might show the baron something recognizable. Hagen was charmed by the elderly gentleman and his wife and listened spellbound as the baron talked about the *Bismarck*. For the first time the story became something more than dry history. It became flesh and blood. The baron had been on that ship and had been changed forever by the experience.

(Below center) What remains of a bilge pump. Deadeyes for the sails lie on the bottom right and in the center of the picture to the right.

(Below) This is the gearlike mechanism we initially mistook for part of a range finding apparatus. It was probably part of a winch.

Müllenheim-Rechberg looked carefully at the pictures Hagen had brought and shook his head sadly. No, there was nothing here that could be identified as the *Bismarck*. Later that day I reached Hagen in Germany to tell him about the wooden rudder. He wasn't surprised.

And so our 1988 *Bismarck* expedition ended on a sour note. When all the evidence was sifted, it was pretty clear we had found a four-masted sailing schooner from the 1880s or '90s, a commercial vessel from the age just before steam took over. But I wasn't prepared to give up just yet. Next spring we would be returning to the Mediterranean for our JASON Project broadcasts. So there would be another golden opportunity to go looking for the wreck that was proving so elusive. Besides, I told myself, it would have been too easy if we had found her so quickly. The *Titanic* did not fall easily—only in the final hours of a grueling five-week search.

In real life the *Bismarck* had turned out to be a devilishly difficult quarry. She had won her first battle with the British, proving to be more than a match for the pride of their fleet. At one point it seemed as though the whole Royal Navy was chasing her. It seemed only appropriate that she should have beaten us this year.

Now, at least, we knew where the battleship wasn't. As I like to tell my sons, "You can't lose if you don't quit." Well, I wasn't quitting now—as long as I could talk my backers into financing another try.

Round one to the *Bismarck*.

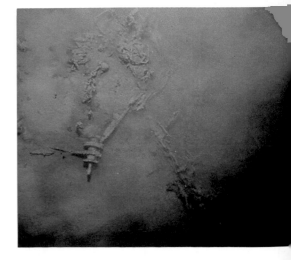

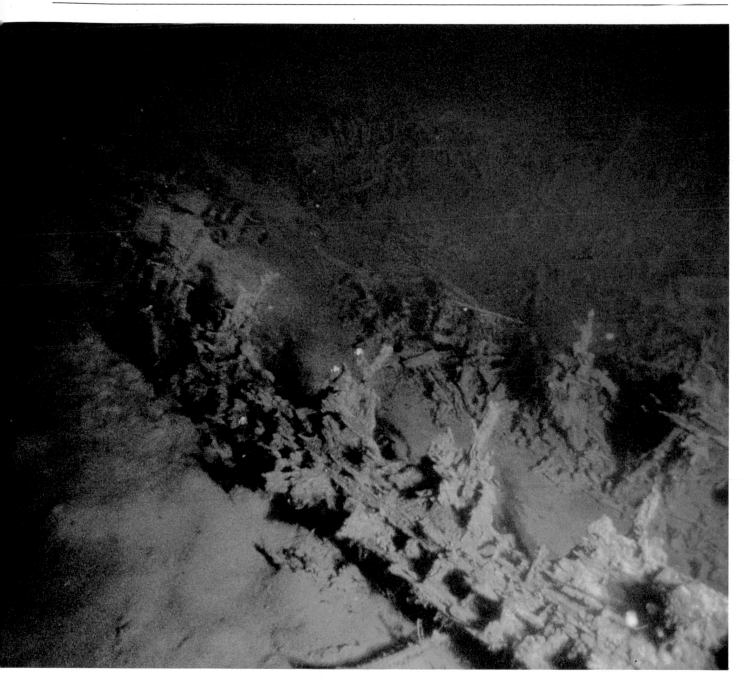

CHAPTER FOUR

Exercise Rhine—
The Opening Moves

Gotenhafen, Occupied Poland—May 19, 1941

Under the cover of a black, starless night the *Bismarck* weighed anchor and headed west. It was 2 A.M. on the morning of May 19, 1941. The months of rehearsal were finally over. Operation Rheinübung—Exercise Rhine—had begun.

As the men of the *Bismarck* sat or stood at their stations or lay dozing in their hammocks, Captain Lindemann announced over the ship's loudspeakers that the purpose of their expedition was to reach the Atlantic and sink as much British shipping as possible over a period of several months. Lindemann's men had no knowledge of the elaborate planning

A photograph taken aboard the *Prinz Eugen* of the *Bismarck* in Grimstadfjord, Norway, on May 21, 1941. Her camouflage stripes and false bow wave have not yet been painted out.

that had led to this moment. They only knew that action was at hand.

For that action to achieve its goal, secrecy was essential. All previous successful commerce-raiders had managed to sneak into the Atlantic undetected. Once the British knew the *Bismarck* was at sea, the far-superior forces of the British Home Fleet could be massed against her. No wonder Admiral Lütjens and his superiors at Group North in Wilhelms-haven had frozen all shipping in the Great Belt (the protected north/south passage that bisects the islands of Denmark) and in the Kattegat between Denmark and Sweden for all of May 19 and half of the following day. These were the narrowest and most congested areas through which the naval task force had to pass, where the *Bismarck* and *Prinz Eugen* would seldom be out of sight of land. It was on this crucial first leg of the trip that they were most likely to be spotted by unfriendly eyes.

The *Bismarck* and the *Prinz Eugen* before their sortie out into the Atlantic.

Prime Minister Churchill did not know the *Bismarck* had sailed, but he and his admirals were sure some fresh German mischief was afoot. During the second week of May there had been more than the usual enemy air reconnaissance between Jan Mayen Island, a tiny island north of Iceland, and Green-land. This could well presage a breakout. If so, the timing was ter-rible. German troops were poised for an assault on Crete (the attack came on May 20). Meanwhile, Britain was barely holding her own against German U-boats in the war at sea. The Battle of Britain had been won, but it would be a hollow victory for Churchill if his people starved and his ships had to remain in port for lack of fuel. He had been thinking about releasing Vice-Admiral Sir James Somerville and Force H, stationed at Gibraltar, to support the defense of Crete. Now this was out of the question.

The *Bismarck* sliced invisibly through the darkness toward a late-morning rendezvous with *Prinz Eugen* off Cape Arkona on Rügen Island in the western Baltic. *Prinz Eugen*, under the command of Captain Helmuth Brinkmann, had departed Gotenhafen the previous evening. The day dawned cloudy and remained overcast, making aerial reconnais-sance unlikely—a good omen. At Arkona the two ships met and were joined by an escort of two destroyers and a flotilla of minesweepers. They sailed west and then north, passing by night through the Great Belt. The next morning, May 20, they entered the Kattegat, the large bay formed by northern Denmark and southern Sweden. The day had dawned under a clear sky and bright sunlight dappled the Danish and Swedish fishing boats that dotted the sea. The good weather meant the Swedish coast was in sight as they sailed north toward the Skaggerak, the strait between Jut-land and southern Norway.

The passage remained uneventful until early the following afternoon, just as they were about to enter Norwegian waters. Around 1 P.M. off

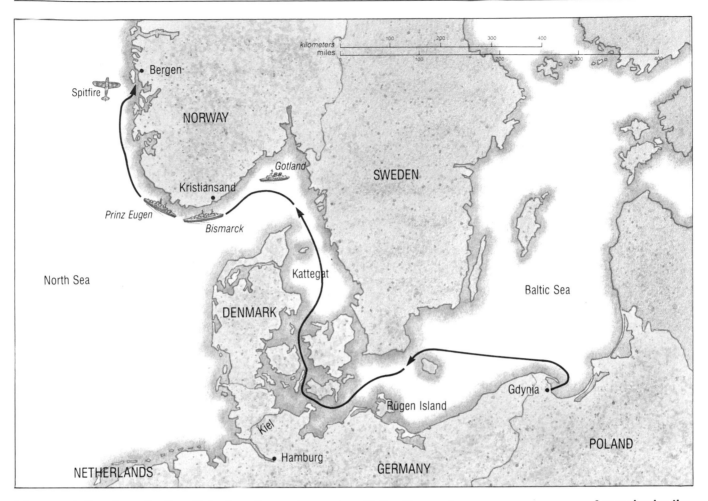

Marstrand, Sweden, the Swedish aircraft-carrying cruiser *Gotland* loomed into view. She steamed along parallel to the German force while she remained in Swedish waters, and then dispatched a radio message.

This was exactly what Lütjens had wanted to avoid. Neutral Sweden was a nest of spies and informers. In the radio room aboard the *Bismarck*, the intelligence staff listened intently for a transmission from the Swedish ship. Sure enough, when *Gotland*'s routine report was decoded, it informed the Swedish admiralty of the German presence. Shortly thereafter, Lütjens notifed Group North that the secrecy of his whereabouts had been compromised. Indeed, it was only a matter of hours before Henry Denham, the British naval attaché in Stockholm, heard the news, which he promptly relayed to London.

Lütjens may have had cause for worry, but most of the ship's company were simply enjoying their first sea voyage and not thinking about what was to come. Those not on duty could wander the decks and watch the mountainous landscape of southern Norway. Near sunset the ships passed Kristiansand near Norway's southernmost point and soon began to veer northwest with the curve of the coast. Once it got dark, Müllenheim-Rechberg and some of the other officers watched a film in the wardroom, *Play in the Summer Wind*, a rather silly love story featuring handsome young men and pretty young maidens disporting themselves in a landscape of green meadows.

As this mindless entertainment unfolded, a second report of the

A map showing the route of the *Bismarck* and *Prinz Eugen* from Gdynia to Bergen. The two ships rendezvoused off Rügen Island then proceeded through the Danish Islands into the Kattegat, where they were sighted by the Swedish cruiser *Gotland*. A second sighting took place off Kristiansand, and near Bergen both ships were spotted by a British Spitfire.

This painting recreates the moment when Flying Officer Michael Suckling of the Royal Air Force Coastal Command, piloting his Spitfire, spotted the *Bismarck* and *Prinz Eugen* in Grimstadfjord on the afternoon of May 21. His reconnaissance camera can be seen on the underside of the fuselage.

Bismarck's position was making its way to the enemy. The agent for this intelligence was Viggo Axelssen, a member of the Norwegian undergound who happened to be strolling with some friends along the cliffs near Kristiansand when the German task force sailed by. He had his binoculars handy and soon a hidden radio transmitter was sending news to London of two German battleships with escorts heading west toward the North Sea. (Until recently, most experts believed that Axelssen's message reached the Admiralty the same day as Denham's, thus corroborating the earlier report. But new research by Norwegian experts has turned up no evidence that Axelssen's intelligence ever reached London at all.)

It may seem surprising that the Germans followed such a vulnerable route into the North Sea, one that kept them within sight of land for several days. In fact their only alternative was nearly as bad. The route to the North Sea via the Kiel Canal and the Elbe—even if partly passed by night—would have put them in a region of regular British aerial reconnaissance and bombing. There was the additional possibility of mines in the canal. And this route would also have taken longer. It was already mid-May, and with each passing day the hours of daylight increased and the chances of good weather improved, making a successful breakout more difficult.

Around noon the next day, May 21, the *Bismarck* and the *Prinz Eugen* entered the protected fjords near Bergen so that *Prinz Eugen* could refuel. This stop was not part of Lütjens' operational orders; the plan was for both ships to refuel from the tanker *Weissenburg* already waiting for them in the northern part of the Norwegian Sea. But *Prinz Eugen* had a much more limited range than the *Bismarck*. Refueling her now gave Lütjens additional flexibility should he decide to break out right away.

Nonetheless, his decision seems ill-considered. The two ships sat all day under clear blue skies in the Norwegian port closest to British airfields, as if waiting to be spotted by British aerial reconnaissance—which is exactly what happened. Around 1:15 P.M., a Spitfire flying over Bergen photographed the ships. Soon the British Admiralty knew exactly where the *Bismarck* was, but what she was doing was another question.

During the warm and sunny afternoon, *Prinz Eugen*'s tanks were topped up while the *Bismarck*'s camouflage—the dazzling black and white stripes and false bow wave and stern wake on her sides (intended to confuse an enemy about her size)—were painted over with a dull gray paint that would help her disappear into the Atlantic. Lieutenant-Commander von Müllenheim-Rechberg, strolling on deck and enjoying the pleasant weather and spectacular scenery, was perplexed. Why didn't Lütjens take advantage of this time to refuel *Bismarck* as well? The junior officer's criticisms have been echoed by many writers. In the Royal Navy it was standard procedure to refuel ships at every opportunity—a policy that makes good sense given the unpredictability of war. *Bismarck* had left Gotenhafen 200 tons short because of the ruptured fuel line. What if Lütjens didn't have time to refuel from the tanker waiting for him in the Norwegian Sea? Once in the Atlantic, every ton became precious. The excuse that such a refueling was not in the day's operational orders shows an incredible inflexibility on the part of a seasoned commander. The

A photograph taken from Suckling's Spitfire. Once it was developed the British Admiralty knew for certain that the *Bismarck* was on the move.

Bismarck left Bergen with her fuel tanks down by about 1,100 tons.

Around 7:30 P.M., the *Bismarck* and the *Prinz Eugen* resumed their northward journey. Lütjens had played his opening gambit in this game of saltwater chess with poor results. It was now clear that the British knew something was up. That morning German intelligence had deciphered a British radio transmission ordering RAF planes to be on the lookout for two German battleships and three destroyers heading north. (A third destroyer escort had arrived by now.) The enemy was on his trail. Fortunately for him, however, the British were still in the dark as to *Bismarck*'s intentions. Nor would they discover for some time that the task force had left Bergen.

Facing Lütjens across the chessboard was Admiral Sir John Tovey aboard his new flagship *King George V.* Tovey was commander in chief of the British Home Fleet based at Scapa Flow in the Orkney Islands just off the northeastern tip of Scotland. Of course, Tovey had many more chess pieces at his disposal than Lütjens, but he had the disadvantage of being on the defensive from the outset, always moving to counter each play made by his adversary. This game was made more complex by the fact that both players could see only part of the board at any one time. Sometimes—in Tovey's case particularly—a player couldn't even be sure where all his pieces were. Bad weather and communication problems were big factors in the war at sea.

Now fifty-six, Admiral Tovey had been in the navy since age fifteen, had commanded a destroyer at the Battle of Jutland in 1916, and had moved steadily up the ranks since then. Diminutive but brimming with self-confidence, he was a warm and humorous man who seldom spoke in anger. A popular commander who inspired great confidence in his subordinates, he wasn't afraid to make a decision or stick to it and was willing to stand up to his superiors if necessary. This did not endear him to Churchill, who fancied himself a naval strategist and preferred admirals who agreed with him. He had found one in Admiral of the Fleet Sir Dudley Pound, his aging and ailing First Sea Lord.

Tovey knew the *Bismarck* task force could have any one of several purposes, including the transporting of military stores for northern Norway. But there were two eventualities he had to guard against. One was a raiding expedition against Iceland; it was of enormous importance that this strategic island remain in British hands. The other and most likely was an

With *Prinz Eugen* in the lead the two German ships left Bergen in the early evening of May 21. That night, British bombs fell harmlessly on the now-empty fjords.

attempt to break out into the Atlantic and prey on ocean convoys.

Early on the evening of May 21, as soon as Tovey received the report that the *Bismarck* and *Prinz Eugen* were in the Bergen fjords, he ordered aerial reconnaissance from Greenland to the Orkneys, covering the area of a potential breakout, and he dispatched additional ships to guard the two main escape routes into the Atlantic. The cruiser *Norfolk* was already patrolling the narrow Denmark Strait. Now he ordered the cruiser *Suffolk*, then in port in Iceland, to join her. The cruisers *Birmingham* and *Manchester*, patrolling the much wider Iceland-Faroes gap, were ordered to refuel immediately and return to their patrol. At the same time Tovey ordered Vice-Admiral Lancelot Holland aboard the battle cruiser *Hood* to leave Scapa Flow with the brand-new battleship *Prince of Wales* and sail for Hvalfjord, Iceland, where they could move to intercept a breakout through the Denmark Strait. The fleet remaining at Scapa was warned to be ready to sail on short notice to reinforce the patrols in the Iceland-Faroes passage. As well as *King George V*, this included the aircraft carrier *Victorious* and would soon include the battle cruiser *Repulse*. If Lütjens attempted an immediate breakout, the Home Fleet would be perfectly positioned to block him.

As night fell, the *Bismarck* left the Norwegian coast and headed north into open water. The great ship's engines throbbed quietly while the ordinary seamen went about their duties. They stood their watches—four hours on, four hours off—with half the ship's guns manned at all times. They ate their rations. They speculated on where the next weeks would take them—the Azores? South America? Most of them had never been so far from home. They were not privy to the strategic thinking of the admirals. Perhaps they wondered what it would be like to get into a real sea battle; but then, who would dare to challenge a ship such as theirs?

In his open-air position at the port midships antiaircraft emplacement, twenty-one-year-old Alois Haberditz shivered, and one of his mates offered him a cigarette. He politely refused. He was a non-smoker because he wanted to keep in good shape for the sports he loved—skiing, mountain-climbing, soccer. But even the tiny warmth of a cigarette seemed tempting at the moment. The air was cold and would get colder as they sailed north of the Arctic Circle. How much better to be stationed below or in one of the big enclosed gun turrets. Well, soon his watch would be over and he could warm up below. He pulled up the collar of his thick wool jacket and wondered when he and his friends would next have a chance to relax together and tell a few jokes. Admiral Lütjens would make an ideal target for his mimicry. Such a serious man, so haughty. He smiled as he imagined how he would have Adi, Franz and Heinz in stitches with his impression of the cold, distant fleet commander.

Admiral John Tovey, commander-in-chief of the British Home Fleet, aboard his flagship *King George V*. A quadruple turret of 14-inch guns is in the background.

Deep in the innards of the ship, Hans Zimmermann was just finishing his shift in the middle boiler room. One last time he checked the pressure gauges to make sure everything was in order. He could almost taste the beer he'd have in the canteen before going to bed. Perhaps he'd go for a brief turn on deck. What a wonderful ship the *Bismarck* was. A technical marvel. He was very proud to be part of the crew. Perhaps some day he would help design and build such ships.

In the dim lights of the captain's bridge, Ernst Lindemann sat staring unseeing into the darkness. As he'd feared, he and Admiral Lütjens were not getting along. Already they'd had several disagreements, but of course Lütjens' view always prevailed. He had determined to break out through the narrow Denmark Strait. Lindemann favored the wider and closer Iceland-Faroes passage. He could not penetrate his superior's thinking nor fathom his moods.

Dinner in the petty officers mess located in the forward section of the *Bismarck*. Visible on the back wall is a portrait of the Führer.

Just before midnight, Müllenheim-Rechberg took a last walk on deck before heading to his cabin. In the distance, over the fast-receding Norwegian coast they'd left a few hours before, he noticed yellow, white and red lights flickering over the mainland. Had he known what they meant, the sight would have chilled his heart. This was antiaircraft fire provoked by the British bombers sent at Tovey's request to attack the ships spotted earlier that day by the Spitfire. The British were on their trail.

Early the next morning, Thursday May 22, the *Bismarck* and *Prinz Eugen* bade farewell to their escort of destroyers and minesweepers. Now they were on their own. On both ships crewmen painted out the Nazi swastikas on the forecastle and the quarterdeck. These were identification for friendly aircraft, but the only planes they would see now would not be friends. All day the weather played into Lütjens' hands: haze and an overcast sky gave way to fog and then rain. With ample cloud cover and low visibility, it would be almost impossible for British planes to spot them. Nonetheless, Lütjens did not increase speed from the easy 24 knots he was keeping, despite protests from the ship's meteorologist, who warned that the favorable weather couldn't last much longer. Perhaps he was conserving fuel because of his decision to head directly for the Denmark Strait without detouring to refuel from the tanker *Weissenburg*. But each hour of delay lessened his chances of reaching his tankers stationed south of Greenland undetected.

While the *Bismarck* steamed northward toward the Norwegian Sea, Admiral Erich Raeder went to the Berghof, Hitler's mountain retreat near Berchtesgaden in southeastern Bavaria, for a naval conference with the Führer. Present at the meeting were Field-Marshal Keitel, chief of the general staff, Captain von Puttkamer, Hitler's naval aide, General Jodl, director of the planning staff, and Joachim von Ribbentrop, foreign minister of the Third Reich. Raeder gave Hitler a wide-ranging briefing on the state of the war at sea: recent U-boat successes against merchant shipping; cruiser warfare in the South Atlantic and the Indian Ocean (one cruiser had been sunk in the Indian Ocean after doing considerable damage to British shipping); the need for Italian submarines to be withdrawn from the Atlantic (Hitler promised to bring this subject up at his next meeting with the Duce). Almost casually tucked into this report was the information that the *Bismarck* and *Prinz Eugen* had left Bergen the day before on a commerce-raiding mission into the Atlantic. This was the first the Führer had heard of Exercise Rhine.

Hitler was visibly upset. What about the danger to his new battleship from British torpedo planes? He and Admiral Lütjens had discussed this very possibility only two weeks before during his visit to the ship. What about the danger of provoking the United States? The *Bismarck* might inadvertently damage an American vessel while operating so close to North America. "Herr Admiral," he asked. "Can't we fetch the ships back?"

This was exactly the question Raeder had been anticipating. He knew his leader feared the blow to his prestige should the *Bismarck* be sunk. Now he carefully explained why it would be a mistake to recall the ships. Such a move would have a terrible effect on naval morale. Months of complex planning had gone into the operation. Besides, given Lütjens' previous successes, there was every reason to expect that this mission would bring even greater glory to the Fatherland. Raeder wisely did not mention that the British had already spotted the ships off Norway and were already looking for the *Bismarck*. After a heated discussion, Hitler reluctantly agreed to let the mission proceed.

All day Thursday Admiral Tovey waited aboard *King George V* at Scapa Flow, his customary good humor stretched to the limit. Only two of the eighteen bombers sent the previous night to attack the German ships spotted in the Bergen fjords had managed to make it to their target because of bad weather. There was no way of knowing if any hits had been registered, but it seemed highly unlikely. All day today the weather over the North Sea and the coast of Norway had remained socked in, preventing high-level reconnaissance flights. He had no way of knowing whether the *Bismarck* had sailed, and if so, where. He was sorely tempted to assume that a breakout was in progress and that he should take to the seas. Any action would be preferable to this damnable waiting. But he knew the wisest policy was to stay put until he knew the enemy had committed itself.

It was not until Thursday evening that Tovey finally discovered that the birds had flown the Bergen coop. Late that afternoon, a daring low-level reconnaissance flight through fog and low-lying cloud had found the two German ships gone from the fjords where they had last been seen. At 10:45 P.M. Tovey led his fleet out of Scapa Flow. Accompanying his flagship were the aircraft carrier *Victorious*, the cruisers *Galatea, Aurora, Kenya* and *Hermione,* and seven destroyers. He ordered the *Repulse* to sail

(Top) Grand-Admiral Erich Raeder, supreme commander of the German navy during the *Bismarck* episode.

(Above) The bow of the *Prinz Eugen* plows through the waves. The swastikas on bow and stern of both ships were painted out along with the hull camouflage as they headed into the Norwegian Sea.

An aerial view of the heavy cruiser *Prinz Eugen*. Although she was smaller than the *Bismarck* her similar design and almost identical silhouette meant that from a distance she was easily confused with the larger battleship.

from the Clyde to join this force, which would take up a position from where it could support the forces covering *Bismarck*'s two possible escape routes. *Hood* and *Prince of Wales* were already lying in wait off Iceland. *Suffolk* was on her way to join *Norfolk* in the Denmark Strait, and *Arethusa* was sailing to strengthen the forces patrolling the Iceland-Faroes gap. Assuming the *Bismarck* was spotted and followed, at least two capital ships, plus various cruisers and destroyers, could quickly move to challenge her.

Before midnight on May 22 Admiral Lütjens received three encouraging radio messages from Group North. The first referred to a communication he had received earlier that day: "Assumption that breakout has not yet been detected by the enemy confirmed." The second reported that Luftwaffe aerial surveillance of Scapa Flow had revealed "four battleships, one possibly an aircraft carrier, apparently six light cruisers, several destroyers. Thus no change from 21 May and passage through the Norwegian Narrows not noticed." This was horribly inaccurate. The Luftwaffe had been fooled by one of the oldest tricks in the book. Two of the four battleships were dummies made of wood and canvas. Had Lütjens known that *Hood* and *Prince of Wales* had already been deployed, he would certainly have thought twice about proceeding with an immediate breakout.

The third message only added weight to the first two. It reported that no operational commitment of enemy ships had been noted and that, in view of the concurrent German invasion of Crete (paratroopers had already landed on the island), an early operation in the Atlantic might do serious damage to the British position. If Lütjens retained any doubt about the course of action he had decided on, this must now have been dispelled. At 11:32 P.M., not knowing that the entire British Home Fleet was now moving to intercept him, he ordered a course change to the southwest, direct for the Denmark Strait.

Winston Churchill was worried. Eleven convoys, including a troop convoy of more than 20,000 men, were about to cross the Atlantic. Massive German paratroop landings were taking place in Crete. And now he had received the news that the *Bismarck* was loose. The timing could not have been worse. It would be up to the Home Fleet to intercept the Germans before they could get out into the Atlantic shipping lanes. If not the consequences would be very serious. But at least it might offer an opportunity to draw the Americans closer to declaring war. Late on the evening of May 22 he drafted a cable to his friend President Roosevelt. In it he described the situation and enlisted his help. "Should we fail to catch them going out, your navy should surely be able to mark them down for us. Give us the news and we will finish the job."

By noon the next day, May 23, the *Bismarck* and *Prinz Eugen* were sailing due north of Iceland and were about to enter the Denmark Strait. The bad weather still concealed them—perhaps Lütjens' gamble would pay off. But the admiral and Lindemann knew this was the most perilous phase of the breakout. A British minefield stretched from the Horn of Iceland toward the Greenland coast, effectively narrowing the aperture at its narrowest point to no more than thirty or forty miles.

The German ships charged southwest through ice-infested waters at a damn-the-consequences speed of 27 knots. Then the weather began to clear. In the distance the glaciers of Greenland shimmered in the sunlight, and the men on lookout momentarily dropped their concentration to gaze at this breathtaking otherworldly beauty. Shortly after 6 P.M. alarm bells sounded. Ships had been sighted to starboard! But these turned out to be ice floes.

In the early evening the weather conditions in the narrowest part of the Denmark Strait favored the patrolling British heavy cruisers *Norfolk* and *Suffolk* under the command of Rear-Admiral Frederick Wake-Walker aboard *Norfolk*. To the north, along the icebound coast of Greenland, the water was clear and the visibility good. But to the south along the Iceland coast lay fog.

The British took full advantage of these conditions as they sailed back and forth along the route the Germans would have to take. These swift, lightly armored ships built in the 1920s—derisively nicknamed "tinclads"— would be no match for the *Bismarck* in battle, but they were well suited to shadowing. Captain Robert Ellis on the *Suffolk* was Wake-Walker's point man, since his ship's new-model radar could sweep a thirteen-mile radius except for a small sector astern. On each northeast leg of this exercise— toward the direction from which any German ships would come—*Suffolk* was out in the open, following the Greenland ice edge, while *Norfolk* lurked in the fog to the south, in case *Bismarck* attempted the risky maneuver of hugging the southern part of the channel and skirting the minefield. On each southwest leg, *Suffolk* stayed close to the fog bank,

Rear-Admiral Frederick Wake-Walker, commander of the *Norfolk* and the *Suffolk*, the two ships patrolling the Denmark Strait when the *Bismarck* was sighted.

ready to slip into its embrace the moment the enemy was sighted.

At 7:22 P.M. the *Bismarck*'s alarm bells sounded again. This time her hydrophones (a primitive underwater listening device) and radar had picked up a ship off the port bow. This was *Suffolk*, also racing on a southwest course but traveling along the edge of the fog bank. Briefly the three-stacked silhouette of the British cruiser came into sight before it plunged into the mist. There was no time to get a bearing and fire.

Able Seaman Newell at his post in the starboard after lookout of *Suffolk*, his position when he spotted the *Bismarck*.

Aboard *Suffolk*, Able Seaman Newell in the starboard after look-out was scanning his sector with his binoculars for what must have seemed like the thousandth time since he had come on watch. In these latitudes the light and ice played tricks, and sometimes the most experienced sailor could be fooled. Newell didn't want to sound a false alarm, but he didn't want to make a mistake, either. Suddenly a great black shape loomed out of the mist no more than seven miles away. "Ship bearing green one-four-o," he shouted. Then a second ship appeared, and he shouted the alarm once again.

Captain Ellis brought *Suffolk* hard over and she heeled heavily to starboard as he headed into the fog, while alarm bells rang and sailors rushed to action stations and china and cutlery clamored to the floor on the messdecks. Once safely in the fog bank, *Suffolk* slowed down and waited for the *Bismarck* and *Prinz Eugen* to pass her before taking up a position to the rear, just within radar range. At thirteen miles, this meant the *Bismarck*'s guns could reach her at any time. The cruiser was roaring along at 30 knots, virtually top speed, and the vibration was tremendous. It was all she could do to keep up with the German ships, which had increased speed. In the plotting room, the *Suffolk*'s plotting officer found it difficult to hold the ruler on the chart because of the way the ship was shaking.

Meanwhile, *Norfolk* had been alerted and was racing back through the fog to join *Suffolk*. But her captain misjudged his relative position and emerged six miles in front of the *Bismarck*, with the great gray leviathan closing fast. Before *Norfolk* could escape back into the mist, five salvoes straddled her. One shell bounced on the water and ricocheted off the captain's bridge. But only shell splinters came on board and no one was hurt.

The jolts from the firing of *Bismarck*'s big guns had put her forward radar out of action. This meant she was now blind to what lay ahead. So Admiral Lütjens ordered Captain Brinkmann aboard *Prinz Eugen* to take the lead, as the two ships raced for freedom. The admiral must have felt discouraged. His breakout had been detected, and in the radio room his intelligence officers had intercepted and decoded a stream of wireless

messages from the British ships, advertising his position. But surely the big British ships that could really threaten him were far away. Late yesterday they had still been at Scapa Flow. If only he could shake these two pesky pursuers, he could continue his mission, take on oil from a tanker south of Greenland and then lie low until things died down.

But as the four ships raced toward the open Atlantic, Lütjens gradually realized that his pursuers were relying on more than visual contact to keep track of him. Hard as he tried, he could not shake them off. Whenever he altered course, the British ships did, too. When he tried a high-speed turn to come back and surprise them, he emerged from a rain squall to find the sea empty. He didn't know it, but the problem was *Suffolk's* radar, which was far superior to anything the Germans had heard of.

Through the eerie half-light of the long Arctic spring evening the chase continued. *Suffolk* held her position astern and to starboard, *Norfolk* astern and to port. On board both the British and German ships, everyone was awake, poised and waiting for something to happen. They filled time by swilling syrupy cocoa or hot soup or coffee. And they wondered what would happen next.

Three hundred miles to the south, Vice-Admiral Lancelot Holland aboard the *Hood* had received *Norfolk's* wireless report that the *Bismarck* had been flushed. Already the *Hood* was racing on a converging course that would bring him within range early the next morning. The *Bismarck's* first battle was about to begin.

CHAPTER FIVE

First Blood

May 24, 1941—
North Atlantic Ocean

A painting of "the mighty *Hood*," the pride of the Royal Navy and the symbol of British seapower between the two world wars.

Midnight passed and the half-hearted Arctic sunset drew nearer, but still the men aboard the *Bismarck* and *Prinz Eugen* had only an inkling that they were sailing inexorably into battle. True, the British cruisers were close on their heels, but surely these worrying hounds could be shaken, and then they would be home free. It was true also that officers had monitored transmissions from enemy ships approaching the area, but which ships, and how far away were they? As far as Lütjens and Lindemann knew, their real adversaries were still hundreds of miles away, having only recently left Scapa Flow. For now the Germans seemed clearly to hold the upper hand.

Lütjens, however, was rattled by the superior British radar. He had put to sea in the most modern battleship afloat; now his state-of-the-art warhorse was being outclassed by older, inferior steeds. (Lütjens believed both *Suffolk* and *Norfolk* were equipped with this new radar and said so in a radio report to Group North.) What other surprises did the enemy have in store? Would this be the mission when his luck finally ran out? Already he had failed to escape into the Atlantic unnoticed.

Whatever his doubts, the admiral did not reveal them to his underlings. But to those around him, he seemed even more dour and withdrawn—almost as if he was resigned to whatever fate held in store. Not for the first time, Captain Lindemann must have wished he had drawn a more compatible commander for the most important voyage of his career.

The mood on board the *Hood* and *Prince of Wales* was one of high anticipation. The German ships were now less than one hundred miles away, and Admiral Holland prepared for battle. He knew that although his two capital ships outgunned the *Bismarck* and *Prinz Eugen* by a margin of eighteen big guns to eight (all on the *Bismarck*), his superiority was very fragile. The *Bismarck* was faster and better armored than either British ship. And she was more sturdily built and far better armored than the aging *Hood*, launched just after World War I.

The *Hood*'s greatest weakness was her lightly armored decks. In her day, this saving in weight had given her a greater speed than other big warships, but a plummeting shell lobbed from long distance had a good chance of penetrating to her vital innards. And while *Prince of Wales* was well armored above, she was a brand-new battleship less than three weeks out of

The 14-inch guns on the quarterdeck of the *Prince of Wales* are swung to starboard. When she took on the *Bismarck* this brand-new battleship had been in commission only two weeks and there were still civilian technicians aboard, working on the big guns.

the shipyard and still working out the kinks in her main armament. In fact, civilian crews from Vickers-Armstrong had been on board when she received orders to sail and were still working on the guns as she went into battle. In real battle conditions the likelihood of major malfunction in her heavy guns was very high. (Throughout the ensuing battle the Germans would continue to mistake her for her slightly older sister ship, the *King George V*, unable to believe so green a ship would be pressed into service.)

To make the most of the forces at his disposal, Admiral Holland hatched a daring plan. If he continued on his current course he would intercept the Germans during the darkest part of the night. But if he altered course to the north, he could intercept the *Bismarck* and *Prinz Eugen* at about 2 A.M., just after sunset in these latitudes in late May. There were two important advantages to this strategy. The *Hood* would approach the enemy ships almost head-on at high speed and so could quickly close the distance (the combined speed of the two vessels would be roughly 56 knots). This would minimize the amount of time when the enemy's shells would be most dangerous (the closer the range, the flatter the shell's trajectory). Equally important, by emerging out of darkness while the enemy was silhouetted against the still-bright sky to the north-northwest, there was the possibility of surprise. The *Hood* and *Prince of Wales* would take on the *Bismarck* while the *Norfolk* and *Suffolk* engaged the *Prinz Eugen*. Even if the Germans were not caught napping, it was a brilliant plan that gave the attackers every possible advantage, but at the price of exposing the onrushing British ships to the full main battery of the *Bismarck* while only able to return the fire with their forward turrets. But

everything depended on the *Bismarck*'s shadowers keeping her on their radar and being able to mirror every change in course and speed.

At 12:15 A.M. Admiral Holland sent out the long-awaited signal: "Prepare for action." Aboard *Hood*, *Prince of Wales* and their escorting destroyers, the big white battle ensigns were raised. Most of the British sailors were going into action for the first time. But they would have to wait somewhat longer. Around midnight the *Bismarck* had disappeared into a snow squall, and the *Suffolk* and *Norfolk* lost contact. Suddenly Admiral Holland's bold plan was in jeopardy.

Because the coast of Greenland prevented the *Bismarck* from turning farther to the west, Holland knew there were three possibilities: the Germans might continue on the current southwest course, they might turn south, or they might double back for the Denmark Strait. It seemed most likely that Lütjens would head south, toward the open Atlantic. On this assumption, Holland turned north and reduced speed. If he was right, he might still surprise the Germans with a head-on approach. If he was wrong, he was still keeping them in range. Meanwhile, he sent his destroyers to continue on the intercept course.

In fact, the *Bismarck* and *Prinz Eugen* had turned slightly to the west to follow the edge of the Greenland ice pack. As a result, Holland's destroyers passed within ten miles of the Germans without spotting them. *Suffolk* finally regained contact at 2:47 A.M., and *Hood* and *Prince of Wales* immediately altered course to intercept and increased their speed. But now the *Bismarck* and the *Hood* were steaming on almost parallel south-

(Top) Framed by the big guns of another ship, the *Hood* sits peacefully at Scapa Flow, home base of the British Home Fleet.

(Above) Vice-Admiral Lancelot Holland, commander of the force that included HMS *Hood*.

westerly courses roughly thirty-five miles apart, with the British to the south of the Germans. Instead of a favorable high-speed, head-on approach, Holland was forced to close with the enemy slowly and from the beam. His other options were too risky. If he tried to outrace the *Bismarck* and *Prinz Eugen*, then come round to meet them head-on, he could lose them altogether. The next time *Suffolk* lost contact might be the last. It now appeared the battle would finally be joined just after dawn.

Most of the men aboard the *Bismarck* and *Prinz Eugen* knew the name of the *Hood*, the bogeyman of their battle practices. But only a few of the more experienced sailors had caught a glimpse of her between the wars, when she came to represent British sea power in every corner of the globe. Until the beginning of World War II, the *Hood* had never fired a gun in battle; her power had been implied, not realized.

This photo taken from the *Prince of Wales* is the last existing image of HMS *Hood*.

Throughout the pale night Lütjens tried to elude his pursuers. He altered course, hid in squalls and snowstorms, even tried making a feint toward them. But each time he thought he had succeeded, there were the *Suffolk* and *Norfolk* on his tail. He was becoming frustrated and increasingly gloomy. How long could it be before other British ships appeared?

Like the rest of the crew on board the *Bismarck*, Burkard von Müllenheim-Rechberg spent half the night on watch, half trying to sleep in his cabin. But the four hours between watches wasn't enough time to rest properly. Besides, who could sleep soundly while their ship was racing with the enemy and some sort of action seemed only a matter of time? His duty station was in the dimly lit after fire control position. Time passed very slowly. Through the stereoscopic rangefinders, which worked quite well at night, he could occasionally catch a glimpse of the British pursuers.

As the Arctic night waned, the sailors on *Hood* and *Prince of Wales*, who had already spent hours at their battle stations, were tense and exhausted, kept going only by adrenalin. They had already ridden an emotional roller coaster. Action was imminent, then delayed. Now they were about to go over the top again. In all, 7,000 officers and men on four great ships were racing toward a fateful meeting.

The captain of the *Prince of Wales*, John Leach, sat in his chair on the dimly lit compass platform and worried. Would his untried crew come through? Would there be effective fire from his balky big guns? He already knew that one of his forward 14-inch guns had proved defective and would likely be good for only a single salvo. How long would the other nine last?

Captain Leach was not the only man on board who was contemplating what was to come. Lieutenant Esmond Knight, Royal Naval Volunteer Reserve, in civilian life an actor and avid birdwatcher, sat in the unarmored antiaircraft fire control. He was bundled against the cold—several sweaters and a warm scarf plus lifebelt—and he wore his tin hat atop the antiflash hood designed to protect him from the effects of a blast. Yet again he peered through his German-made Zeiss binoculars, a souvenir of a prewar vacation in Austria. Whatever bit part he played in the coming events, it would be seen by few, applauded by none. It was simply a matter of duty. And quite likely of dying.

As the day brightened, on the bridge of the *Hood* all was business. Signalman Ted Briggs, acting as flag lieutenant's messenger, found it all a bit unreal. They were about to go into battle, for God's sake, but the officers behaved as if it was just another war game. There was Admiral Holland, lounging in the captain's chair in front of the compass binnacle, the picture of self-repose. This was where he had chosen to direct the action, rather than from the admiral's bridge one deck below. Behind him stood Captain Phillips, conning the ship according to the admiral's verbal orders. Briggs watched and listened as the officers gave commands and received reports, trying to detect the excitement that he knew lay just under the surface of their professional calm.

Just after 5 A.M., Holland turned to the flag lieutenant next to him and gave the order: "Signal instant readiness for action." The lieutenant walked back to where Briggs was standing at the rear of the bridge and repeated the command. Briggs promptly turned and shouted down the voice pipe: "Instant readiness for action." Moments later, the *Hood* flashed the message to the *Prince of Wales*.

Captain Lindemann nodded gravely as he read the message from Captain Brinkmann: shortly after 5 A.M., the *Prinz Eugen*'s hydrophones had picked up the sound of high-speed propellers. It seemed that more British ships were about to arrive on the scene. What would Admiral Lütjens do? Lindemann asked himself. Would he try to outrun the enemy, or would he turn and fight? As the alarm bells indicating general quarters sounded through the *Bismarck*, Lindemann walked to the port wing of the captain's bridge and stared at the southern horizon. After a few minutes, dark smudges of smoke appeared—a sure indication of big ships making top speed. Then, at about 5:45, mast tips came into view and began to grow rapidly into the unmistakable forms of warships. But what ships were these? And where had they come from so quickly?

From the bridge of the *Hood*, the dark shapes of the German ships could now be seen on the horizon. The weather was calm, but there was a fair swell. To Signalman Ted Briggs, the *Bismarck* "was a very black and sinister-looking effort," but it is unlikely he knew which of the two ships was in fact the battleship. Because of the similarity of their silhouettes, it was almost impossible to tell German ships apart from such a distance. Admiral Holland himself was temporarily fooled, assuming the lead ship, *Prinz Eugen*, was his primary target.

At 5:44 the enemy was fourteen miles away. On their present slowly converging course, the lightly armored decks of the *Hood* would remain exposed for far too long. So Holland ordered a sharp turn to the west,

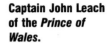

Captain John Leach of the *Prince of Wales*.

toward the Germans. This meant he would close more quickly, but neither he nor *Prince of Wales* would be able to use their after turrets on the enemy. The number of heavy guns he could bring to bear would thus be reduced from eighteen to ten. The First Sea Lord, Sir Dudley Pound, later described this as "going into battle with one hand when you have two." But Holland felt he had no choice. At 5:49 he signaled Captain Leach to concentrate fire on the lead ship, which he still believed was the *Bismarck*.

Just forward of turrets Caesar and Dora, in the *Bismarck*'s after fire control station, Müllenheim-Rechberg watched and listened intently as the enemy ships came into view. Through the port director, a periscope-like device that peeked above the armored roof of the control station, he watched the *Suffolk* and *Norfolk* to see if they would make a move to launch torpedoes. Through the telephone headset clapped over his ears he could hear the *Bismarck*'s officers issuing orders and exchanging information. It was like being on a party line, but this was no party. He listened as Adalbert Schneider, the first gunnery officer and, next to the captain, the most respected officer on the ship, commented on the approaching enemy. From his higher station in the foretop fire control, Schneider had a better view. He agreed that the enemy ships looked like cruisers, as everyone had first supposed.

Such questions became academic when the British opened fire at 5:52 A.M. The sky above was overcast but the rising sun lit the horizon. From the size of the flashes followed by great clouds of dark-brown cordite smoke, it was obvious to any gunnery officer that the adversaries were indeed capital ships. But why didn't Lütjens respond? Was he hoping to outrun them? As the first salvoes from the enemy arced across the thirteen-mile gap, the gunnery crews aboard the *Bismarck* and *Prinz Eugen* waited in a kind of suspended animation for permission to fire.

"The *Hood*—it's the *Hood*!" Müllenheim-Rechberg heard one of the officers shout. But still Lindemann did not give the order. Admiral Lütjens was hesitating.

"Enemy bearing two-ten-o. Distance 20 kilometers." Schneider's voice was still calm, confident.

The first salvo from the *Hood* fell harmlessly astern of the *Prinz Eugen*, throwing up great geysers of water close to the ship. But Captain Leach aboard *Prince of Wales* had realized their mistake before Admiral Holland, and without awaiting permission, opened fire on the *Bismarck*. The *Hood* and *Prince of Wales*, in close formation, were closing rapidly.

"I will not let my ship be shot out from under my ass," Lindemann was heard to mutter.

Still the admiral waited.

Finally, with tension among the gunnery officers and crews about to explode, the order came.

"Permission to fire!"

At his position in the after gunnery computer room, Heinz Jucknat also heard the conversations of the gunnery officers through his headphones, held his breath in anticipation for the order to fire, felt relief when Lindemann finally spoke the words. All the while, he, Adolf Eich and Franz Halke feverishly computed the variables that determined the

A *Bismarck* crewman in his lifejacket mans a communications telephone.

gunners' aim: wind speed, air temperature, ship speed, distance and bearing of the enemy. The information poured in from the fire control stations, but their minds were half on the task at hand, half on events they couldn't see. Even deep within the heavily armored "citadel" of the *Bismarck*'s middle platform deck, they could hear and feel that first salvo as the eight 15-inch guns fired in close succession. There was a distant rumble and an accompanying vibration, something like an earthquake.

"Short," muttered Schneider. Adjusting the angle and bearing of the guns, he ordered another salvo. "Long."

Even deeper inside the *Bismarck* the battle was also being waged. Hans Zimmermann in the after middle boiler room was just as important to the ship's success as were the gunners. During the tense pause before the order to fire was finally given, Zimmermann and his workmates joked nervously that the admiral was playing war games more suited to their

(Below and bottom) A *Bismarck* salvo viewed from two different angles during the battle with the *Hood*. The battleship is moving at high speed as the large bow wave and thin stream of smoke from her funnel in the topmost photograph attest.

exercises in the Baltic. But once the guns began firing, it was all business. He and his colleagues kept a constant eye on the oil and water supply for their two boilers. It was essential the ship have maximum steam—power and maneuverability—for the battle. As he checked his feed lines and pressure gauges, Zimmerman felt the vibration of the guns, wondered how well the gunners had aimed, and noticed as he had during sea trials how the whole ship plunged with the recoil from the force of a full salvo.

For those on the bridge, in the fire control stations or, worst of all, in the turrets themselves, each salvo was a bone-rattling, mind-numbing experience—something like being next to a bomb going off. The roar was deafening, the sudden increase in air pressure made it almost impossible to breathe, and the thick cordite smoke choked and blinded. Unlike most modern forms of warfare, where the senior officers are far from the sting of battle, on board a battleship admirals and captains are more exposed than most of the ordinary sailors—and their positions are extremely vulnerable to an enemy hit.

The battle, but a few minutes old, was going poorly for Admiral Holland. Because he continued to keep his two ships in close formation, they presented a single target for the German gunners who were rapidly homing in. He had realized after his first salvo that he was concentrating his fire on the wrong ship, while both German vessels were blasting away at him for all they were worth. But it took his inexperienced gun crews inordinately long to switch fire. Meanwhile the *Prince of Wales* kept firing; her seventh salvo straddled the *Bismarck*.

The first German salvo had fallen just ahead of the *Hood*. The second fell just astern, and the splashes from the plunging shells blinded the for-

Turrets Caesar and Dora fire on *Prince of Wales*.

ward rangefinders on the *Prince of Wales*, which followed close behind. Then a shell from *Prinz Eugen*'s second salvo exploded at the base of the *Hood*'s mainmast, touching off UP projectiles stored there. These 3-inch rockets loaded with cordite propellant started a spectacular fire that soon spread to nearby ammunition. As the fire continued to blaze, a blue pendant shot out the *Hood*'s yardarm, signaling a 20 degree turn to port. Holland had decided he could wait no longer to bring all his heavy guns to bear.

On the *Bismarck*, Adalbert Schneider's men, helped by the fire on the *Hood*, had found their range with their third salvo, which straddled. The fourth proved deadly accurate. As the *Hood* was still turning to port, one or more shells from this barrage—no one will ever know for sure—hit the pride of the British navy forward of her after turrets, pierced her thin deck armor and exploded somewhere inside the ship, probably in the 4-inch magazine that then set off the 15-inch ammunition stored nearby. What followed was horrifying to friend and foe alike.

In the *Bismarck*'s after fire control position, Müllenheim-Rechberg still kept watch out the starboard director—away from where the battle was taking place—in case the *Norfolk* and *Suffolk* attacked from that quarter. (It is one of the puzzles of this famous battle that Admiral Holland failed to communicate his intentions to Admiral Wake-Walker on the *Norfolk*, who therefore never ordered his two ships to engage the enemy and simply watched the horrible events from a distance.) Müllenheim-Rechberg thus missed seeing the fire on the *Hood* after the first hit, or the fireball that followed the hit from the *Bismarck*'s fourth salvo. But he knew something big was happening when Schneider's even, emotionless voice intoning range and direction corrections suddenly blurted out, "My God, was that a misfire? That really ate into him." Schneider's voice was abruptly lost in an excited crescendo as other eyewitnesses involuntarily voiced their astonishment at what was happening to the enemy ship. Müllenheim-Rechberg could stand it no longer. He turned his position over to a petty officer and rushed over to the port director. Before he could train it on the *Hood*, he heard an astonished shout: "She's blowing up!" The young

officer would never forget the sight that now met his eyes:

"At first the *Hood* was nowhere to be seen; in her place was a colossal pillar of black smoke reaching into the sky. Gradually, at the foot of the pillar I made out the bow of the battle cruiser projecting upwards at an angle, a sure sign that she had broken in two. Then I saw something I could hardly believe: a flash of orange coming from her forward guns! Although her fighting days had ended, the *Hood* was firing a last salvo."

On the bridge of the *Hood*, Signalman Ted Briggs didn't hear an explosion (a number of witnesses said the *Hood* blew up without a sound), but suddenly a sheet of flame shot around the front of the compass binnacle a few feet away, and he was thrown off his feet. As he and the others on the bridge scrambled to regain their footing, the ship leaned sharply to starboard, then righted herself momentarily before listing even more heavily to port. Meanwhile the quartermaster reported that the steering had gone, and the captain calmly ordered emergency steering, a command by then impossible to execute. There was no time to order abandon ship; the ship was abandoning them. As he headed for the starboard exit from the bridge, Briggs noted that Admiral Holland was making no move to leave his position. Briggs himself had just started down the ladder when the water swallowed him and he was dragged under. He swam frantically to get away from the plunging superstructure, felt himself being sucked down and down, had virtually given up when suddenly he seemed to shoot to the surface. Although he'd gone over the starboard side, he came up on port. Fifty yards away from him, the bow of the ship was poised vertically in the water. Then he turned and swam for dear life.

(Above) Behind the *Prince Wales*, the *Hood*'s bow juts upwards from the force of the explosion in her magazine.

(Overleaf) A dense column of black smoke rises from the sinking *Hood* as the *Prince of Wales* alters course to dodge the wreckage.

He didn't see her sink.

Able Seaman R.E. Tilburn was at his antiaircraft position on the *Hood*'s boat deck when the *Bismarck*'s fatal salvo hit. A shell tore through the deck beside him, turning his neat and ordered world into a maelstrom of twisted steel and flying splinters. Hardly had he managed to get back on his feet than he was engulfed in a cloud of dense black smoke and then blasted by a furnace of flame. There was nothing to do but make for the icy water. As he tore off his gas mask and tin hat, he saw an ammunition locker flying in his direction and jumped just in time to avoid it. As he fought the sinking ship's suction, one of the radio aerials lassoed his boots. He managed to get out his pocketknife and cut his feet free. When he surfaced, the *Hood* was gone.

Midshipman W. J. Dundas had the most amazing escape of all. From his position in the spotting top, the highest manned point on the ship, he was literally washed through one of its windows and into the sea as the *Hood* sank.

On the British and German ships, regardless of their rank or experience at sea, the few men who saw the last moments of the *Hood* were transfixed and would take the scalding images to their grave. First a huge pillar of flame shot up toward the sky, followed by a mushroom cloud of smoke. Then pieces of the ship were visible sailing through the air. (That final salvo observed by Müllenheim-Rechberg was probably involuntary, the last gasp of the legendary ship as circuits closed by themselves.) Captain Brinkmann aboard *Prinz Eugen* saw shells exploding like fireworks in the midst of the billowing smoke, showering white stars. It reminded him of a celebration for the Führer's birthday.

Accounts differ, but none is more graphic than that of Esmond Knight aboard the *Prince of Wales*, who had a ringside view from his antiaircraft fire control station: "There had been a rushing sound which had ominously ceased, and then, as I looked a great spouting explosion issued from the centre of the *Hood*, enormous reaching tongues of pale-red flame shot into the air, while dense clouds of whitish-yellow smoke burst upwards, gigantic pieces of brightly burning debris being hurled hundreds of feet in the air. I just did not believe what I saw—*Hood* had literally been blown to pieces." From the *Hood*'s opening salvo, the battle had lasted just six minutes.

Having split in two, the stern and bow sections of the mighty *Hood* momentarily pointed vertically in the air before disappearing beneath the waves. Captain Leach aboard the *Prince of Wales* had to do some fancy maneuvering to dodge the *Hood*'s wreckage, and in doing so put himself directly in the sights of the *Bismarck*'s guns. But Leach's gunners had found their range also. As his ship charged toward the Germans, his eighth or ninth salvo found the mark. But there was no time to savor this minor triumph. A shell from the *Bismarck*'s next blast bowled through the captain's bridge, killing everyone save Leach, his chief yeoman of signals and his navigating officer, who was wounded. Because the shell did not explode, few people on board were immediately aware of this catastrophe. Even one deck below in the plotting room, no one realized anything was amiss until blood dripped onto the chart from the voicepipe that commu-

Lieutenant Esmond Knight was temporarily blinded by the shell that hit the bridge of the *Prince of Wales*.

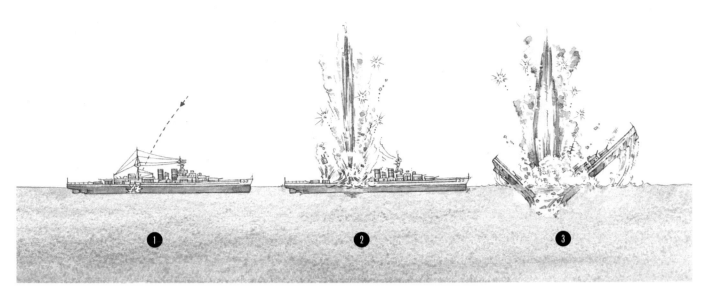

nicated with the bridge.

Esmond Knight fell victim to the debris sent flying by the shell that mauled the bridge. He remembered hearing "a great rushing noise, like the approach of a cyclone, and having quite an irrelevant dream about listening to the band in Hyde Park, and then being conscious of a high ringing noise in my head and slowly coming to." When he regained consciousness he could hear voices but could see nothing. "Stretcher bearer!" someone shouted. "Clear the way there!" The "horrible smell of blood" filled his nostrils as dead bodies were lifted off him and he was helped down to sick bay. A shell splinter had blinded him. (He did recover his sight and resumed his acting career after the war, appearing in a minor role in the movie *Sink the Bismarck!*)

Seeming undaunted, the *Prince of Wales* soldiered on into the withering fire from the *Bismarck* and *Prinz Eugen*. But she suffered more and more hits—seven in all—while her own guns, still going through teething pains, malfunctioned. Never did she have all ten working at once. First the forward turret jammed and was unable to function, causing Captain Leach to choose discretion over suicide and turn his ship away, laying down smoke to camouflage his retreat. As he did so, his after turret jammed, leaving only one of his ten guns in action. He had lost eleven men, nine were wounded, and his ship was in bad shape. There was damage topside and flooding where shells had hit aft, one along the waterline, another just below the waterline near one of the boiler rooms.

On the bridge of the *Bismarck*, Captain Lindemann could barely contain his rage. But his long years of service overcame his urge to throttle Lütjens, admiral or not. As soon as *Prince of Wales* had turned away, the fleet commander had ordered his two ships to cease firing. He was allowing the wounded British battleship to get away rather than closing in for the kill. Lindemann protested in vain, his anger straitjacketed in formal military tones. Every fiber in the captain's being told him to give chase. This was what he had been trained for all his life. But Lütjens was unmoved. His orders were to engage British capital ships only if unavoid-

(Above) The three stages of the destruction of the *Hood*:
1) A 15-inch shell from the *Bismarck* penetrates the lightly-armored deck and ignites an ammunition magazine.
2) An exploding fireball erupts from the ship and a pillar of fire shoots into the sky.
3) The ship breaks in two and quickly sinks.

able. His mission was to raid commercial shipping, not get into pitched sea battles. Besides, the *Bismarck* herself was wounded, and that had to be his primary concern.

In the din of battle only a few on board the German battleship realized she had been damaged. Hans Zimmermann and his mates in the after middle boiler room felt the impact when one shell from the *Prince of Wales* hit beneath the armored belt, penetrating to the torpedo bulkhead where it exploded. This caused flooding in the forward generator room on the port side and some slow seepage of water into the forward port boiler room. (The port boiler room was subsequently shut down as a precautionary measure, reducing the ship's maximum speed to about 28 knots.) Soon damage reports reached the bridge, and with each report Admiral Lütjens grew gloomier and gloomier.

Most serious was the hit forward, where a shell had passed clean through the ship. The holes in the hull were just above the waterline but not above the wave thrown up by the bow, and water was pouring in. The shell had damaged the main transverse bulkheads separating these adjacent compartments, and both began to flood rapidly. By the time *Bismarck* ceased firing, a thousand tons of seawater had flowed into the ship, putting considerable pressure on the bulkhead separating compartment 20 from 21, which had to be shored up. The holes in the bow were patched with collision mats, which inhibited but did not stop the flow of water. Because of the flooding, the *Bismarck* was down at the bow and listing to port, at times lifting the starboard propeller partly out of the water. To correct the trim, two ballast tanks were flooded aft. But when Lindemann suggested reducing speed and temporarily heeling the ship so that the holes could be patched properly, the admiral flatly refused. He didn't want to risk any delay.

But there was nothing the damage control teams could do about the main problem: the flooding and other damage had cut off access to the forward fuel tanks containing one thousand tons of fuel. Suddenly Lütjens' decision not to refuel at Bergen loomed ominously large.

The *Prinz Eugen*, with her much thinner armor, had escaped almost untouched—nothing short of a miracle. Virtually the only evidence that she had been in a battle was a large shell splinter—a remnant of the *Prince of Wales'* first salvo—that had landed on her deck near the funnel. On neither German ship had there been a single casualty.

When the damage control teams had completed their work, the German battleship was handicapped but still formidable. Her top speed was reduced to 28 knots, she was still taking in water, and her available fuel was seriously reduced, but enough remained to get her to ports more than one thousand miles away. The damage to her electric plant cut her reserve capacity in half, but she was still able to operate with full electrical power. Seawater in the electrical plant threatened to seep into the other two forward boiler rooms, further reducing her top speed. She was also trailing oil in her wake, which would make her easier for aerial reconnaissance to spot and also reveal to enemy eyes that she had been damaged. But all her artillery was intact. Her gunnery had proved extremely accurate, and the crew had performed with the greatest of skill.

**The *Bismarck*
shows the effects of
her battle wounds:
she is seriously
down by the bow.**

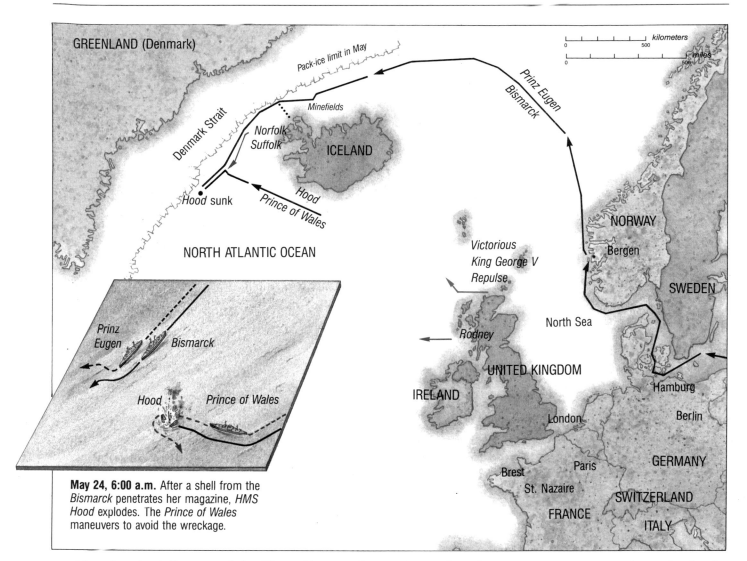

GREENLAND (Denmark)

Pack-ice limit in May

Prinz Eugen
Bismarck

Denmark Strait

Minefields

Norfolk
Suffolk

ICELAND

Hood sunk

Hood

Prince of Wales

NORTH ATLANTIC OCEAN

NORWAY
Bergen

SWEDEN

Victorious
King George V
Repulse

North Sea

Rodney

Hamburg

UNITED KINGDOM

Berlin

IRELAND

London

GERMANY

Brest
St. Nazaire

Paris

FRANCE

SWITZERLAND

ITALY

Prinz
Eugen

Bismarck

Hood

Prince of Wales

May 24, 6:00 a.m. After a shell from the *Bismarck* penetrates her magazine, *HMS Hood* explodes. The *Prince of Wales* maneuvers to avoid the wreckage.

A map showing the route from Bergen to the Denmark Strait with an inset showing the disposition of the two British and two German ships during the sinking of the *Hood*.

Now that the full extent of the *Bismarck's* wounds was clear, Admiral Lütjens was faced with a tough decision. Immediately following the battle he'd elected to steer a course toward St. Nazaire, France. For now, commerce-raiding was out of the question. The damage was too serious to be repaired at sea, but if he could get to France, future operations would be much easier. His fuel reserves were seriously reduced—just how much was not yet clear. Should he turn back toward the Denmark Strait, or make a run eastward through the Iceland-Faroes gap? Either way he would likely be met by more British ships, which he could now safely assume were already gathering like pack wolves for the kill. The open sea offered more room to maneuver and more chances of escape than the shorter, narrower route back to Norway. As he moved south, the nights would become longer, providing more chance for evasive maneuvers. If he could shake his shadow, perhaps he could still link up with one of his tankers, then lie low until the British were forced to leave the field to refuel. He decided to continue for France. Had he known where the British ships actually were, he would undoubtedly have changed his mind.

Among the bits of wreckage and the film of fuel oil where the *Hood* had gone down, three men still clung to life—three men out of the ship's company of 1,419. After their ship sank they each managed to climb into one of three small life rafts that had floated free of the wreck. For a time they grappled together, cheering each other with talk of imminent rescue. But cold and fatigue finally forced them to let slip their grasps. Soon they lay slumped in a kind of numb half-sleep, drifting toward hypothermia as their rafts floated aimlessly in the swells.

Two hours after the battle, the destroyers that had been left behind by the *Hood*'s dawn charge finally arrived on the scene. When HMS *Electra* spotted the three lonely rafts, one of the officers on board, Lieutenant-Commander J.T. Cain, wondered where the rest of the survivors could be: "Where were the boats, the rafts, the floats. And the men, *where* were the men? I thought of how we'd last seen *Hood*; I thought of her impressive company. Like a small army they'd looked, as they mustered for divisions. Then I thought of my words to Doc. 'We'll need everyone we've got to help the poor devils on board.' " The very fortunate poor devils were Signalman Briggs, Able Seaman Tilburn and Midshipman Dundas.

It had not been a good week for British sea power. Four destroyers and two cruisers had been sunk in the Mediterranean as the Royal Navy tried to prevent the Germans from consolidating their beachheads on the island of Crete. And May had been another terrible month for mercantile shipping: 511,042 tons in all went down. But the loss of the *Hood* was the worst blow imaginable, for it was psychological.

It is difficult for anyone not living in Britain then to comprehend the impact of this event on British pride and morale. It was as much of a shock and humiliation as the Japanese attack on Pearl Harbor would be to Americans seven months later. In his book *Pursuit*, Ludovic Kennedy, at sea on a British destroyer at the time, pulls no punches: "For most Englishmen the news of the *Hood*'s death was traumatic, as though Buckingham Palace had been laid flat or the Prime Minister assassinated, so integral a part was she of the fabric of Britain and her empire. Admiral Wake-Walker, announcing the tragedy to the Admiralty and the world with his laconic signal '*Hood* has blown up,' felt compelled to classify it 'Secret,' as though somehow this might prevent the dreadful news reaching Hitler. Many people simply did not believe it."

The news reached Winston Churchill at Chequers, the country home of British prime ministers. Among his houseguests was Averell Harriman, then American ambassador to the United Kingdom. Churchill was awakened at 7 A.M. Saturday morning with the awful news. He got up, went to the end of the corridor where Harriman was staying and told him, "The *Hood* has blown up, but we have got the *Bismarck* for certain." This was a typical bit of Churchillian bravado, for he was anything but confident of the outcome. All day Saturday he buried himself in paperwork, but the German battleship was never far from his mind. "Only one scene riveted my background thoughts," Churchill later wrote, "this tremendous *Bismarck*, forty-five thousand tons, perhaps almost invulnerable to gunfire, rushing southward toward our convoys, with the *Prinz Eugen* as her scout. As long as we held fast to the *Bismarck* we could dog her to her doom. But what if we lost touch in the night? Which way would she go? She had a wide choice, and we were vulnerable almost everywhere."

Able Seaman R. E. Tilburn after the sinking of the *Hood* and his rescue from the North Atlantic.

Signalman Ted Briggs, another of the three *Hood* survivors.

The news of the *Hood*'s sinking reached Churchill considerably sooner than it reached the German leader (Lütjens' first two radio signals never made it to Berlin). Late on Saturday Admiral Raeder phoned Hitler and told him what had happened. The news was a tonic for the ever-anxious Führer. He was elated and praised the navy to the skies. This was a great victory for the Reich, which Dr. Goebbels and his propaganda machine could exploit to maximum effect. Raeder wisely didn't report to Hitler the damage to the *Bismarck* and his concern about Lütjens' decision to steer for France, which he judged risky. Raeder even considered issuing a recall order that would have forced Lütjens to head immediately for Norway. But finally he decided to let the man on the scene make the decision.

The general euphoria aboard the *Bismarck* and *Prinz Eugen* at their spectacular victory soon gave way to a more sober mood. The flagship was damaged and they were still being shadowed by the *Suffolk* and *Norfolk*, now joined by the damaged and temporarily gun-less *Prince of Wales* (the technicians had nine guns back in working order by 7 A.M.). They had seen what had happened to the *Hood*, and knew it was a graphic demonstration of the fate that could be in store for them.

The ship's company of HMS *Hood* in Malta in 1939. Out of over 1400 officers and men only three were saved (two are shown opposite.)

Meanwhile, Admiral Lütjens was left to make the next moves, the moves that would constitute the middle game of this chess match on the high seas. If he retained any faith in German intelligence, it must have been dashed by the unexpected apparition of his attackers that morning. Perhaps other ships were just over the horizon, ready to pounce. If only he could elude that infernal British radar. But it seemed hopeless.

Four hundred miles away, Admiral Tovey also contemplated his next play. The Admiralty had already begun to place new pieces on the board, detaching battleships and cruisers from patrol or convoy duty and sending them to join the chase. But the nearest of these were still much farther away than his own fleet, which consisted of the battle cruiser *Repulse*, the aircraft carrier *Victorious*, his flagship *King George V*, four cruisers and nine destroyers. This force was more than a match for the two German ships, but first they had to be caught. This presented Tovey with a problem; he still didn't know which way the Germans would go.

At last report Admiral Wake-Walker was in close pursuit as the *Bismarck* and *Prinz Eugen* continued to sail at top speed southwestward along the edge of the Greenland pack ice. Was a tanker waiting for them somewhere southwest of Greenland? Perhaps they would head back to Germany as soon as the opportunity presented itself. Most likely they would make for France. But he could assume none of these possibilities, and had to allow for all of them. He could only hope that the *Bismarck* would not lose her shadowers before he could bring his own force to meet her.

CHAPTER SIX

The Chase

Saturday May 24, 1941—
North Atlantic

After the sinking of the *Hood*, the *King George V*, the carrier *Victorious* and the *Repulse* (in background) pursue the *Bismarck*.

As the morning wore on, the stalemate continued. Each move made by the Germans was immediately countered by the British shadowers. Toward noon the weather got worse—rising winds and seas accompanied by frequent squalls interspersed with haze and the occasional fog bank—so that visibility seesawed from as much as seventeen to as little as two miles. But still Lütjens could not shake the three ships that dogged his tracks. Despite this situation, morale aboard *Bismarck* and *Prinz Eugen* remained high. After all, that morning they had sunk the mighty *Hood*, escaping with minor damage and without the loss of a single man. The *Bismarck* was still making good speed—27 to 28 knots, but laboring with a heavy bow trim and a slight list to port (both problems were gradually corrected by counterflooding). There was talk that the admiral planned to lure the British into an ambush of U-boats waiting just south of Greenland.

In the warmth and comfort of the heated and enclosed admiral's bridge, the mood was not nearly so upbeat. There seemed to be problems with the ship's radio—Lütjens had received no answers from Group North to his repeated messages of the last several hours. He had reported the victory over the *Hood* and had indicated his intention to part company with the *Prinz Eugen* and then head for France and the dry-

HMS *Rodney* battles heavy seas as she races to intercept the *Bismarck*.

docks of St. Nazaire that could handle his repairs. At noon, as he passed south of 60 degrees north, the line of latitude that touches the tip of Southern Greenland and the Northern Hebrides, operational control of his mission would switch from Group North in Wilhelmshaven to Group West in Paris, but would he be able to keep Paris informed? His concern increased when he discovered that over the previous two days *Prinz Eugen* had received a number of important radio messages from Group North that he had not. These communication problems only reinforced his pessimism. First the British radar, now his radio.

More serious was the fuel situation. He was still waiting for a final report from his chief engineering officer, but he expected it to be bad. Best to hedge his bets, to slow down and adopt a compromise course until he knew the worst. Shortly after 12:30 P.M., Lütjens ordered a reduction in speed to 24 knots and a course change to the south.

Five hundred miles to the southeast, the *Nelson* class battleship *Rodney*, with four destroyers, was escorting the troop ship *Britannic* to Halifax. From there *Rodney* would continue to Boston for a long overdue refit. On board were an additional 500 passengers, most of them draftees for the Falklands and naval cadets for Bermuda. But among them were several American officers, including thirty-eight-year-old Lieutenant-Commander Joseph H. Wellings. For the past ten months Wellings had been observing operations and tactics of the British Home Fleet, gaining information of considerable value to the U.S. Navy if it entered the war. His tour had included a stint on a destroyer in the North Atlantic. (In a report to Washington, he'd written, "Out of five days in the general area of Iceland there were only about five hours in which visibility was as much as five miles. I can now see how the German ships get through.")

Now he was on his way home, eager for a reunion with Dolly, his wife of four years, and their daughter, Anne, whose third birthday had just passed. Only one day out from Scotland, the trip was already beginning to seem interminable.

Wellings' thoughts of home faded, however, when the *Rodney* received the news that the *Bismarck* and *Prinz Eugen* had been spotted in the Denmark Strait. They receded entirely when news of the *Hood*'s sinking arrived over the ship's wireless. All morning on the 24th he read the *Rodney's* incoming radio signals with Lieutenant-Commander Gaffney Gatacre, the ship's navigator. From the radio messages they pieced together the movements of the Home Fleet and speculated on the likelihood of *Rodney* getting in on the fun.

Then, just before noon, they read the signal they had been waiting for. It was from the Admiralty to *Rodney*: "Enemy's position 62, 25' N., 33, 00' W., course 210, speed 26 at 0900/24. Steer best closing course. If *Britannic* can't keep up let her proceed alone with one destroyer." Around 2 P.M., the battleship and three destroyers headed north at full speed. As *Rodney's* engines strained, and her battered hull plates rattled with the vibrations, Wellings tried to imagine what it would be like to face the fearsome new German battleship.

Similar thoughts were in the minds of British sailors on other ships even more distant from the scene, who received orders from the Admiralty to join the chase. The battleships included the *Revenge*, in Halifax, and the *Ramillies*, on convoy escort to the south. Also called were the cruisers *Edinburgh*, patrolling near the Azores, and *London*, escorting another convoy. Finally, and most important, was Force H, which had already left Gibraltar and moved into the Bay of Biscay to cover a troop convoy. Force H, consisting of the carrier *Ark Royal*, the battle cruiser *Renown* and the cruiser *Sheffield*, along with six destroyers, could have been of great use in the Mediterranean, where Crete was falling and Malta was hard pressed. The *Bismarck*'s breakout overrode those concerns.

Aboard *King George V*, the commander in chief of the Home Fleet knew his job was to bring the *Bismarck* to account any way he could. Although Admiral Tovey had received reports that the *Bismarck* was trailing oil, he had to assume the damage was not serious. He interpreted her change of course to the south and reduction in speed to 24 knots as evidence Lütjens was unaware that a powerful British force was moving to intercept. But he worried that at any time the Germans might put on a burst of speed, shake their shadow and disappear into the void of the mid-Atlantic. However risky, he felt he had to try to slow her down.

The only weapon at hand that was capable of accomplishing this goal was the aircraft carrier *Victorious*. But so human a commander as Tovey, a deeply religious man, must have held grave doubts about using this newly commissioned ship and her untested crew in such a dangerous fashion. Had Exercise Rhine not intervened, the carrier would now be on her way to Gibraltar with a load of crated Hurricane fighters. She had only fifteen operational aircraft on board—nine three-seater Swordfish torpedo bombers and six two-seater Fulmar fighters. Most of the aircrews had never flown at sea, were still learning the ropes. Now, on their first

At the time of the *Bismarck*'s breakout there seemed little chance that Force H, based in Gibraltar, would take part in the chase. Events proved otherwise. Above from top to bottom: the aircraft carrier *Ark Royal*; the battle cruiser HMS *Renown*; the light cruiser *Sheffield*.

A cluster of Swordfish biplanes awaits orders to take off from the deck of the *Victorious*, May 24, 1941.

A Swordfish with wings folded is brought on deck from its storage hangar.

high-seas mission, they were being asked to take off in unpredictable weather, fly to the extreme limit of their range and attack an enemy that had just sunk the most famous warship in the Royal Navy. And they were being asked do this in slow-moving Swordfish—known as "stringbags" because of their carrying capacity and apparent fragility—fixed-wheel biplanes with open cockpits that looked like relics of World War I and whose top speed when armed was barely 100 knots.

Just after 3 P.M., Tovey issued the order for *Victorious* and four cruisers, under the command of the flagship *Galatea*, to leave his battle fleet and steer a course that would get the carrier within 100 miles of the *Bismarck* and *Prinz Eugen* before dusk. As Tovey watched the untried aircraft carrier fade into the gray distance, he must have wondered whether he was sending the young flyers on a suicide mission.

Alois Haberditz had been cold for hours; now he was getting tired. He and the rest of the *Bismarck*'s port midships antiaircraft crew had been in a state of constant alert since they had entered the Denmark Strait a day and half ago, had not left their battle stations since early that morning. Whenever they tried to catch a few minutes' shut-eye, they were inevitably jolted awake by the aircraft alarm bells, as yet another Catalina flying boat from Iceland flew over to reconnoiter. Occasionally one came close enough for them to get in a few good shots, but no hits were scored.

Haberditz was beginning to think the British were just toying with them. Then a gust of wind whipped through the open gun mount, and he pulled his leather jacket around him more tightly as he returned to scanning the empty horizon.

Aboard *Prinz Eugen*, Captain Brinkmann took a pull on his ever-present cigar and wondered just what Admiral Lütjens was thinking. Early that afternoon the admiral had signaled his intention to stage a breakaway, to be executed on the code word, "Hood." While the *Bismarck*, which was still in position astern of *Prinz Eugen*, altered course and diverted the enemy, *Prinz Eugen* would continue southward until she was out of range, then hook up with a tanker and continue commerce-raiding independently. But the first attempt around 3:30 P.M. had failed, and nothing further had been heard. Perhaps the admiral had changed his mind? It seemed logical to Brinkmann for the task force to stay together.

Shortly after 6 P.M., as the two ships entered a fog bank, Brinkmann was surprised to see the *Bismarck*'s signal light frantically winking at him: "Execute Hood." Immediately the battleship turned to starboard and faded into the mist. A few minutes later he heard the sound of *Bismarck*'s heavy guns. Sometime later he and the others on *Prinz Eugen*'s bridge caught one last glimpse of their "big brother" far off to the northwest, flashing fire and smoke from her guns, coloring the sea and clouds dark red. Then she disappeared into a rain squall.

The *Prince of Wales* with three of her forward guns elevated.

Lütjens' sudden maneuver temporarily caught the British ships off guard (the *Suffolk* had briefly turned off her radar to rest it), but by the time the German battleship loomed out of the mist at a range of ten miles, the *Suffolk* was ready. In the ensuing long-range battle, many salvoes were fired by the British, fewer by the Germans, but no hits were registered. During the action two of *Prince of Wales'* 14-inch guns jammed—further proof that the ship was not ready for action.

The *Bismarck* resumed her course to the south and the chase went on, but with a crucial difference. Admiral Wake-Walker decided to keep his forces together in case of another attack. (At this point he didn't realize *Prinz Eugen* had broken away, and his radar crew would continue for many hours to report two ships on their screens.) He ordered all three of his ships to take up a position in a line on the *Bismarck*'s port quarter (astern and to port). *Suffolk* and her priceless radar set took the lead, *Prince of Wales* the middle, and Wake-Walker's flagship *Norfolk* the rear. This concentration of force may have been sound battle tactics, but it was flawed for the primary purpose at hand—maintaining contact with the *Bismarck*. The best way to do that was to keep his ships spread out to cover both quarters astern of the *Bismarck*, so that a turn in either direction would quickly be spotted.

The *Suffolk* fires her 8-inch guns at *Bismarck* during the German feint that allowed the *Prinz Eugen* to escape.

Matters deteriorated further when warnings of U-boats in the area forced the shadowers to adopt a zigzag course. Since the *Bismarck* continued on a straight line south, this meant that on each port (southeast) leg of the zigzag, the *Suffolk* passed out of radar range, only regaining the *Bismarck* on the way back to starboard. For the time being, however, this tactic worked well, and the *Suffolk's* radar operators became used to losing their target for roughly fifteen minutes during each complete zigzag.

Admiral Lütjens broke into a rare smile as Lindemann and the other officers on the bridge congratulated him. The breakaway of the *Prinz Eugen* had worked flawlessly, proving yet again his mastery of sea tactics. But the smile was soon gone as chief engineer Lehmann arrived with his final damage report. The fuel situation remained critical. There seemed

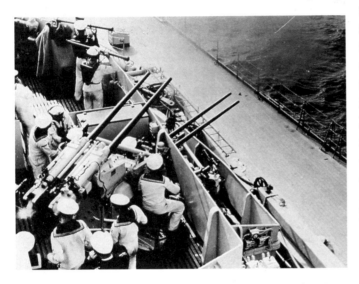

The *Bismarck's* 37–mm antiaircraft guns had difficulty hitting the slow-moving Swordfish.

no prospect of getting access to the thousand tons of fuel trapped in the bow. Lütjens now knew that any thought of leading his pursuers into the hornets' nest of German U-boats stationed south of Greenland had to be abandoned. His only option was to head directly for France, at the most economical speed. Just before 9 P.M. he radioed Group West: "Shaking off contact impossible due to enemy radar. Due to fuel steering direct for St. Nazaire." He ordered Lehmann to reduce speed to 21 knots. For the time being he held course due south. He hoped to disguise his intentions for as long as possible.

At 10 P.M. the aircraft carrier *Victorious* was still 120 miles away from the *Bismarck*, darkness was coming on, and the weather was deteriorating. Time was running out for Captain Bovell. Could his pilots find the Germans, attack and then return to land in darkness without running short of fuel? He realized the whole mission was operating with no margin for error, not to mention on a wing and a prayer. But he had his orders. And so did the flight crews who were even now clambering into the nine flimsy Swordfish biplanes that were lashed to the heaving flight deck. Those who had only flown from land before looked at the tiny runway that rose one minute with the swell, then plunged the next as if it would sink into the sea, and wondered whether they would manage to take off at all, let alone find their quarry. Landing was an almost unthinkable prospect for these novice aviators.

An hour and a half later eight aircraft (one had got temporarily lost in transit) were homing in on their target. But the heavy cloud cover was proving a problem; it caused them to lose their bearings until the *Norfolk* set them back on the correct course. Finally, the primitive radar on the squadron leader's aircraft again picked up a ship. Without hesitating, its pilot, Lieutenant-Commander Eugene Esmonde, led the charge down through the clouds only to discover that they had picked the wrong target. This was the United States Coast Guard Cutter *Modoc*, which had strayed into the area while searching for survivors from a convoy recently attacked by U-boats. Those on board the *Modoc* had a distant view of the battle that followed. It must have looked to them as though eight mosquitoes were trying to bring down a grizzly bear.

Lieutenant Percy Gick, leading one subflight of three Swordfish, realized the *Modoc* was not the *Bismarck* when distant guns started firing. "Damn," he muttered to himself. So much for catching the Jerries by surprise. He banked his aircraft sharply toward the German battleship still several miles away. The other two planes in his subflight followed suit, then climbed with him to about 2,000 feet. None of the flak bursting around touched them, and it looked harmless enough, leaving nothing more than dark puffs of cloud through which they flew.

Now Gick had the *Bismarck* in his sights and decided to come in at the port bow. Swooping down until he was barely missing the twenty-foot wave tops, he led his planes in. The Germans were throwing everything at him—even their heavy guns were firing. As the big shells splashed, they threw up huge waterspouts in his path, any one of which would have knocked his plane out of the air. Then, as they approached critical distance, Gick decided he wasn't satisfied with their position and signaled his subflight to swing around and try again. Courageously he led his tiny force back into the unremitting barrage. This time they released their "kippers" (torpedoes) at one thousand yards, only to see the *Bismarck* turn in time to avoid a hit. As he flew away, dodging flak and waterspouts, Gick's observer insisted that he increase altitude so he could take a photograph. As he was doing so one of the splashes got them, literally lifting the aircraft up in the air and ripping out its bottom. Somehow Gick flew on.

A squadron of Swordfish each equipped with a single torpedo, or "kipper."

Alois Haberditz's guns were so hot from firing that he and the other men were forced to wrap wet cloths around the barrels to keep them working. He couldn't believe the risks these crazy Englishmen were taking as they swarmed in so close he could almost have reached out and touched them. But still they couldn't score a hit. It was hard to keep the enemy in your sights when your own ship was constantly changing course and heeling heavily first to port, then to starboard, as the helmsman steered to "rake" the paths of the oncoming torpedoes. It was certainly frustrating for the antiaircraft crews. Their only consolation was that the attackers seemed to be having no more success than they were.

In the after fire control station, Burkard von Müllenheim-Rechberg heard a sound like a muffled cannonshot and felt the ship shudder slightly. He realized instantly that an enemy torpedo had struck, but because of his position he couldn't see what had happened. He concluded the hit must have occurred forward and looked immediately at the speed and rudder indicators to see if the damage was serious. Apparently it wasn't. A few minutes later he overheard Gerhard Junack's damage control report to the bridge: the ship was unharmed. The torpedo, running shallow, had only struck at the armor belt, just below the waterline, pushing the armor in an inch or so.

As the Swordfish lumbered off into the growing darkness, the *Bismarck* quickly returned to normal. Men relaxed at their stations, smoked cigarettes, boasted about their marksmanship. No one really knew for sure how many enemy planes had attacked them, and the number grew with each telling. No one had actually seen a plane crash, but before long the story went that the enemy had lost numbers exceeding the entire attacking force. All laughter ceased, however, when they heard that Kurt Kirchberg, a crew member who had been handling ammunition on the deck above where the torpedo had hit, had been thrown against the ship structure and killed instantly. Six other men, all stationed below, had broken bones.

Heinz Jucknat, Adi Eich and Franz Halke were stunned when the news reached the after computer room down below, where they had barely felt the torpedo's impact. They had known Kirchberg well. He was a member of their Third Division; they had trained with him from the day of their arrival in Hamburg when the ship was still being completed. More than the damage from the battle off Iceland, the first death on the *Bismarck* brought home the tenuousness of their position. With the departure of *Prinz Eugen* they were now completely alone in enemy territory. English ships were close at hand. Their position was known. With the return of daylight more attacks would inevitably come, whether from planes or ships or both, they could not know.

While the *Bismarck* settled in for the short night, the adventure was far from over for Percy Gick and the other crew members of the "stringbags"

(Below) A Swordfish returns safely and prepares to land at the end of its mission.

(Right) Swordfish pilots on the deck of the *Victorious*. The squadron leader during the *Bismarck* attack, Lieutenant-Commander Eugene Esmonde, is second from left.

limping the hundred miles back to the *Victorious*. Miraculously no planes had been lost, but several had been damaged, and all would need every pint of fuel to complete the return journey. Gick's air gunner, now sitting with his feet dangling over empty space, periodically broke in over the intercom, "Bloody drafty back here." But this was a minor problem compared to finding their carrier, whose homing beacon had stopped working. The fliers were getting desperate when squadron leader Esmonde caught sight of a red signal lamp aboard the *Galatea*. Three pilots had never made a night landing at sea. If they missed with the first try, they would likely have no fuel for a second. One by one they landed safely. The engine on one of the planes cut out the instant it was safely snagged by the arrester wires. Gick's air gunner was half frozen and could hardly walk.

Victorious' five Fulmar fighters had been sent out some time after the Swordfish took off. Their mission, in Admiral Tovey's words, was "to shadow and to distract the enemy." Of these only two actually found the *Bismarck* and only three returned safely to the *Victorious*. This was almost to be expected given the rawness of the pilots. As Tovey later wrote, "The crews were inexperienced, some of the observers finding themselves in a two-seater aircraft for the first time, with wireless set tuned only on deck and no homing beacon. Night shadowing is a task which tries the most experienced of crews and it is not surprising in these difficult conditions that they failed to achieve it." The two missing planes went down in the sea, but the crew of one of them was ultimately rescued by a passing merchant ship.

This picture of the *Bismarck* was taken by one of the Swordfish from the *Victorious* during the attack.

Although the torpedo had done little direct damage, the shock from its detonation, combined with the *Bismarck*'s high-speed evasive action during the attack and the jarring constant firing from all the guns had reopened her earlier wounds. The collision mats protecting the shell holes forward had come loose, and water was again pouring in, causing the bow to go down farther. The packing in the damaged bulkheads was loosened, leading to the complete flooding of the forward port boiler room, which had to be abandoned. There was now a danger of seawater getting into the boiler feed water and shutting down the whole system. Lütjens ordered the speed slowed to 16 knots while the mats were repaired. The engineering crews worked feverishly to ensure a supply of fresh water to the boilers. The admiral must have wondered how much more his ship could take. He simply had to slip his shadow before morning.

In the early hours of May 25, the British forces were beginning to close in. *Revenge, London* and *Edinburgh* were still too far away, but *Victorious* was ready to launch another air attack at dawn. And Admiral Tovey's battle fleet, *King George V* and *Repulse*, was steaming westward at full throttle. If the *Bismarck* maintained her current course and speed, he would make contact around 8:30 A.M., shortly after sunrise. *Rodney*, with three destroyers, was now roughly 350 miles southeast and would intercept at about 10 A.M. *Ramillies*, steaming from the south, was due to arrive around 11 A.M.

And now a new chess piece was placed firmly on the board. This was Force H, under Vice-Admiral Sir James Somerville, already in the Bay of Biscay. At 3:30 A.M. the order went out for Somerville to make a course at full speed to intercept the *Bismarck*. At this juncture it still seemed highly unlikely that Force H, consisting of the old battle cruiser *Renown* flying Somerville's flag, the aircraft carrier *Ark Royal* and the cruiser *Sheffield*, with their attendant destroyers, would have any role in the unfolding drama. It was more than one thousand miles to the southeast. But the fates had put Somerville in difficult circumstances before and shown him to be a professional sailor of iron determination. It was he who had fired on the French fleet off Algeria following the fall of France, when the French admiral in charge had refused his ultimatum to either scuttle or come over to the British side. It had cost the French 1,300 men and many ships and left a bitter feeling between the two allies, but it had to be done and Somerville did it.

May 25 was Admiral Lütjens' fifty-second birthday, and he was about to give himself the best possible present. It had not escaped his notice that all three British ships were remaining in formation on his port quarter, as if inviting him to attempt a getaway to starboard. He was also aware that his shadowers were maintaining a zigzag course that took them well away on the port leg. So he waited until the opportune moment, and then shortly after 3 A.M., ordered his helmsman to turn hard over to starboard. He timed it perfectly. Although he didn't know it—*Suffolk*'s radar signals were still being picked up by the Germans—the *Bismarck* had just disappeared from the *Suffolk*'s radar screens.

Once he'd opened up the distance, Lütjens began a wide loop north and then east that took him across the wakes of his pursuers and left him on a direct southeast course for France. He doubted the stratagem had succeeded, but it had been worth a try.

The exhausted radar operators on *Suffolk* were not particularly surprised when they failed to make contact with *Bismarck* as expected at 3:30 A.M., after the latest southeast leg of their zigzag. Obviously the Germans had altered course slightly to the west. They would find them soon enough, as they had on countless other occasions. (They still believed the two German ships were together.) But the minutes ticked by and still there was no blip on the radar screen, even though they headed farther and farther southwest. Finally, at 5 A.M., Captain Ellis reluctantly signaled Admiral Wake-Walker: "Have lost contact with enemy."

Admiral Tovey was not amused. In the plotting room aboard *King George V*, he and his officers stared glumly at the chart on which were marked the approximate positions of all the ships that had joined in the chase. To maintain maximum secrecy from the Germans, British ships rarely broadcast their positions, so Tovey had only a general idea where his forces were. (For example, *Victorious* was actually 200 miles south of where he thought she was.) But until now he had always known exactly

Vice-Admiral Sir James Somerville, commander of Force H, on board *Ark Royal* at Malta.

where the *Bismarck* was. Now she had vanished into thin sea air. Which way had she gone? Various theories were suggested as to Lütjens' intentions. Tovey listened, but for once said nothing to lighten the mood. This was no time for jokes. As commander in chief of the Home Fleet, he bore the ultimate responsibility. It fell to him to decide how to deploy his inadequate forces. Back on shore, First Sea Lord Dudley Pound and Winston Churchill were second-guessing his every move. Tovey knew he would have to face Churchill's wrath and would probably lose his job if he allowed the *Bismarck* to slip through his grasp.

Since Tovey did not know how seriously the *Bismarck* was damaged, he had to consider the possibility that she would rendezvous with a tanker, then go after merchant shipping. If a tanker was her goal, her most likely course was either northwest to the Davis Strait (a good hiding place for an oiler) or south into the mid-Atlantic where a German fuel ship was suspected to be operating. If, as he thought most likely, a safe port was Lütjens' goal, he might now be steering northeast toward the Iceland-Faroes gap or southeast for Brest, Gibraltar or even Dakar. But he did not have sufficient forces in the area to cover 360 degrees on the compass. He concluded that he must move to forestall the most damaging possibility—a refueled *Bismarck* loose in the Atlantic shipping lanes.

The *Norfolk* and *Suffolk* under Admiral Wake-Walker were already searching to the southwest (*Prince of Wales* was detached and ordered to join up with *King George V.* Later, running low on fuel, she was sent back to Iceland.) Reluctantly, Tovey now ordered *Victorious* and the accompanying cruisers to cover the route to the northwest. He had no way of knowing that this meant the few precious planes he possessed would be searching in exactly the opposite direction from the way the *Bismarck* was now heading. Other units were ordered to take up the patrols of the Denmark Strait and the Iceland Faroes Gap. The route to France—the least damaging possibility—was left unsearched. Only Force H, steaming up from Gibraltar, and *Rodney*, much closer but still well to the south, were in position to intercept the Germans if they were heading in that direction—and were rediscovered in time. As the sun rose on the morning of May 25, the British were everywhere the *Bismarck* wasn't.

Lieutenant-Commander Wellings, USN, and his friend Gaffney Gatacre were sure they knew where *Bismarck* was heading—a Bay of Biscay port—and they tried to convince *Rodney*'s commander of their view. Captain F.H.G. Dalrymple-Hamilton was a stubborn, down-to-earth Scot who had quickly won Wellings' respect. The captain invited Wellings to join the Operations Committee formed at the news of the *Bismarck*'s breakout. Now assembled in the chart house, the committee wrestled with the question of which way *Rodney* should go. After considering all the arguments, Dalrymple-Hamilton elected to hold his present position for two or three hours. If the German ship was not resighted, he would then act on the assumption that the *Bismarck* was headed for Brest. That morning Wellings recorded in his personal diary: "No further word from *Bismarck*. Will she get through? All kinds of excitement."

Even as far away as the White House there was consternation when the news of the *Bismarck*'s escape was received. President Roosevelt had

The First Sea Lord, Admiral of the Fleet Sir Dudley Pound, Admiral Raeder's opposite number in the Royal Navy.

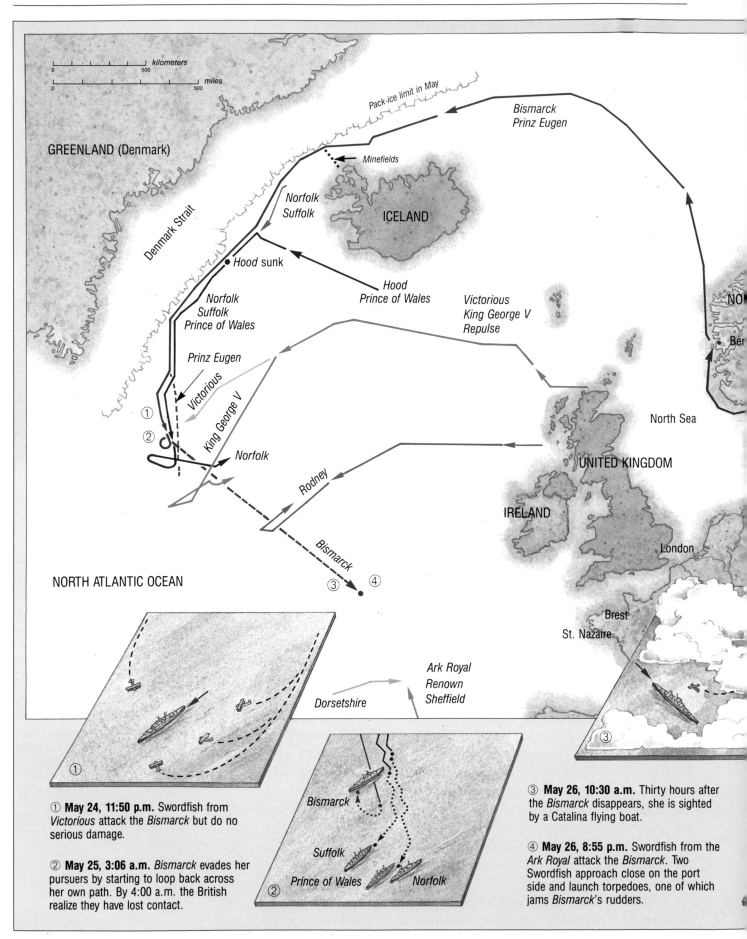

kilometers
0   500

miles
0   500

GREENLAND (Denmark)

Pack-ice limit in May

Bismarck
Prinz Eugen

Minefields

Denmark Strait

Norfolk
Suffolk

ICELAND

Hood sunk

Norfolk
Suffolk
Prince of Wales

Hood
Prince of Wales

Victorious
King George V
Repulse

Prinz Eugen

Victorious

King George V

Norfolk

Rodney

Bismarck

① ②

③ ④

NORTH ATLANTIC OCEAN

North Sea

UNITED KINGDOM

IRELAND

London

Brest
St. Nazaire

Ark Royal
Renown
Sheffield

Dorsetshire

① May 24, 11:50 p.m. Swordfish from *Victorious* attack the *Bismarck* but do no serious damage.

② May 25, 3:06 a.m. *Bismarck* evades her pursuers by starting to loop back across her own path. By 4:00 a.m. the British realize they have lost contact.

Bismarck

Suffolk

Prince of Wales   Norfolk

②

③ May 26, 10:30 a.m. Thirty hours after the *Bismarck* disappears, she is sighted by a Catalina flying boat.

④ May 26, 8:55 p.m. Swordfish from the *Ark Royal* attack the *Bismarck*. Two Swordfish approach close on the port side and launch torpedoes, one of which jams *Bismarck*'s rudders.

③

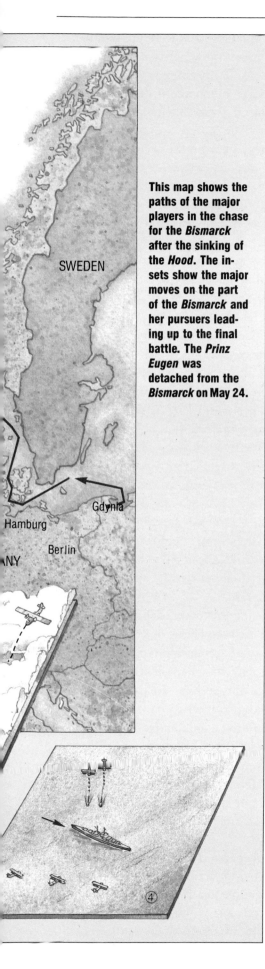

This map shows the paths of the major players in the chase for the *Bismarck* after the sinking of the *Hood*. The insets show the major moves on the part of the *Bismarck* and her pursuers leading up to the final battle. The *Prinz Eugen* was detached from the *Bismarck* on May 24.

been following events closely since the monster battleship had appeared in the Atlantic. He was worried the German ship might end up in the Caribbean, where he would be in a position to order her sunk by American submarines. "Do you think the people would demand to have me impeached?" he asked his advisers, trying to determine the effect at home of such an action. Only if the navy fired and missed, they replied.

While the British were in a fuddle, Admiral Lütjens, heading southeast for France at a speed of 20 knots, believed he was being followed. Perhaps he was still picking up distant radar impulses from the *Suffolk*, and these swayed him. Perhaps after being followed for more than two days, he simply couldn't believe he'd eluded the British radar and chose to ignore the positive evidence. Possibly Lütjens' grip on his command was already slipping. Whatever the reasons, he made what appears in retrospect to be a very careless mistake: he broke radio silence. Even after 8:46 A.M., when Group West radioed him that the British seemed to have lost contact, he insouciantly sent off two further radio messages.

For the time being, however, Lütjens' birthday luck held. The British did get bearings from the *Bismarck*'s radio transmissions, but Admiral Tovey's navigator misinterpreted them. The bearings clearly showed the *Bismarck* to be southeast of her last reported position—suggesting strongly that she was indeed heading for France. However, instead of sending Admiral Tovey the new position they had worked out, the Admiralty relayed only the bearings. Apparently Tovey wanted to do the calculations himself, since this would allow him to factor in any additional bearings from his own destroyers equipped with radio signal direction finders (D/F), and so get a more precise fix. Unfortunately and inexcusably, on board *King George V* the bearings were miscalculated, yielding a position ninety miles north of where the *Bismarck* was. This convinced Tovey the *Bismarck* had turned north and was aiming for Norway through the Iceland-Faroes gap. He altered course to the northeast and sent out this fateful message at 10:47 A.M.: "By D/F estimate enemy position at 0952/25 was 57 N., 33 W. All Home Fleet forces search accordingly." Thus, as midday passed, the closest British forces were racing away from the Germans.

To Heinz Jucknat, Franz Halke and Adolf Eich, life had closed down to four gray walls. Occasionally, Lieutenant Heinz Aengeneyndt would give them permission to smoke. At meal times a steward arrived with food, usually a steaming pot of stew and some black bread. The only time they left their confinement was to relieve themselves. They hadn't been on deck for days, or so it seemed. Once in a while someone would start into a story—usually Heinz, who was a good talker. But they had heard almost all of his tales now, knew his entire childhood in East Prussia by heart. In the long silences, several men would usually nod off.

Captain Dalrymple-Hamilton was perplexed. He had just received Admiral Tovey's 10:47 message, and he found it most extraordinary. It told him the *Bismarck* was sixty miles north of the position his own navigator had plotted using the Admiralty bearings. Fortunately he was a practical fellow, assumed the message was a mistake and would be corrected shortly, and directed *Rodney* on a course to intersect the route he still believed the *Bismarck* was following—to Brest. But what would he do if no correction came? He was absolutely sure the Germans were not aiming for Norway. He experienced great relief, therefore, when at 11:58 A.M. he received the following message from the Admiralty: "Act as though the enemy is proceeding to a Bay of Biscay port." Lieutenant-Commander Wellings and Lieutenant-Commander Gatacre were also delighted. They'd been right all along.

"Achtung, achtung. Stand by for a message from the admiral." It was almost noon as the loudspeakers blared, and instantly everyone in the *Bismarck*'s after computer room was wide awake. The men had recently heard the rumor that contact had finally been broken with the enemy. Most now assumed Lütjens was about to confirm this wonderful news. Then came the admiral's formal clipped tones, devoid of emotion. This is how Burkard von Müllenheim-Rechberg has reconstructed what Lütjens said:

Crewmen of the *Bismarck* at mess. After Admiral Lütjens' fatalistic speech the mood was grim throughout the ship.

"Seamen of the battleship *Bismarck*! You have covered yourselves with glory! The sinking of the battle cruiser *Hood* has not only military, but also psychological value, for she was the pride of England. Henceforth, the enemy will try to concentrate his forces and bring them into action against us. I therefore released *Prinz Eugen* at noon yesterday so that she could conduct commerce warfare on her own. She has managed to evade the enemy. We, on the other hand, because of the hits we have received, have been ordered to proceed to a French port. On our way there, the enemy will gather and give us battle. The German people are with you, and we will fight until our gun barrels glow red-hot and the last shell has left the barrels. For us seamen, the question now is victory or death."

Victory or death. Heinz, Franz and Adolf looked at each other. What chance did a single ship have against the massed forces of British sea power? In the aft middle boiler room, Hans Zimmermann and his friends wondered if Admiral Lütjens was going mad (they had all been amazed when he failed to follow up his advantage and go after the damaged *Prince of Wales*). Throughout the ship, young men who knew little of war at sea listened to their admiral's words and felt a sinking feeling. In the after fire control station, one of Müllenheim-Rechberg's petty officers summed it up: "The admiral says we haven't a hope, sir." Even this late on May 25, nine hours after he had shaken off the hounds, Lütjens still believed he was being followed. This despite messages from Group West that told him the opposite. With success staring him in the face, he seems already to have given himself over to fate.

Morale was partially restored by a speech an hour later from Captain Lindemann, who presented a much more optimistic picture of their chances. He spoke of the U-boats that would come to their aid, the German planes that would give them cover as soon as they got closer to France. But despite the respect in which he was held by the entire crew, he could not completely reverse the effects of Lütjens' speech. Gerhard Junack later recalled that afterward, some officers were seen wearing lifejackets, in strict contravention of standing orders.

Did the admiral even notice? He was in no mood to care. He was already certain that his fifty-second birthday would be his last. He read the birthday congratulations from Admiral Raeder and Hitler without pleasure. At least Raeder's message was warm. The Grand Admiral had not abandoned him now that failure loomed. But the Führer's was curt and passionless. It read: "Best wishes your birthday. Adolf Hitler." Lütjens crumpled the paper and stuffed it in his pocket. He cared little for the megalomaniac German leader, but he loved Germany. When he died, he would die for Germany.

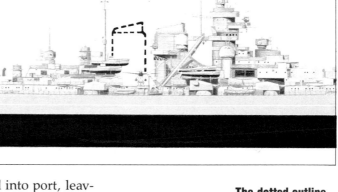

By the time Admiral Tovey realized the error in his calculations and turned his ship southeast toward Brest, the *Bismarck* had opened up a 150-mile lead. Most of the forces at his immediate disposal were running so short of fuel that they had to be ordered into port, leaving him virtually alone to continue the chase. *Prince of Wales, Victorious, Repulse* and *Suffolk* all left the field. *Ramillies,* which would now never catch up, was dispatched to take over the escort of the *Britannic.* That left him with *Rodney,* which had never deviated from its northeast course to bring it between *Bismarck* and Brest. He could also count on *Norfolk*—for now. Admiral Wake-Walker's fuel was also low, but he could not bear the thought of abandoning the chase after he had let the *Bismarck* slip away when interception seemed certain. He, too, turned southeast toward France.

Captain Lindemann and his senior officers kept dreaming up schemes to keep their men's minds occupied, their hands busy. That afternoon the project was building a dummy funnel, which when rigged would help disguise the ship by changing her silhouette. Building the funnel boosted morale on the *Bismarck,* which had gradually recovered as the news that they had indeed broken contact sank in. (From about noon on Lütjens maintained strict radio silence.) The degree to which good spirits had returned to officers and crew is suggested by the jesting order from the chief engineering officer, Lieutenant-Commander Walter Lehmann, that circulated through the ship as the dummy stack neared completion: "Off duty watch report to the First Officer's cabin to draw cigars to smoke in our second stack!"

We will never know how convincing it would have looked, since the dummy funnel was never rigged. Although many thought the idea somewhat silly, it might well have made a difference at the most critical juncture in the whole story. It would not have fooled a surface ship for long, that's certain. But given the difficulty of identifying ships from the air, it might have confused a rookie airplane pilot.

As night gathered the *Bismarck* into its protective cloak on Sunday

The dotted outline shows where the dummy stack was to have been erected. Whether or not it would have fooled a British plane is another question.

May 25, it looked to everyone, except perhaps Admiral Lütjens, as if the Germans were going to make it. They continued to elude contact; Admiral Tovey couldn't catch up, and in another day would himself be perilously short of fuel. Force H continued to steam northward; at 9 P.M. *Rodney*, which had been sailing northeast all day, altered course to the east to intersect the *Bismarck*'s probable course. Both Force H and the *Rodney* would be in range if the *Bismarck* could be found. Now, almost in desperation, the Admiralty placed new pieces on the board: six destroyers.

Rodney still had three destroyers in company, but these were getting

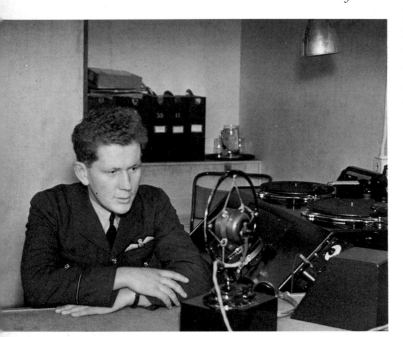

Flying Officer Dennis Briggs, pilot of the Catalina flying boat that rediscovered the *Bismarck* after she had eluded the British for more than thirty hours.

low on fuel, and *King George V* was sailing unescorted into U-boat waters. The only destroyers close enough to join them were escorting troop convoy WS8B, and were under the command of the captain of the destroyer *Cossack*, Philip Vian, a tough and daring sailor. Vian was ordered to leave his convoy with minimal escort and join the battleships. *Cossack*, *Sikh* and *Zulu* were to join *King George V. Maori* and the Polish destroyer *Piorun* were to accompany *Rodney*. The British were throwing every ship at their disposal into the *Bismarck* chase.

At 3:30 A.M. on Monday May 26, a Catalina flying boat took off from Lough Erne in Northern Ireland, and with it one of the least likely heroes in the *Bismarck* saga. He was twenty-six-year-old Ensign Leonard B. "Tuck" Smith of the United States Navy, one of a contingent of navy pilots sent over to help the British to fly their Lend-Lease Catalinas and to gain wartime experience. Ensign Smith's presence as copilot aboard the airplane was a wartime secret—Congress permitted America to lend material to the British war effort, not men. Nonetheless, as Smith sat buckled into the copilot's seat, cotton plugged into his ears to muffle the engine racket, he wore his U.S. Navy uniform. If the plane were shot down and the crew picked up by a German craft, Herr Goebbels would have a field day. So would isolationist elements of the American press.

The friendly Yank from Higginsville, Missouri, had become popular with the ten-man Catalina crew. Now Smith napped in the copilot's seat while Flying Officer Dennis Briggs steered the plane west toward where the *Bismarck* was believed to be. The first three hours of these flights were always the worst—everyone was still bleary-eyed from leaving in the middle of the night. Things looked up around dawn, when the smell of bacon and eggs filled the cabin, and there was finally enough light to see where you were going. Ensign Smith woke up and ate his breakfast. This morning the weather was hazy, visibility poor. A strong wind whipped the sea below into whitecaps.

Neither commanding officer Briggs nor copilot Smith really expected to spot the *Bismarck*. What were the chances of finding one ship in the middle of this empty vastness? "George," their nickname for the autopilot, was flying the boat at about 500 feet. One minute they could see the water, the next it was obscured. At 10:30 A.M. a dark shape "the size of a

cigar box" appeared in the mist ahead of them. "What in the devil's that?" asked Smith. Then, excitement entering his voice, "Looks like a battleship." But could it be the *Bismarck*? There were no destroyers in sight as you would expect if the ship were British. "Better get closer. Go round its stern," Briggs ordered as he headed aft to the wireless operator's table and began to write out a signal. Smith took the Catalina up into the clouds, then circled to come in closer. But he misjudged and broke out of the clouds right above her, to be greeted by all guns firing. Black puffs of smoke surrounded them, and they could hear bits of shrapnel hitting the plane's hull. The flying boat shook with the explosions of flak; one off-duty crewman was knocked out of his bunk.

That was the *Bismarck*, all right, but would they live to send the word? Briggs finished scribbling out the coded message for the wireless operator while Smith banked hard and did violent S turns as the Catalina shot up into the cover of the clouds. When Briggs returned to his pilot's seat he caught sight of the ship below them. It looked like "one big flash," he recalled. A piece of shrapnel hit between the two pilot seats as Briggs was taking over the controls. Smith looked down and saw a chink of daylight. Once they were out of range an inspection revealed half a dozen holes in the aircraft, but no injuries to the crew. The rigger, who had been washing the breakfast dishes when the firing happened, was a bit shaken up,

(Above) An artist's recreation of the encounter between the Catalina and the *Bismarck*. The airplane was damaged by flak, but managed to climb out of range in time.

(Below) Ensign Leonard B. "Tuck" Smith, (right) co-pilot of the Catalina, shown here with two other American airmen serving with R.A.F. Coastal Command.

and some of the dishes were broken.

When the *Bismarck's* actual position—roughly 700 miles from Brest—was broadcast to the British fleet (a signal also picked up and decoded by the Germans), Admiral Tovey discovered just how close his ships had come to running right into her. Captain Vian's destroyers had passed only 30 miles astern. *Rodney* had missed by 50. Now both *Rodney,* 125 miles to the northeast, and *King George V,* 135 miles to the north, were too far away to catch up. Only Force H, which was 100 miles away and stood between the *Bismarck* and Brest, was in a position to slow her down. But Tovey dared not send Force H's *Renown* and *Sheffield* against the *Bismarck.*

In a shootout, the cruiser and the venerable battle cruiser would be no match for the Germans' superior firepower and protective armor. *Renown* was older than the *Hood,* and was even more lightly armed and armored. No, it was up to *Ark Royal,* now roughly 50 miles away from the *Bismarck* and on a parallel course, to deliver the blow. That meant he must rely once again on Swordfish biplanes, the same type of one-torpedo aircraft that had tried and failed to slow the German battleship two days earlier. At least, Tovey reflected, these pilots were among the most seasoned flyers in the British navy. If the *Bismarck* could be slowed, he and *Rodney,* which had joined him early in the afternoon, could move in for the kill.

Swordfish lined up on the deck of the *Ark Royal* preparatory to take-off.

Around 4 P.M. Tovey received the news that fifteen Swordfish had left the *Ark Royal* armed with torpedoes. As he waited and hoped, he paced the bridge and cursed himself for his earlier miscalculation. The odds now were impossibly long. He was hoping for a miracle.

Müllenheim-Rechberg braced himself as the *Bismarck* heeled over and slid sideways in the heavy sea that pushed them toward France. She was still sailing well, despite her injuries. At least the weather was growing truly awful, the seas more precipitous—and that couldn't help the British. Many of the inexperienced crew were sick, having never encountered stormy conditions in an open sea. Once again he wondered why the dummy stack had never been rigged, asked himself whether that subterfuge, however feeble, might have fooled the reconnaissance plane that had spotted them that morning. Because he spoke English well, he had volunteered to prepare English Morse code messages to send in the event that they were found. These might have duped the first airplane. And even a few hours might have made the difference. Instead, Lütjens had opened fire, giving them away immediately.

Once contact was reestablished, morale on the *Bismarck* plummeted. Death, not victory, once again occupied the men's minds. The first British airplane was relieved by another. By the time that one disappeared, a Swordfish (minus torpedo) arrived on the scene and shadowed the Germans. That meant an aircraft carrier could not be far away. Then why, the crew wondered, did the British not attack? For the rest of the day, as they steamed toward Brest, still trailing oil at the painfully slow speed of 20 knots, at least one Swordfish was always on their tail, never coming close

enough for them to get a good shot. If they had had more fuel they could have sailed faster, and by now would have been within the range of German bombers. How Lütjens must have cursed himself for not topping up at Bergen or in the Arctic. Then, just before 6 P.M., a distant ship hove into view. This was the *Sheffield*, detached from Force H to shadow the *Bismarck* and direct the air attack, the first British ship to make visual contact in forty hours. But still there was no British attack. Before long it would be dark—by morning they should be home free. German spirits rose yet again.

The fifteen Swordfish flew in formation for the *Bismarck*, found a ship on radar, dived and attacked. Only a few of the pilots wondered why the ship failed to return fire or noticed that their target had two funnels, a feature no German warship possessed. Only three recognized the *Sheffield* and held onto their torpedoes. Many of the pilots only discovered their mistake when they returned to their carrier—they had attacked one of their own. Vice-Admiral Somerville, aboard the flagship *Renown*, used every four-letter word in his considerable arsenal of expletives when he learned what had happened. Somerville was a big hearty man, and when

Robert Taylor's painting of a Swordfish leaving *Ark Royal* on its way to attack the *Bismarck*.

he swore he did so with gusto.

With relief it was pointed out that no damage had been done. Many of the torpedoes, armed with magnetic firing pistols, had exploded on contact with the water. The captain of the *Sheffield* had managed to evade the others. Somerville ordered another attack to be launched as soon as possible. But with the steadily deteriorating weather, this would take several hours. At least one useful lesson had been learned: the faulty magnetic firing pistols were replaced with the old, reliable contact-firing variety.

The *Bismarck* is sighted, trailing oil, but still a deadly adversary for the British biplanes.

Lieutenant Herbert Wohlfarth on the bridge of *U-556* couldn't believe his eyes. Out of the gathering dusk loomed the silhouettes of two great warships. On the port bow was an aircraft carrier; to starboard was a battleship. The bridge party scrambled below, and the submarine submerged to periscope depth, but there was nothing the seasoned U-boat commander could do except curse in frustration and watch the *Ark Royal* and the *Renown* parade serenely by. They would have been easy pickings, but Wohlfarth had no torpedoes left. He had used the last one on convoy HX 126, was now low on fuel and heading for Brest, just like the *Bismarck*.

The irony of the situation was not lost on him. Wohlfarth well remembered Captain Lindemann's good-humored response to his suggestion that *U-556* "adopt" the *Bismarck*. He knew that even now the cartoon showing "Parsifal" warding off enemy torpedoes hung in the officers' wardroom as a reminder of his jesting promise to guard her from all adversaries. Fate had placed him in the perfect position to fulfill that promise, and fate had deprived him of the means to do so. Wearily he turned away from his periscope, composing in his mind the report he would send off to Group West. Where was the *Bismarck* now, he wondered. And where were the other U-boats that might have come to her aid?

Meanwhile, Number 2 subflight's three Swordfish had lost contact with the rest of their squadron. Somewhere below them, barreling forward with a following wind and sea under the leading edge of a cold front, was the *Bismarck*. Together they climbed to 9,000 feet without escaping cloud. Finally, the subflight leader, Lieutenant Godfrey-Faussett, noticed ice forming on his wings and turned down to attack. Sub-Lieutenant Kenneth Pattison saw the thumbs-up sign given by his leader, banked, and dove right behind him. Moments later they came hurtling out of the clouds less than 1,000 feet above the water. There was the *Bismarck* to port, spitting fire. Pattison took a hit just under his seat, but wasn't hurt. Down they went until they were less than 100 feet above the sea, drove to within range, dropped their torpedoes and slalomed away. Although he had other things to think about, Pattison couldn't help admiring the German battleship—the largest he'd ever seen. She was rather a fine—if terrifying—sight.

The third pilot of Number 2 subflight, Sub-Lieutenant Tony Beale, spotted the *Bismarck* while he was in a climb, then dove in on her port side. The monster ship remained eerily quiet as they came in at 50 feet and dropped their kipper 800 yards away. Apparently the *Bismarck*'s gunners didn't see them—until they had turned sharply away and were attempting to make their escape. Then the "whole ship exploded into the flash and crackle of the close range guns firing." As they wove a crazy evasive pattern away from the ship, two members of the Swordfish crew thought they saw a column of water rise amidships on her port side. "You've hit her!" someone exclaimed, and Beale looked over his shoulder in time to see the end of the splash.

With the constant British shadowing since morning, Alois Haberditz and the rest of the *Bismarck*'s port antiaircraft crew had been at their station all day. Although they had traveled many hundreds of miles south from the Denmark Strait, the air was still cold and the salt spray even colder. When one of them needed to warm up, he walked to the nearby deck vent and stood in the blast of hot air from the engines. But only for a minute. They expected a swarm of enemy biplanes to swoop out of the clouds at any moment. This time they were sure they would hit some of them—even if the seas were rough and getting rougher, which would make aiming difficult. But as dusk approached they had begun to let down a little. If the Brits hadn't attacked by now, they must have other plans. A nighttime gunnery battle perhaps? Then, just before 9 P.M., when it seemed certain they would be able to go below for some food and warmth, the aircraft alarm bells began jangling. Then planes were coming at them from every direction, in ones and twos and threes, their wheels almost skimming the waves. Mad dogs, these Englishmen—suicidal.

A Swordfish pulls up after its "kipper" has been sent on its way.

Lieutenant-Commander Gerhard Junack was down in the middle engine room when the explosion happened. He saw the deck plates rise and fall "at least a meter." Others closer to the stern felt it even more acutely. One seaman was lifted off his feet and hurled into other members of his crew. Another crew member said the ship made "a movement like an accordion." Even Müllenheim-Rechberg, high in his after gunnery control station, felt the ship tremble. As with the previous torpedo hit, his eyes automatically turned to the rudder indicator, which showed "12 degrees to port." The impact had come in the midst of a high-speed turn to port. Would the indicator change? He waited but nothing happened. The *Bismarck* continued her high-speed turn, stayed heeled heavily to starboard, and then began to slow down. Her rudder remained locked to port. Müllenheim-Rechberg felt sick.

In the end all fifteen Swordfish managed to launch their torpedoes, get away and return to the *Ark Royal*, but not without damage. Three planes crashed on landing and were completely wrecked. Many had been hit by flak, but only two crew members were wounded.

One of the planes from Number 2 subflight, either Pattison's or Godfrey-Faussett's, was probably responsible for the mortal hit in the starboard quarter that disabled the *Bismarck*'s steering mechanism and jammed the rudders. The only other hit, likely made by Tony Beale, struck just outside the port engine room and slightly below the edge of the armor belt (one of the most heavily-armored parts of the hull), causing minor structural damage and some flooding.

Admiral Tovey was skeptical. He had just received a report from the *Sheffield*: "Enemy steering 340 degrees." If true, this meant the *Bismarck*

The fatal hit: a recreation by artist Wesley Lowe of the launching of the torpedo that damaged the Bismarck's rudders.

The two Swordfish of Number 2 subflight from the Ark Royal, piloted by Lieutenant "Feather" Godfrey-Faussett and Sub-Lieutenant Kenneth Pattison, are shown approaching the Bismarck on her port side. The two planes were less than 100 feet above the waves—too low for the Bismark's guns to bear on them.

had reversed course and was sailing back toward her pursuers. But preliminary messages from Force H indicated no hits during the Swordfish attack (the squadron leader had left the scene without seeing any). Tovey had already resigned himself to the *Bismarck*'s escape and Churchill's ire. Impatiently he dismissed this latest report. Either the Germans were still maneuvering to avoid the torpedo bombers, or the *Sheffield* had been fooled by the *Bismarck*'s silhouette and assumed the bow was the stern. It could easily happen. And the *Sheffield* had been busy avoiding a salvo from *Bismarck* at the time. But confirming reports soon followed. Something was seriously wrong with the German battleship. She had slowed down and seemed to be traveling in a big, slow circle. Tovey's miracle had come to pass.

Not far from where Tovey stood, a staff officer named Bingley fingered the piece of paper in his pocket and smiled to himself. He had made the right decision. On the piece of paper was a message for the commander in chief from the First Sea Lord, Sir Dudley Pound, but it smacked of Churchill's hand. Pound had never been able to stand up to the pugnacious prime minister. Earlier that evening Tovey had informed the Admiralty that his fuel situation would force him to turn back to port at midnight if the *Bismarck* was not slowed down. Pound's reply would have made him apopleptic: "We cannot visualize the situation from your signals. *Bismarck* must be sunk at all costs, and if to do this it is necessary for KGV [*King George V*] to remain on the scene she must do so, even if it subsequently means towing KGV." That would have made the admiral's flagship an easy target for enemy subs. Bingley imagined how Tovey would have reacted to this extraordinary order, not only putting at unnecessary risk the most powerful new battleship in the whole British fleet, but impugning Tovey's courage and resolve as well.

Tovey knew that with the *Bismarck* crippled, *King George V* and *Rodney* could be in a position to attack in a few hours. Captain Vian and his destroyers were already on the scene. Force H was poised to offer air and sea support. Tovey had the *Bismarck* in his grasp. He gave orders for the destroyers to keep track of the wounded ship but to make no foolish attacks. He would wait until dawn, when he could approach the German ship from the northwest with the wind behind him and the light outlining the enemy for his gunners. Then he would make his final move. Checkmate.

CHAPTER SEVEN

The Final Salvo

May 26, 1941—Eastern Atlantic Ocean

Aboard the *Bismarck*, Captain Lindemann listened calmly to the damage control report. The British torpedo had blasted a hole near the stern below the steering gear rooms, flooding these compartments and jamming the rudder mechanism. Lindemann believed that all was not lost. With luck, the locked rudders could be freed. If not, it might be possible to steer the ship using only the propellers, which had not been damaged.

A painting of the *Bismarck* firing a broadside.

But Admiral Lütjens quickly accepted the worst. As Lindemann and his engineering officers discussed ways to restore the ship's maneuverability, Lütjens composed a gallant farewell message for the German people: "Ship unmaneuverable. We fight to the last shell. Long live the Führer." Half an hour after the torpedo hit, but long before the full ramifications of the damage could be known, he gave this note to the radio room for transmission. As usual, the admiral was putting the worst possible construction on the evidence before all the facts were in.

The damage control crew's first order of business was to shore up the bulkhead above the steering compartments and pump the water out of the port engine room. This could not be done because the start mechanism for the pump failed. Sending men into the breached steering compartments was out of the question: water was violently surging in and out, and anyone would have been killed in an attempt to reach the damaged steering mechanism. And when two seamen opened the hatch to the upper platform deck to try to disconnect the rudder from above, they were met by a violent geyser of water.

The twin rudders of the *Bismarck* that were jammed by the torpedo hit from the Swordfish attack are clearly visible in this picture taken while she was still under construction in the Blohm and Voss shipyard in Hamburg.

Now more desperate solutions were proposed: put divers over the side; try to blow the rudders off with explosives; rig a hangar door as a temporary rudder that would offset the permanent rudders' jammed position. But all these schemes were ultimately rejected. The sea was far too rough. Lindemann would have to steer as best he could using only the propellers, something that had proved near impossible during sea trials.

As darkness closed in, the weather began working up to a real northwest gale. The heavy sea and wind that had been pushing the *Bismarck* toward France now contributed to her undoing. No matter what combination of forward, stopped or reversed propellers Lindemann tried at whatever combination of speeds, the wind and waves in concert with the locked rudders worked to turn her into the sea and wind, back toward the pursuing enemy. Finally Lindemann gave up. The ship slowed to a speed of 7 knots on an erratic course. For once Admiral Lütjens' pessimism was entirely justified. All Lindemann could do now was wait for morning.

Around 11 P.M., as the *Bismarck* limped through the waves, her course an involuntary zigzag into the wind, Captain Vian and his flotilla of five destroyers made contact. Vian's orders were to keep track of the Germans until daylight, when the two big battleships would move in. But he was an aggressive officer, not satisfied merely to stand sentinel. Perhaps he could sink the *Bismarck* himself. He later sent this message to his commander in chief explaining how he had construed his duty: "Firstly, to deliver to you at all costs the enemy, at the time you wished. Secondly, to try to sink or stop the enemy with torpedoes in the night if I thought the attack should not involve destroyers in heavy losses."

Given the worsening weather, Vian's "duty" was easier to enunciate than to execute. Destroyers are much smaller than battleships, much less stable in heavy seas—in this case waves fifty feet high and growing. Vian's four Tribal class destroyers, *Cossack*, *Maori*, *Zulu* and *Sikh*, were among the largest in the British fleet, but being on board was like riding a roller coaster. Sometimes the ships would heel so far over it seemed as though they were sure to capsize. When they were heading into the wind, green seawater washed over their foredecks, and their open bridges were drenched with spray. It was even worse aboard the fifth member of the flotilla, the slightly smaller Polish destroyer *Piorun*. But despite the adverse circumstances, Vian managed to get his five ships into a net around the *Bismarck*, and he ordered a synchronized torpedo attack.

This initial attack only succeeded in proving once again the accuracy of *Bismarck*'s gunnery control. At first the brilliant flashes of the German guns that lit up the black night seemed harmless, since the wind carried

(Below left) The Tribal class destroyer *Cossack*, one of the five destroyers under the command of Captain Philip Vian, seen (below)

on board the *Cossack*. Vian and his ships were escorting a troop convoy when they were summoned by the Admiralty to join in the pursuit of the *Bismarck*.

the sound away. But as the destroyers attempted to close in, blazing away with their pitifully small guns, the enemy's shell splashes landed all around. They were driven off without managing to launch a single torpedo. In the process, a sub-lieutenant in *Zulu*'s gunnery control tower had his wrist severed by a shell fragment, and a shell landed on the ship's forecastle but didn't explode; another shell sheared off *Cossack*'s radio antenna.

By around midnight all of the destroyers had lost touch with the *Bismarck*, and the combination of complete darkness and filthy weather convinced Vian that a coordinated attack was no longer possible. So he ordered his captains to fire as opportunity arose. *Maori* was the first to relocate the ship and moved in, launched torpedoes and retired. One after another the others followed suit. (*Piorun* never did regain contact and was finally obliged to head for Plymouth to refuel.) Numerous hits were reported by wishful captains, and for a while the German ship lay stopped dead in the water, but continued to spit fire whenever a destroyer came too close. After about an hour she got underway again.

In the ever wilder weather, it was proving difficult to keep track of the enemy. Admiral Tovey aboard *King George V*, still to the northeast of the *Bismarck*, became concerned that he would run smack into her as he moved to take up his position to the west before dawn. So he ordered starshells to be fired. These illuminated not only the Germans but the positions of the destroyers, a great help to the *Bismarck*'s gunners. Again the destroyers were forced to retreat. At 3:35 A.M., Captain Vian aboard

During the long night of the final battle few men on the *Bismarck* left their battle stations, subsisting on caffeine and cigarettes in place of the hearty fare that was usually ladled out in the galleys.

Cossack moved in to a range of about two miles, launched his last torpedo and withdrew. By 4 A.M., no British ship was in sight of the *Bismarck*, but from the radio messages she continued to send they knew she remained close at hand.

To the exhausted crew of the *Bismarck*, this night battle served at least one useful purpose: it kept their minds off what lay ahead. But in the hours after midnight, as action became more sporadic, the men of the great battleship had time to consider their probable fates. Reassuring messages from Group West were broadcast over the ship's loudspeakers. Submarines were on their way; eighty-one bombers would take off from France at first light. The men clung to these crumbs of encouragement and told each other that Germany would not abandon them, but in their hearts, they doubted. These doubts were not helped when they received the Führer's coldly formal message: "All Germany is with you. What can be done, will be done. Your performance of duty will strengthen our people in the struggle for its destiny."

As Alois Haberditz tried to sleep, his mind kept turning over the Führer's words. He had heard stories of a British captain who had machine-gunned German sailors in the water. German propaganda had told him that the British treated their prisoners badly. Perhaps it would be better to die than to be captured?

Burkard von Müllenheim-Rechberg was too experienced a sailor to give much credence to promises of salvation. He knew that in this weather at this distance from France, aid was highly unlikely, that the odds were now stacked heavily against them. But he kept these thoughts to himself. There was no sense in doing anything to depress his men.

Through the stereoscopic rangefinders he could clearly see yet another British destroyer move in to launch torpedoes. Mercifully none had hit so far—the British were firing at long range, and the *Bismarck* was swinging so erratically that she was a difficult target in this weather. Star-shells burst far away, ghoulishly illuminating the wild seascape. Then the bursts of light came closer. One exploded over the ship, exposing her silhouette to the enemy; it made him feel naked, defenseless. Then, after quite a long pause in the firing, a flare dropped on the forecastle, and there were shouts of fire. The decking was singed, but no serious damage was done. Still the *Bismarck* hobbled on through the night.

Down in the engine rooms and boiler rooms, where the ventilator outlets had been shut for hours because of the battle, the air was unbearably stale and hot. The stokers and engine room workers in their leather clothing were near the point of total collapse. Hans Zimmermann and the others had been on duty in the after middle boiler room since 4 P.M. the previous afternoon and had not sat down since then. Now saltwater was getting into the boiler feed lines—if this kept up, the boilers would definitely explode—and the reverberations from the continued firing of the big guns had everyone worried about cracks in the main steam pipes. As the night dragged on and their exhaustion increased, the only nourishment they were given was some pure dextrose and special chocolate laced with caffeine. The men were also issued cigarettes, but it was strictly forbidden to smoke in the boiler rooms, so they took to smoking in a corner when the boiler master wasn't looking—even though they knew that being caught meant an automatic twenty-eight days in the brig. It was strange being down here in the bowels of the ship, so far from what was going on above, and frightening. If their ship started to sink, would any of them be able to get out in time?

The most helpless observer of this eerie and inconclusive night battle was Herbert Wohlfarth in *U-556*. On his way home to France after a successful mission, he had overheard the *Bismarck's* radio signals indicating

A German Type VII U-boat, the class of submarine commanded by Herbert Wohlfarth, (inset) shown here wearing the Knight's Cross he received from Admiral Dönitz on his return to France.

that her rudder was hit and that she was crippled—not far away from his position. Just before midnight he was almost run down by one of Vian's destroyers, but was able to submerge just in time. When he resurfaced he saw the distant orange flashes of the *Bismarck's* guns, but could do nothing to help her. He signaled to Group West that the weather was getting worse—the wind stronger, the seas higher. Periodically he radioed his estimate of the *Bismarck's* position so that German planes or submarines could find her. There was nothing else he could do. His fuel was running low. Soon he would have to leave his adopted ship to her fate.

As an American, Lieutenant Commander Wellings would be only a witness during the coming action, but he was as excited as any man on board *Rodney* at the prospect of participating in his first sea battle. He knew his wife Dolly would be horrified had she known he was about to come under fire—she was expecting him in Boston in a day or two. Had she been informed that his arrival would be delayed and why? He thought briefly of his baby daughter whom he hadn't seen in almost a year. Would she even remember him? Then he pushed all thoughts of home from his mind as he listened to Captain Dalrymple-Hamilton address the crew. It was a simple, direct speech, just what you would expect from such a straightforward man. He told them they would be in action shortly after dawn, urged them to act in a manner befitting their uniforms, and wished them success. Then the chaplain said a short prayer: "We make our address to Thy Divine Majesty in this our necessity, that Thou wouldst take the cause into Thine own hand and judge between us and our enemies." It was the same prayer that had been used for centuries on British ships of war before a battle.

On the admiral's bridge of *King George V,* Sir John Tovey and his officers "sat, stood or leant like a covey of disembodied spirits," in the words of Lieutenant-Commander Hugh Guernsey. There was little talking, with nothing to be done but wait for morning. If anyone broke the silence it was likely to be Guernsey, who stood by the voice pipe to the wireless room and relayed all radio messages received on the flagship. Guernsey and most of the others had been there since 8:30 the previous evening, but the stretched-out tension kept them all wide awake. They would remain at their posts until the battle was lost or won. At some point steaming cocoa was passed around. "We drank it gratefully, but it might equally have been pitch tar—no one would have noticed," he later wrote.

Elsewhere, on the fleet of British ships and on one German, several thousand men dozed fitfully at their action stations or stared wonderingly into the future. Some, mostly those who had been sunk before, had nightmares. Others pulled out pictures of wives, mothers, girlfriends and children and stared at them longingly. A few boasted about their exploits to come, thinking of glory and their place in history. But most of the men on board the *Bismarck* were too tired or too afraid to boast. And on all the ships most of those who were awake were silent, their thoughts distracted only by the sounds of a ship in bad weather: a loose hatch clanging until someone made it fast; pans clattering in the galley; the distant whine of turbines; the wail and whistle of the wind; the crash of waves and the creaks and groans of hull plates too long at sea.

Adolf Eich left the after gunnery computer room and made his way through the empty passageways of the quiet but wakeful *Bismarck* toward the deck and fresh air. The destroyers seemed to have backed off, and Lieutenant Aengeneyndt had given each man under his command permission to go topside for half an hour. Now it was Eich's turn. As he stepped on deck, the blast of wind that hit him was cold and full of spray, but it felt good after countless hours below. He walked forward, past the airplane catapult and the great single funnel, past the antiaircraft mounts and their half-frozen men, and then went back inside and climbed up to

(Below) The after gunnery computer room where Adi Eich, Franz Halke and Heinz Jucknat served. This photograph was taken while the *Bismarck* was still under construction.

(Below) Adolf (Adi) Eich in 1941.

the bridge. If no one stopped him, perhaps he could pick up the latest news. He, for one, had not given up hope. Captain Lindemann was too fine a commander, Admiral Lütjens too experienced a strategist.

Nonetheless, when he reached the bridge, Eich was surprised to find the mood almost jolly. Lindemann was shaking his first gunnery officer Adalbert Schneider by the hand and offering him hearty congratulations. The Führer had just bestowed on Schneider the Knight's Cross, in recognition of his role in the sinking of the *Hood*. Schneider was beaming, and even Admiral Lütjens looked pleased. When Eich returned to his comrades below, he told them what he had seen. Things obviously could not be so bad; for a time, their spirits lifted.

Sometime before dawn the order went out to open the ship's stores and let the men help themselves. This was a sure sign that those in command believed the *Bismarck* was finished. Discipline slackened. Then the order came from the bridge: "All engines stop." Lieutenant-Commander Gerhard Junack, the ship's chief turbine officer on duty as usual in the center turbine room, waited for further orders. The ship rolled heavily in the seas. He became worried that the turbines would overheat and warp if this situation lasted much longer. Finally he called the bridge and requested an "ahead slow." He never forgot Lindemann's reply; it was so unlike the man he knew: "Ach, do what you like."

As the night waned, a new player was closing in from the south. This was the cruiser HMS *Dorsetshire*, under Captain Benjamin Martin. When he had heard the *Bismarck* had been rediscovered the day before, Martin, without seeking or receiving permission from the Admiralty, had detached himself from the convoy he was escorting and steamed to intercept the Germans. Martin craved action; he was fed up with the monotonous work of convoy escort. It was not what he had joined the navy for. Every dawn he read his men a selection from the Royal Navy's fighting instructions as if it were an inspirational passage from the Bible. Now he would have his chance to put the instructions into practice.

Seventeen-year-old Midshipman Joe Brooks, one of the ship's torpedo firing officers, was at his battle station in the torpedo fire control position above the *Dorsetshire*'s bridge when Captain Martin's voice rang out over the loudspeakers. "Well, men," he announced. "I've been told to intercept the *Bismarck* and sink her. We'll go in with our main armament firing and when we get close, we'll turn and fire torpedoes at her, and then we'll ram her amidships." This fire and brimstone oration may have been intended to inspire, but it had the opposite effect on many members of the crew, Brooks included. To a man they had been shocked at the news of the sinking of the *Hood*. Few fancied the notion of taking on the German battleship single-handed, as their captain implied. Later Brooks went off watch and strolled along the deck toward the stern of the ship, chatting to the gun and torpedo crews along the way. When he reached the stern, he stared at the white foam of the wake against the blackened sea, he couldn't help wondering how far it was to swim to Brest.

Pale morning light seeped onto the bridge of *U-556*. A short distance away Herbert Wohlfarth could see the friendly shape of *U-74*, which had answered his call and followed his beacon to the spot. As daylight

(Below) The cruiser *Dorsetshire*, which left its convoy and raced to the scene of the *Bismarck*'s last battle.

Captain Benjamin Martin, the *Dorsetshire*'s skipper.

(Below) The after fire control station where Lieutenant-Commander Müllenheim-Rechberg spent the final battle.

(Above) Burkard von Müllenheim-Rechberg as a young naval officer in 1934.

strengthened he signaled the other U-boat his best estimate of the *Bismarck's* position (he had never actually seen her, only the fire from her guns). *U-74* had been damaged by depth charges and could not use her torpedoes, but she had enough fuel to assume the job of keeping in contact and helping to guide any relief forces to the spot. At 6:30 A.M. Wohlfarth submerged and proceeded at his most economical speed toward France. It would be close, but he thought he could make it to Lorient without running out of fuel. He had done all he could.

Thus Wohlfarth was submerged when Admiral Lütjens radioed Group West for any U-boat in the area to come and pick up the war diary. He wanted to save the log of all the decisions he had taken and all the action the *Bismarck* had experienced since Exercise Rhine had begun. Earlier, an attempt to send off the diary aboard one of the Arado aircraft had failed because it turned out the catapult had been damaged by fragments from the boats hit by a shell from the *Prince of Wales*. Now Lütjens' last hope that this precious record would reach shore rested with a U-boat. But no U-boat came. And as the day grew brighter and ragged patches of blue appeared among the scudding clouds, the *Bismarck* seemed to be completely alone on the wind-ravished sea.

It was almost 8 A.M., it had been daylight for over an hour, and Müllenheim-Rechberg could not understand why the British had not attacked. What was the enemy waiting for? Well, there was nothing useful for him to do in the after fire control station where he had spent most of the night. A stroll would do him good. His first stop was the wardroom, where less than twenty-four hours before, with the British still out of contact, he and his fellow officers had looked forward to their first meal in France. Now the atmosphere was funereal. After some minutes, when the only sound to be heard was that of the ladles sloshing back and forth in a tureen of gruel, someone spoke mournfully of the wife he would never see again. Things were bound to be more optimistic on the bridge, Müllenheim-Rechberg thought as he left the dismal scene.

When he reached the bridge he was sadly disappointed. Gone was the jocularity Adolf Eich had witnessed only a few hours before. No one

talked, and people stood or sat almost motionless. Müllenheim-Rechberg looked for the captain, then saw to his astonishment that Lindemann was wearing an open lifejacket. He walked over and saluted smartly, expecting some word from the man he had served as personal adjutant when the ship was still being finished at the Blohm and Voss dockyard in Hamburg. He had come to know the captain well, respected him deeply. But Lindemann did not even return his salute, would not look at him, stared blankly as he ate his breakfast in silence. He wondered if Lindemann were consciously detaching himself from the *Bismarck*'s final moments, disassociating himself from the inevitable loss of his ship. More likely the captain had finally caved in under the strain of command, his conflicts with Lütjens and long hours without sleep. As Gerhard Junack had discovered earlier, the captain of the *Bismarck* had seemingly relinquished all pretense of command.

On his way back to his station, Müllenheim-Rechberg encountered the admiral and his staff officer heading for the bridge. At least Lütjens

(Above) The Arado float plane that was intended to carry the *Bismarck*'s war diary to safety is dumped overboard. The compressed air line to the catapult was bent and thus the plane could not be launched. To make sure it would sink, its wings were folded and holes were punched in the floats.

Admiral Tovey's flagship, *King George V*, steams into battle with its big 14-inch guns ready to fire.

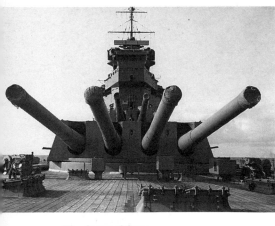

The forward four-gun turret on *King George V*.

met his gaze and returned his salute as he brushed past. But he, too, said nothing. Thus, as the *Bismarck* approached her final battle, the two men most responsible for her fate had withdrawn into their private worlds. No one could know what they were thinking or feeling. Then the alarm bells rang out urgently and Müllenheim-Rechberg's morbid thoughts vanished. The battle was about to begin.

As day broke over the angry Atlantic, Admiral Tovey considered the conditions and decided to wait a while longer before attacking. The weather was the problem: "patchy rain squalls, flickering sun, tearing wind from the northwest and a rising sea," was how Hugh Guernsey, who had stood on the bridge with the admiral all night, described it. Tovey had held off this long against the advice of many of his anxious subordinates, who feared the *Bismarck* would repair the damage and slip through their grasp yet again. But Vian's destroyers had done their job; Tovey knew where the *Bismarck* was. This time he would play all his pieces perfectly, wait for full daylight and good visibility. Unlike Admiral Holland, he would let his two attacking ships maneuver independently. He would not let the *Bismarck* do to him what she had done to the *Hood*.

Tovey's plan was simple, yet sound. *King George V* and *Rodney* would approach from the west with the wind at their backs, into the faces of the Germans. The *Bismarck* would be backlit in the early morning light, making her an easier target for his range finders. His two battleships would close quickly to sure-hitting range, approaching end-on to present the smallest target. Tovey hoped, as he later wrote, that "the sight of two battleships steering straight for them would shake the nerves of the range-takers and control officers, who had already had four anxious days and nights." If needed, he had *Ark Royal*'s torpedo bombers close at hand (the sea and weather conditions had prevented Admiral Somerville from sending them off, as planned, at dawn). *Norfolk* would arrive at any minute from the north, and *Dorsetshire*, charging up from the south, would now appear in time for the battle.

At 7:37 A.M., the *Bismarck* was twenty-one miles east-southeast of the two battleships, as they altered course and headed directly toward the Germans. At 7:53 *Norfolk*, which was much closer to the enemy, sighted the *Bismarck*, but mistook her for *Rodney*. Admiral Wake-Walker only realized his mistake when the battleship did not return his visual signal. Expecting to be under German fire immediately, the *Norfolk* retreated to a safe distance to the northwest but kept in visual contact. Thus Wake-Walker, who had let the *Bismarck* slip away in the mid-Atlantic, found himself again shadowing the German ship. It was some measure of vindication. Meanwhile the two British battleships continued their approach from the west, sighting *Norfolk* at 8:20, their first visual link with the *Bismarck*. Wake-Walker signaled that the German ship was sixteen miles southeast of Tovey's position. *King George V* and *Rodney* altered course accordingly. In a matter of minutes the battle would begin.

Admiral Tovey put on his "battle bowler" tin hat and found himself drenched with rainwater that had collected there overnight. "He just grinned," Guernsey later wrote, "quite undisturbed by that or indeed by any other incident of this five-day chase," during which he had seen his hopes raised and dashed time and again. Who could help but love such a commander? The other officers on the bridge smiled with him. Everything was going to be all right. A few minutes later, at 8:43, Tovey and the others finally saw the sight they had been longing for and dreading during these recent endless days and nights. As the *Bismarck* emerged from a distant rain squall, she looked to Guernsey like "a thick, squat ghost of a ship, coming straight towards us end-on." A ghost of her former self, perhaps, but not dead yet. By no means.

The two British battleships charged the wounded German titan, coming in on the port bow as the *Bismarck* struggled to turn to starboard so she could deliver a full broadside. It was *Rodney*, the old lady of the three, who should have been in the refit docks and not in the midst of a historic battle, who fired first, at 8:47. The first salvo from her 16-inch guns shook her from stem to stern; to many on board it seemed as though her aging hull plates would separate. But she furrowed forward as her gun crews busily prepared to fire again. Then the flagship, *King George V,* fired her first round. Still there was no response from the *Bismarck*.

The first salvo from *King George V'*s 14-inch guns caused the bridge compass to bound out of its binnacle. Guernsey's tin hat tipped over his nose and clattered down on the deck while a pile of signal papers shot up like a fountain, then swirled away "in the tearing draft made by the great guns." Then orange flashes could be seen from the *Bismarck*'s two forward turrets, and on the bridges of both *Rodney* and *King George V* those in command held their breaths, waited to see where the shots would fall. All of them knew the German reputation for accuracy. "It took two hours for those shots to fall," wrote Guernsey. They fell one thousand yards short of the *Rodney.* Clearly the *Bismarck*'s first gunnery officer, Adalbert Schneider, was directing his fire at the older, weaker ship—hoping for a repeat of his success with the *Hood*. When Guernsey realized his ship was not the target, he couldn't help thinking, "Thank heavens she's shooting at the *Rodney.*"

The advancing British chargers continued to close the range as salvo answered salvo and the Germans held their own. *Norfolk* joined in, firing her 8-inch guns from ten miles away and to the east of Tovey. *Bismarck*'s third salvo straddled *Rodney*, but only shell splinters hit the ship, damaging the antiaircraft director but causing no casualties—it was then evacu-

Turret Caesar fires a salvo.

ated. Lieutenant-Commander Wellings found that battle concentrates the mind wonderfully. In his personal diary he later wrote that if that salvo had "landed about 20 yds. further aft our entire bridge structure would have been pierced & probably wrecked with the captain and other key personnel." In that event the executive officer would have assumed command and Wellings—an American—would have found himself very suddenly the second-in-command of a British warship—or so he believed.

A few minutes after 9 A.M., the *Dorsetshire* arrived on the scene, galloping up from the south. Since leaving his convoy, Captain Martin had steamed non-stop for nearly six hundred miles. Now he ordered his 8-inch guns to begin firing, but the range was so great there was little chance of hitting the target. The *Bismarck* was now beset by four ships. The odds against the Germans, whose locked rudder prevented any maneuvering, were well nigh impossible. Nonetheless, had the *Bismarck* made an early hit as she had in the battle off Iceland, the day might have gone very differently. But even had she won this battle, other ships would inevitably have arrived to finish her.

According to those on board the watching destroyers, the early stages of the battle had a terrible beauty about them. Sub-Lieutenant Ludovic Kennedy, aboard the destroyer *Tartar*, described the engagement thus:

"In all my life I doubt I will remember another hour as vividly as that one. It was the colour contrasts I recall most, so rare in the eternal greyness of voyaging at sea. The sun appeared for the first time in days, shining from a blue sky between white, racing clouds; and the wind, still strong, was marbling and stippling the green water, creaming the tops of the short, high seas. There was the somber blackness of the *Bismarck* and the grey of the British ships, the orange flashes of the guns, the brown of the cordite smoke, shell splashes as tall as houses, white as shrouds.

"It was a lovely sight to begin with, wild, majestic as one of our officers called it, almost too clean for the matter at hand. It seemed strange to think that within those three battleships were five thousand men; it seemed almost irrelevant, for this was a contest between ships not men. And who was going to win?"

The first real blood was drawn by the British. At 8:59, with the battle only twelve minutes old, a 16-inch shell from *Rodney* exploded near Anton and Bruno, knocking them both out of action. Almost at the same instant an 8-inch shell from *Norfolk* destroyed the foretop fire control director, taking with it Commander Schneider and his newly awarded Knight's Cross. In one of war's endless ironies, it was a hit as fortunate as the one that had done in the mighty *Hood* three days before. The battle had barely begun, but already the *Bismarck* was fighting with one eye blind and one hand broken.

Müllenheim-Rechberg listened to Schneider's calm voice directing fire at *Rodney* and wondered why it took the British so long to score their first hit. To him it seemed much longer than the twelve minutes that actually elapsed between the first salvo and the abrupt disappearance of Schneider's voice from the telephone. Then Sub-Lieutenant Friedrich Cardinal, in command in the forward gunnery computer room, informed him that turrets Anton and Bruno were out of action and that there was

no communication with the main gunnery control station. Müllenheim-Rechberg was to assume control of the after turrets. Suddenly the young officer found himself in sole command of the ship's remaining heavy artillery. The defense of the *Bismarck* was now in his hands.

Müllenheim-Rechberg could no longer see the *Rodney* through his port director (Captain Dalrymple-Hamilton had fallen out of line and turned north to assume a better attacking position), but the *King George V* was clearly in view at about 2.5 miles, and moving quickly on a reciprocal course. As the *Bismarck's* own course continued to seesaw between north, northeast and northwest, the young German officer now in control of the *Bismarck's* fate ordered one salvo, then another, then another. His third straddled *King George V*, his fourth was long. All the while his eyes were glued to the port director as he rattled off instructions to the aft computer room, which relayed corrections to the turrets. Just after the fourth salvo, the director shook violently and banged hard against his face. When he looked again into the eyepiece, all he could see was a blue blank: the director had been shattered. The *Bismarck* was now completely blind. There was nothing for Müllenheim-Rechberg to do but let turrets Caesar and Dora fire independently. It was roughly 9:15 A.M. and the battle was not quite half an hour old.

By this time the *Rodney* and *King George V* were close enough to bring their secondary armament to bear. They had already scored numerous hits on the German ship, but Tovey was unsure just how much damage he had done. And so the death-dealing hail of fire continued. In Guernsey's words, the shells "bored their way through the armour belt like a piece of cheese." "After half an hour of action," Tovey later wrote, "the

(Above) Salvos from the British ships fall around the *Bismarck* as her turrets return some of the punishing fire, in this painting by Jörg Wischmann.

The *Rodney*, entering the picture from the right, fires at the *Bismarck* in this view from the *King George V*.

Bismarck was on fire in several places and virtually out of control. Only one of her turrets remained in action and the fire of this and her secondary armament was wild and erratic. But she was still steaming."

Deep inside the *Bismarck*, where the crews in the boiler rooms and engine rooms were fighting their last battle with steam and turbines, it was impossible to distinguish between the thud of the *Bismarck*'s guns and the explosion of British shells hitting the ship. However, whenever a salvo straddled, water poured in through the air intakes, so they could guess that the enemy was frequently hitting the mark. In other below-

***Rodney* firing her 16-inch guns.**

(Below) Aboard *King George V* and *Rodney* gun crews in the big turrets load shells and prepare for the next salvo.

decks positions—in the computer rooms, the infirmaries, the magazines, the galleys—the men only knew what their officers told them. Each battle station was isolated from the next one, and their only contact with other parts of the ship was by telephone. As communication broke down, this isolation increased. But still the men toiled on or waited for orders that never came. For many in the forward part of the ship where damage was the greatest, death came swiftly.

Rodney and *King George V* were now at such close range that their guns were at maximum depression, and the battle was turning into target practice for the British. Shell after shell slammed into the *Bismarck*. Soon the forward part of the ship was an almost total wreck, with gun barrels pointing crazily skyward or drooping "like dead flowers," according to one observer. At 9:21 a heavy-caliber shell hit turret Caesar. Although the men inside were unharmed, their starboard gun would no longer elevate. At 9:27 one of the forward turrets managed to fire a last salvo. Then around 9:30 the left barrel of turret Dora burst, whether from a shell hit or internal explosion is not known, shredding like a peeled banana. At 9:31 the *Bismarck* fired her last salvo; then her great guns were silent.

But still the British poured their fire into the stricken battleship. Tovey's orders were to sink the *Bismarck*, to gain full revenge for the sinking of the *Hood*, even if it meant using every ounce of ammunition. The expenditure was enormous. In all, 2,876 shells were fired at the Germans— 719 from the big guns alone. Perhaps as many as 400 struck the ship. But because the range was so close, the trajectory so flat (many bounced off the water before hitting), they did little damage below the waterline. The *Bismarck* was a blazing wreck, but still she would not sink. At one point, in exasperation, Tovey remarked, "Get me my darts! Let's see if we can sink her with those."

The firing continued, even though the *Bismarck* was now a battered hulk with fires burning in many places. Her bow plates rose and fell so sharply that they sent up great blasts of spray. Then the impersonal steel leviathan that had haunted the British for the past week acquired a human dimension. "There, racing across her quarter-deck were little human figures," wrote Lieutenant-Commander Guernsey aboard *King George V.* "One climbed over the wire guard rails, hung on with one hand, looked back, and then jumped into the sea. Others just jumped without looking back at all. A little steady trickle of them, jumping into the sea, one after the other." A Canadian lieutenant aboard *Tartar*, George Whalley, later put into words what many were feeling: "What that ship was like inside . . . does not bear thinking of: her guns smashed, the ship full of fire, her people hurt; and surely all men are much the same when they are hurt." Around 10:15 A.M. Tovey ordered the firing to cease and withdrew with *Rodney* following. The battle had lasted almost an hour and a half.

Salvos from the *Rodney* land all around the *Bismarck* in this photograph taken from the *Dorsetshire.*

Shells were still hitting the *Bismarck* when the order to scuttle and prepare to abandon ship was issued by Commander Oels from his position in the heavily protected command post directly under the conning tower. As the ship's executive officer, it was he who assumed command when communication with the bridge ceased. Then Oels and his staff left and headed aft. He knew that forward the ship was a disaster area with many fires raging.

Gerhard Junack was at his station in the middle engine room when he received the order to scuttle, relayed to him by his superior Walter Lehmann, the *Bismarck*'s chief engineer. Then the telephone went dead. Junack dispatched his best petty officer to ask for further orders, but the man failed to return. Finally he decided to act on his own. He inspected the engine room to make sure that all the doors were open (so that water could pass between compartments), then ordered his chief machinist to ignite the fuses to the scuttling charges that would blow open the seacocks in the boiler room and the cooling water inlets to the condensers, causing water to flow rapidly into the boiler and engine rooms. He left his station with the last of his men.

The order to scuttle was also received near the stern of the ship by Warrant Officer Wilhelm Schmidt, in charge of Damage Control Team No. 1. He had his hands full. Four or five shells had hit near the stern, knocking out lights and the ventilation system and killing a number of his men.

Nitrogen gas had started fires on the decks above, and one group of men that he had sent to fight the blazes had not returned. Given the situation, it was a relief to hear the words, "Execute Measure Five." Immediately he reversed all the pumps to flood his area and led his remaining men toward the upper deck—through a shell hoist, as all other passages were blocked.

In the after computer room the men sat silently at their positions, waiting for Lieutenant Heinz Aengeneyndt to do something. The telephone had stopped working, but the ship's alarm bells continued their insistent ringing. The lights flickered occasionally, but continued to function. They knew their own guns had stopped firing, but the reverberation of each enemy shell hit could be heard—a distant thunder. The air was becoming stuffy and the men anxious. Heinz Jucknat felt a ticking in his ears. The air pressure was increasing, he thought. Perhaps the ship was already sinking. He fought back the feeling of panic, and without asking permission lay down on the floor; the ticking stopped. Finally Aengeneyndt sent someone to find out what was going on. A few minutes later the man reported back that the order had already gone out to scuttle and abandon ship.

Shell splashes continue to fall near the *Bismarck* as she burns on the horizon.

When the young lieutenant tried to lead his men to the upper decks, he found their way blocked by fire and wreckage. He seemed at a loss. Heinz Jucknat proposed attempting to escape through the communications tube linking the computer room with the fire control station. He found the hatch and climbed in. Right behind him was Adolf Eich, then came Franz Halke. The lieutenant hesitated and then climbed in after Franz. So did one more of their comrades, Herbert Langer.

In darkness they climbed until they could climb no farther. Heinz tried to open the hatch above his head. It wouldn't budge. So he took the housing from his gas mask and banged on the metal. If someone was alive up there, he would hear him. It was getting hot in the narrow shaft. Breathing was becoming difficult, sweat poured down his face. Then he heard the sound of scraping (bodies were being moved out of the way), the latch was released, and the hatch opened. The first thing he noticed was slimy liquid that poured down on him, making it difficult to pull himself into the room. Then he realized that he was drenched in blood. The awful smell of it filled his nostrils as he looked around the crowded room.

Other refugees from the lower decks of the ship had already found shelter in the fire control station, which had remained almost undamaged since the initial hit that had put the directors out of action and left the *Bismarck* blind. The cupola had been torn off the roof, exposing a fragment of sky, but the lightly armored walls were intact, and the men huddled there waiting for Müllenheim-Rechberg, the senior officer present, to tell them what to do next. At one point acrid yellow smoke filled the room, and men automatically reached for their gas masks. Franz Halke realized with sudden terror that he had forgotten his. But Heinz one away from a dead man and handed it to him. Finally Müllenheim-Rechberg allowed the men to open two small hatches for air. The British continued to fire.

While the men waited, some of them began to talk. At one point a junior officer pulled out his wallet and opened it to a picture of his wife and daughter. He looked at the picture and said mournfully, "Today you are going to be a widow."

When Commander Oels and his men left the ship's internal command post, one of their number, machinist Josef Statz, remained behind. He

(Below) This cross-section diagram shows the escape route up the communications tube followed by Adolf Eich, Franz Halke and Heinz Jucknat from their battle station in the after computer room to the after fire control station.

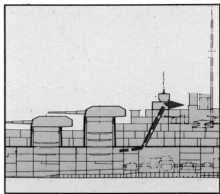

(Above far left) The door to the after fire control station, through which the three men exited after their climb up the narrow shaft.

(Above from left) Adolf Eich, Franz Halke and Heinz Jucknat

(Overleaf) The last moments of battleship *Bismarck* as painted by war artist Charles E. Turner.

felt safer here, even though he knew from the lights on the control panel that the ship was filling with water. He made one attempt to head aft, but was discouraged by the smoke and pitch-blackness, so he returned to the seeming safety of the still-lighted room. Then the telephone rang.

It was Müllenheim-Rechberg wanting to know who was in command, what new orders were in effect. Statz told him that the order to abandon ship had been issued and hung up. The living voice from above decks roused him to action. Somehow he would find his way out.

Suddenly two men materialized in the command post. They led him up a frighteningly narrow shaft—the heavily armored communications tube between the armor deck and the conning tower—and emerged just as a shell hit the already badly damaged bridge area. The shell splinters killed his two comrades and tore a gash in his shoulder. Then he heard a familiar voice greeting him in friendly tones. It was Friedrich Cardinal, the chief computer officer of the ship who had so proudly showed Hitler the workings of his state-of-the-art equipment when the Führer had come on board on May 5—only twenty-two days before.

Together they surveyed the scene of devastation. Fires were raging and thick smoke swirled: it was a scene from Dante's *Inferno*. No other living soul was in evidence. Turrets Anton and Bruno were silent wrecks. Antiaircraft guns pointed skyward but did not fire. Somehow, however,

the big binoculars mounted in the middle of the bridge were intact. And higher still, the admiral's enclosed bridge appeared to be unhurt, its windows still in one piece. But there was no sign of Lütjens or his entourage.

Then the British firing ceased. Silently the two men made their way aft through the no-man's land of destruction and death toward where the survivors of the *Bismarck*'s final battle had gathered as the ship heeled ever more sharply to port and began to sink by the stern.

One of the last shells to hit the *Bismarck* penetrated to the battery deck in Compartment 10, just aft of the funnel, where a few hundred men had gathered and were surging forward toward the companionway to the open deck above. Commander Oels had just arrived on the scene and was frantically urging the men to save themselves. Instead he was killed along with more than one hundred others; many more were wounded.

Herbert Blum was one of the few who survived unhurt. He had been with Walter Lehmann at the engineering command post when the order came to abandon ship. Then he had watched his superior officer replace the telephone receiver "as carefully as if it were the most fragile glass" and tell his men calmly to get out while they could. Now Blum picked his way through the unspeakable carnage of mutilated bodies, of men vomiting or holding in their blasted guts with blood-soaked hands, or screaming in pain. Somehow he managed to reach the upper deck. But the scene there was almost as horrible: gaping shell holes into which panicked men fell, twisted and burning superstructure, piles of the dead and dying.

Hans Zimmermann had also been on the battery deck when the shell hit, and he had also seen the death of Commander Oels. When the smoke cleared somewhat, he and a few others managed to find their way onto the upper deck behind the first starboard 5.9-inch gun mount. Although the order to scuttle had already been given, one crazy gunner was firing flak at planes that existed only in his imagination. Hans headed aft to the airplane deck. There he met his old school chum Hermann Emmerich, whom he hadn't even known was also on the *Bismarck* until their chance meeting at home over his New Year's leave. How many centuries ago that seemed. The friends grasped hands and solemnly vowed that if either of them survived, he would take a final message to the other's family. By the time they went overboard the ship was lying almost on her side, and the starboard part of the keel was visible.

The British firing was tailing off now, but in the after fire control station Müllenheim-Rechberg waited. After his brief conversation with Statz he knew the order to abandon ship had been given. Still, there was no point in running the gauntlet until he was sure the British had finished firing. At last the enemy guns ceased. He noticed the ship was listing more heavily to port as he ordered the men to move toward the stern and await orders. Meanwhile he ventured forward.

"The scene that lay before me was too much to take in at a glance and is very difficult to describe. It was chaos and desolation. The antiaircraft guns and searchlights that once surrounded the after station had disappeared without a trace. Where there had been guns, shields, and instruments, there was empty space. The superstructure decks were littered with scrap metal. There were holes in the stack, but it was still standing.

Midshipman Joe Brooks (above) of the *Dorsetshire* drew this color sketch of the burning *Bismarck*.

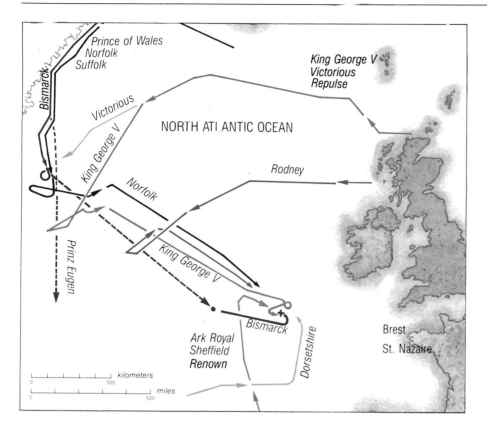

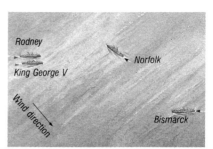

May 27, 8:08 a.m. *Rodney* and *King George V* sight *Norfolk* which had been shadowing *Bismarck*.

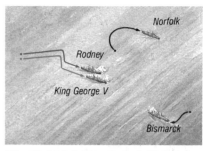

May 27, 8:08–8:49 a.m. At 8:47 *Rodney* opens fire on *Bismarck*, followed by *King George V* at 8:48. *Bismarck* returns fire at 8:49 as *Norfolk* turns away.

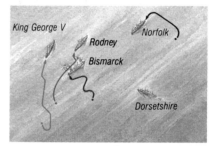

May 27, 9:17–9:40 a.m. At 9:17 a.m. *Rodney* drops out of position behind *King George V* and closes in, firing on the *Bismarck*. The burning *Bismarck* fights on but her salvos are intermittent and inaccurate. The *Norfolk* loops back, and by 9:40 the *Dorsetshire* arrives on the scene.

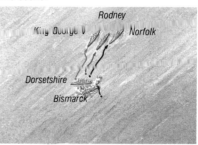

May 27, 10:22–10:39 a.m. At 10:22 the British cease firing. The *Dorsetshire* closes in, fires her first torpedo at 10:29, crosses *Bismarck*'s bow and then at 10:36 fires another. At 10:39 the *Bismarck* sinks and *Dorsetshire* stands by to pick up survivors.

Whitish smoke, like a ground fog, extended from the after fire control station all the way to the tower mast, indicating where fires must be raging below. "Out of the smoke rose the tower mast, seemingly undamaged. How good it looked in its grey paint, I thought, almost as if it had not been in battle. The foretop and the antiaircraft station also looked intact, but I well knew that such was not the case. Men were running around up there—I wondered whether they would be able to save themselves, to find a way down the mast."

Heinz Jucknat had become separated from his comrades. He was somewhat dazed, unsure what to do as the smoke swirled around him. He was too tired now to feel panic—things were ghostly, unreal. The blood that made the deck slippery, the dead bodies, the screams and moans no longer affected him. He found a sheltered spot and sat down to have a smoke. Not far away he noticed another sailor sitting on a bollard. The man called out to Heinz, asking him to bring a smoke. As Heinz approached, he realized he knew the fellow; then he saw that his legs were gone. Where his feet should have been a pair of empty boots sat, but no blood dripped from his leg stumps. As if in a dream Heinz handed the man a cigarette, leaned over and lit it for him. Then he returned to his own spot and smoked in silence.

Another man walked by, this one with a bottle in his hand. The legless sailor asked the newcomer for a drink; it was proffered. Then he asked Heinz and the other man to help him get off the ship, to throw him overboard. He said, "I can't move, but I feel no pain." As he spoke he grabbed onto the third man, clung to him desperately and begged. Finally the man carried his wounded comrade to the rail. Heinz looked away, unable to watch.

The Discovery of the Bismarck   135

As Heinz sat smoking his cigarette, more and more people were leaving the ship. Some were jumping off to starboard, some were sliding down the sloping deck. But others seemed reluctant to exchange the precarious security of the sinking *Bismarck* for the uncertainties of the cold ocean. Not far away a group of men were singing sailor songs—dirty ditties about girls and booze—as they passed a bottle around.

Finally Heinz decided it was time. The slope of the deck was becoming alarming. If he didn't leave the ship soon, it would leave him. Calmly he removed his boots and took off his uniform so that he was only wearing his socks and his longjohns. He put on his lifejacket and inflated it. Then he slid into the water.

Franz Halke was reluctant to leave the shelter of the gun control station when Müllenheim-Rechberg gave the okay, but he started to follow his friend Adi Eich. After a few yards he changed his mind; he wanted to go back. Adi argued with him and they went back and forth until Eich finally ran out of patience. If Franz wanted to go down with the ship, that was fine with him, but he was going to save himself. He headed for the stern. Near turret Dora he met his friend Hans Riedl, a loader from the crew of turret Caesar, among a group of survivors. They waited for a while. Then he and Hans jumped together over the port side.

"Three Sieg Heils, then we jump," shouted Gerhard Junack. Several hundred men were gathered between the two after turrets, among them Herbert Blum and Franz Halke, who had finally found his resolve and ventured aft through the dead bodies and the decks washed with blood. The sun shone, the British guns had gone silent. "Don't worry, comrades. I'll be taking a Hamburg girl in my arms again, and we'll meet once more on the Reeperbahn." More than one of those who heard this remarkable speech must have wondered how Junack could think of the prostitutes of Hamburg's red light district at a time like this. But they all cheered and headed for the water. The smart ones slid down the starboard hull to the keel and jumped from there. Some fools dove head first and broke their necks. Others who tried to slide down the deck and go in on the port side were washed back against the ship and knocked unconscious.

Friedrich Cardinal and Josef Statz heard the cheers and saw Junack's group leave the ship. They rested by a port turret, but soon it was partly under water. They would go no farther. Cardinal jumped first, then Statz followed. They were the only men to escape the forward part of the ship.

Müllenheim-Rechberg briefly considered going to his cabin to collect some personal belongings, then dismissed the thought. His duty was with the men. He joined a small group gathered just forward of turret Dora, told them to wait a while before going over. The ship was sinking slowly, and every extra minute on board meant one less in cold water. He was sure that British ships would rescue the survivors. But where were they? *Rodney* and *King George V* had sailed away, leaving an apparently empty ocean. He waited until the list to port and the sinking of the stern became extreme, then ordered the men with him to inflate their lifejackets and prepare to jump over the starboard side. The *Bismarck's* battle standard was still flying from the mainmast. "A salute to our fallen comrades," he called out. The men saluted the flag and then they jumped.

By the time *Ark Royal*'s Swordfish arrived on the scene they could only watch the battle from afar.

As *Rodney* and *King George V* withdrew, Tovey signaled any ship that still had torpedoes to close in and finish the *Bismarck* off. The destroyers had already left the scene, heading home to refuel. That left the *Dorsetshire*. Now Captain Martin had his chance to win the prize. He moved in to a range of about 1.5 miles on the *Bismarck*'s starboard beam and launched two torpedoes. One hit right under the bridge area. Then he moved around to the other side and launched a third. It, too, found its mark.

A few minutes later, the *Bismarck*'s stern sank under the waves, her jaunty, flared bow pointed briefly into the air, and then disappeared. From his station on the *Dorsetshire*, Midshipman Joe Brooks watched her go down, found it a most unpleasant sight, and thought how such things turned one against war in general. He was close enough to see the men jumping overboard and swimming in the water. To Admiral Tovey, who watched through fieldglasses from farther away, the *Bismarck*'s final moments seemed more noble: "She put up a most gallant fight against impossible odds, worthy of the old days of the Imperial German Navy."

Above the scene, a squadron of twelve Swordfish torpedo bombers circled. They had arrived when the battle was well in progress, and couldn't risk being caught in the British cross fire, but had stayed to watch the show. Observer Edmond Carver could see down into the "absolute cauldron of fires" on the *Bismarck*'s deck. He saw men jumping overboard, then watched as the ship rolled over to port, capsized and sank. He saw the hundreds of survivors bobbing in the oily water, strung out in the wake of a ship that was no more.

This photograph shows a sea of heads floating in the oily water just after the *Bismarck* sank. For some reason the British censor has blotted out most of the faces.

Although the two British battleships had been very lucky, escaping without a hit, both were considerably the worse for wear after more than an hour of continuous firing and several near misses from the *Bismarck*'s shells. A number of *King George V*'s heavy guns had become inoperative at various times during the battle, but her secondary armament had picked up the slack as the range closed.

The venerable *Rodney* had fared much worse. The force of the explosion from a shell that landed in the water close by had jammed her port torpedo tube doors. But this was minor compared to the side-effects of the continuous firing of her big guns, several of which actually jumped their cradles. There was damage throughout the ship. Another U.S. passenger on board, a Chief Petty Officer Miller, described the devastation in his report: "Tile decking in washrooms, water closets and heads were ruptured throughout the ship.... Longitudinal beams were broken and cracked in many parts of the ship having to be shored. The overhead decking ruptured and many bad leaks were caused by bolts and rivets coming loose. All compartments on the main deck had water flooding the decks.... Cast iron water mains were ruptured and in many instances broke, flooding compartments....Bulkheads, furniture, lockers, and fittings were blown loose causing undue damage to permanent structures when the ship rolled." Given this evidence, the damage from even one well-placed 15-inch shell would likely have been enormous.

While most of the British ships, which were desperately short of fuel, left the scene, the destroyer *Maori* and the cruiser *Dorsetshire* remained to pick up survivors.

Gerhard Junack swam for all he was worth to get free of the sinking ship. When he was safely away he turned to watch her go. As she rolled over to port he looked along the starboard side for any sign of torpedo holes and saw none. Then the *Bismarck*'s bow pointed into the air and she slid straight down by the stern. Without thinking, Junack looked at his watch, which was still working. It was 10:36.

The *Dorsetshire* was one of the two British ships that rescued survivors.

Heinz Jucknat and the other swimmers who could see the bow of the ship were astonished to observe Captain Lindemann standing on the forecastle in front of turret Anton. With him was a young seaman, his messenger. Everyone had assumed their beloved captain was dead. How had he survived the raging inferno that had enveloped the forward part of the ship? As the slope of the deck increased, the two figures moved toward the bow. It was obvious from Lindemann's gestures that he was trying to persuade the young man to save himself and jump, but he refused. As the ship turned on its side, the two walked out onto the hull and then, as it turned over, stood on the keel. Finally, in a gesture worthy of a Wagnerian hero, Lindemann saluted, and the two went down with the ship.

Once he was in the water, Josef Statz looked for his friend Friedrich Cardinal. The next wave washed the two together. Statz started to speak, then realized something was wrong. Cardinal's head hung limply and blood oozed from a bullet wound. Inexplicably the officer he had admired so much had first saved himself and then committed suicide. Statz turned and swam furiously away.

More than one thousand men now found themselves swimming for their lives. But from what quarter would succor come? Surprisingly, many didn't notice the cold (13 degrees Celsius). Those who did felt it first in their hands and feet. Heinz Jucknat had kept his socks on, but was beginning to regret his decision to strip down to his longjohns. Far worse than the cold was the fuel oil, which lay in a horrible stinking slick over the waves. According to Müllenheim-Rechberg, "the odour stung our noses. It blackened our faces and forced its way into eyes, noses and ears."

The men had been in the water for an hour when they saw the welcome silhouette of a three-stack cruiser—the *Dorsetshire*. They began to swim toward salvation as lines were lowered, since it was too rough to

launch boats. Soon the sheltered lee side of the British ship was crowded with hundreds of men. It was mayhem. Men fought for the same line while others dangled unattended. The oil made the ropes slippery and the cold cramped their hands—it was almost impossible for most to hold on unless the rope was tied in a bowline so you could get a foot or an arm through the loop. Müllenheim-Rechberg found one such loop, stepped in and was within a few feet of safety when he released one hand to reach out for another line. Before he could grab on, his other hand gave way, and he fell back into the sea. The second time he held tight the whole way. When he reached deck level he said politely in his best English, "Please pull me on board."

Franz Halke did not fare so well. He tried and failed to grab a line

Bismarck survivors struggled to reach the safety of the *Dorsetshire*. Many were too injured or too exhausted to pull themselves up the ropes thrown over the side.

from the *Dorsetshire*, which was still in motion when he reached her; then he saw the *Maori* off in the distance and swam for dear life. It took him three tries to get on board, and he was so exhausted that it took two sailors to drag him over the railing.

Many were less lucky. One man whose arms had been blown off, but had somehow made it this far, was trying to grab a line in his teeth. On *Dorsetshire*, Midshipman Joe Brooks climbed over the side in an attempt to get a bowline around him. But the ship began to move forward and Brooks lost him, only barely managing to climb back on board himself. The ever-vigilant Captain Martin promptly put Brooks under arrest for leaving the ship without permission—and had him confined to his cabin.

(Below right) Captain Martin addresses the *Dorsetshire*'s crew after the battle.

(Above) Splinter damage in the wardroom of the light cruiser *Sheffield* which was fired on when shadowing the *Bismarck* on May 26.

The destroyer *Maori* was beginning to pick up survivors when the signal came from the *Dorsetshire* of a possible U-boat sighting. Both ships were to leave the area immediately. As they got underway, some men clung desperately to lines as long as they could, others scratched uselessly at the gray paint, salvation slipping from their grasp. Only those who were already partway up a rope had a chance. Hundreds of others watched in disbelief as their only hope quickly faded into the distance. Theirs would be a slow, creeping death.

This is how Ludovic Kennedy portrayed the grisly scene: "In *Dorsetshire* they heard the thin cries of hundreds of Germans who had come within an inch of rescue, had believed that their long ordeal was at last over, cries that the British sailors, no less than survivors already on board, would always remember. From the water the *Bismarck*'s men watched appalled as the cruiser's gray side swept past them, believed then the tales they'd heard about the British not caring much about survivors were true after all, presently found themselves alone in the sunshine on the empty, tossing sea. And during the day, as they floated about the Atlantic with only lifebelts between them and eternity, the cold came to their testicles and hands and feet and heads, and one by one they lost consciousness, and one by one they died."

In all, 110 men, so blackened with oil they looked like coal miners, were pulled from the water: 85 were on *Dorsetshire*, 25 on the *Maori*. They were stripped, wrapped in warm blankets and bundled below. There they were given dry clothes, perhaps a cigarette and put to bed. Hot sweet tea

with lots of milk was poured down their throats. The ships' doctors examined them. Those with wounds were attended to. Many were offered a slug of rum to warm their insides, but few could keep down the first swallow; although this had the inadvertently beneficial effect of purging them of fuel oil and saltwater.

Lieutenant-Commander Müllenheim-Rechberg was the highest-ranking of the four officers to survive. Lieutenant-Commander Gerhard Junack (ranked lower because turbines were lowlier than guns) also made it to safety. Antiaircraft gunner Alois Haberditz, along with his friends Heinz Jucknat and Adolf Eich, ended up on the *Dorsetshire*. It would be some time before they discovered that their comrade Franz Halke had also been saved by the *Maori* and that, along with Herbert Langer, they were the only four survivors from the after computer room. Hans Zimmermann managed to get on board the *Dorsetshire* after three tries; his friend Hermann Emmerich, who had gone overboard with him, did not make it to safety. Josef Statz from the damage control command center was the only man to survive from the forward part of the ship.

Herbert Wohlfarth in *U-556* surfaced at noon, a time when radio signals from Group West were repeated. Only then, many miles from the scene of the *Bismarck*'s sinking, did he hear the order for him to pick up the *Bismarck*'s war diary. He radioed back and requested that this order be transferred to *U-74*, which he assumed was still on the scene. Then he submerged again and headed for Lorient. By the time he arrived, his fuel tanks would be almost empty.

(Above) The men of the *Dorsetshire* celebrate their role in the victory.

(Above) Captain Martin receives congratulations for delivering the final blow to the *Bismarck*.

The Discovery of the Bismarck   141

In this contest of titans there were many bit players, many unsung heroes. War has a way of thrusting ordinary men into extraordinary situations, of pulling from them reserves of courage and endurance that would otherwise go untapped. But there are also extraordinary men whose peacetime lives seem like dull interludes awaiting the challenges of war. Such perhaps was Admiral Tovey, who in retirement became a sad shadow, replaying his wartime exploits in crotchety isolation. Such certainly was Winston Churchill. Despite the British prime minister's often counterproductive meddling in naval strategy, there is no doubt his ability to lead and to inspire helped the British survive. And he knew how to

capitalize on this triumph, just as Hitler would have done had the *Bismarck* somehow escaped unsunk. Churchill was a master of political discourse. He also knew how to underplay his rhetorical hand when the situation suited.

On the morning of May 27, Churchill rose in the House of Commons to report on the battle in Crete, which was going badly, and the *Bismarck*. "This morning," he said, "shortly after daylight the *Bismarck*, virtually at a standstill, far from help, was attacked by the British pursuing battleships. I do not know what were the results of the bombardment. It appears, however, that the *Bismarck* was not sunk by gunfire, and she will now be dispatched by torpedo. It is thought that this is now proceeding, and it is also thought that there cannot be any lengthy delay in disposing of this vessel. Great as is our loss in the *Hood*, the *Bismarck* must be regarded as the most powerful, as she is the newest battleship in the world."

Hardly had Churchill resumed his seat when a note was passed to him. He promptly rose again. "Mr. Speaker, I crave your indulgence," he said. "I have just received news that the *Bismarck* is sunk." Nothing more. Then he sat down. He later wrote of the reaction: "They seemed content."

The sinking of the *Bismarck* was welcome news for Prime Minister Winston Churchill.

The following day Churchill penned a top-secret memo to Sir Dudley Pound, the First Sea Lord. Its subject was the *Prinz Eugen*, still at large somewhere in the Atlantic. The thrust of this communication was Churchill's desire to involve the United States in the capture of the German cruiser, thus perhaps precipitating America's entry into the war. "It would be far better, for instance, that she should be located by a United States ship, as this might tempt her to fire upon that ship, thus providing an incident for which the United States government would be so thankful." Unfortunately for Churchill, *Prinz Eugen* did not oblige. After sailing 7,000 miles and managing twice to refuel from German tankers, but without engaging a single convoy or enemy vessel, she slipped safely into Brest on June 1. She would never roam the Atlantic again.

At noon, Adolf Hitler was informed that the British government had announced the *Bismarck*'s sinking an hour before. How humiliating to learn of this blow from the enemy and not from his own intelligence. This was just what he had feared. He should never have allowed Raeder to send the battleship to sea in the first place. Walther Hewel, Ribbentrop's liaison to Hitler's staff, described the Führer's reaction thus: "Mood very dejected. Führer melancholy beyond words. Uncontrollable fury at naval staff." The next day Raeder answered Hitler's anger with reason. Although her loss was indeed a blow to German prestige, she had served an important purpose. Five battleships, three battle cruisers, two aircraft carriers, thirteen cruisers, thirty-three destroyers and eight submarines had been engaged in her pursuit and destruction. Such a diversion had unquestionably contributed to the successful conclusion of the invasion of Crete. But Raeder knew that the German leader would be reluctant to approve any further commerce raiding in the Atlantic. Indeed, for the duration of the war the Germans never mounted an operation on the scale of Exercise Rhine.

While the British fleet returned to port, a few survivors still clung to life on the tossing sea. Three of them lay in a rubber life raft they had managed to launch while the British guns were still firing. They were Herbert Manthey, Georg Herzog and Otto Höntzsch. None had seen the *Bismarck* go down; by that time they had already drifted too far away and the seas were too high. All day they had bobbed on the waves, shivered in the wind. Herzog was suffering the most from a serious wound to his calf. Now with darkness coming on, they had pretty much given up hope of rescue. Then, just before 7 P.M. they saw a U-boat—unmistakably it was German. But had it spotted them? They waved and shouted, but the streamlined shape slid by only a couple of hundred yards distant. They had almost given up hope when it began to turn around into the wind.

Life rings were thrown overboard from the German sub, but Höntzsch and Manthey were reluctant to abandon their wounded comrade, who couldn't swim. Finally, seeing that the space between them and safety was widening, they jumped and swam. To their relief, Herzog was eventually rescued, too. All three recovered and were able to tell their story to the German Admiralty.

The submarine was *U-74*, the same vessel Herbert Wohlfarth had left to stand watch over the *Bismarck* when he could stay no longer. *U-74* searched in vain for other survivors through the night and all the next day. Finally, reluctantly, near midnight on May 28, she headed for her home port in France.

But the German weather ship *Sachsenwald* had better luck that same evening. About 10:35 P.M. she sighted two red lights on the port side. As she came closer two men could be seen on a life raft. When they were brought on board they reported that other survivors were on a raft close by. But although the *Sachsenwald* continued to search the next day and the next, she found only one empty rubber dinghy.

The Spanish cruiser *Canarias*, which had sailed to the sinking area at the German Admiralty's request, found only wreckage and floating bodies. On May 30 she gave up. When the last ship had left the scene, 115 men had been pulled from the sea alive, out of a crew of 2,206.

The German sailors who fought the *Bismarck*'s last battle were not the

In Britain, newspaper headlines celebrated the naval victory.

(Below) Crewmen of the *Sheffield* point to splinter holes caused by a near-miss from the *Bismarck*,

only ones who wondered what had happened to the German bombers supposedly dispatched to the rescue. All the British ships returning to port, most of them short of fuel and zigzagging to avoid submarines, were on the alert for air attack. But on the 27th, only the *Ark Royal* encountered enemy airplanes—she was bombed but not hit by two Heinkel bombers. In fact, bad weather prevented the many planes that took off from France that morning from reaching the scene. The next day, however, the weather was much better and a big wave of bombers went out in search of British warships and some measure of revenge.

On the morning of the 28th, *Tartar* and *Mashona*, two of the destroyers that had escorted *Rodney* but taken no actual part in the battle, were steaming north toward Londonderry at an economical 15 knots. Suddenly the lovely summer morning was shattered by the appearance of Focke-Wulf bombers. They kept coming, wave after wave, as the destroyers dodged the bombs and the antiaircraft guns tried to drive them off. *Tartar* was lucky; *Mashona* was not. Around noon she took a hit in the boilers and began to list heavily. Steam could be seen rising amidships. In no time she was right over, and men were sliding down her hull into the sea. To Sub-Lieutenant Ludovic Kennedy, who had arrived on *Tartar's* bridge just as the first plane was spotted, it was all too much like a gruesome replay of the *Bismarck's* sinking, but with the roles reversed. However, thanks to a fortuitous lull in the air attacks, *Tartar* was able to rescue all but 45 of the 250 men on board.

To the *Bismarck* survivors on board *Dorsetshire* and *Maori*, the events of the previous five days were already beginning to seem unreal. They were warm and well fed, and the British treated them kindly. Soon a camaraderie developed between captives and captors (in later years many of the survivors would count former enemies among their closest friends). The British sailors warned the Germans that they would not be treated so well when they reached shore. (They were right.)

On May 28, machinist Gerhard Lüttich died on board the *Dorsetshire*. He had been badly burned and had lost an arm: it was amazing he had made it far enough to be rescued. The next day British and German sailors who had so recently been trying to kill each other gathered on the deck. At first Hans Zimmermann, who didn't speak any English, didn't know what was going on. But then he saw the body wrapped in an ensign of the Imperial German Navy, noticed the honor guard from *Dorsetshire*, and saw the chaplain in his robes. All at once he realized that the British were according a full military funeral to his friend. He and Lüttich had been recruited together, had suffered through the same eight weeks of basic training on the island of Rügen in the western Baltic. They had belonged to the same platoon, slept in the same room, and they had been transferred to Hamburg the same day, June 4, 1940. Hans and his fellow prisoners stood solemnly at attention on the deck while a bugler played the last post. They were permitted to give the Nazi salute. Then one of the *Bismarck's* crew played a sad sailor's lament on a borrowed harmonica: "Ich hatt' einen Kamaraden." "I had a comrade." Zimmermann had already lost so many friends—this one was simply too much. He was not the only one with tears in his eyes as the body was committed to the waves. He

Burial services are held on the *Sheffield* for three men who lost their lives in the *Bismarck* operation.

(Above, middle and bottom) British sailors wounded during the *Bismarck* battle are brought ashore in England.

noticed that many of the British sailors were openly weeping, too.

For the rescued Germans, the fighting was over. During the next few years their lives would be led in a progression of POW camps—some harsh, others relatively pleasant. Many would end up in Canada. It would be a long time before any of them would see home.

For most of the British sailors, the war was just beginning. After a brief leave in port they would be back at sea—most to the tense tedium of convoy duty. Admiral Tovey and the main warships of the Home Fleet would soon be back in Scapa Flow, awaiting the next challenge to Britain's control of the Atlantic. Force H, including the *Ark Royal* that had struck the crucial blow at the eleventh hour and delivered the *Bismarck* into Tovey's hands, returned to Gibraltar to a tumultuous welcome.

Midshipman Joe Brooks spent the next three months a prisoner on his

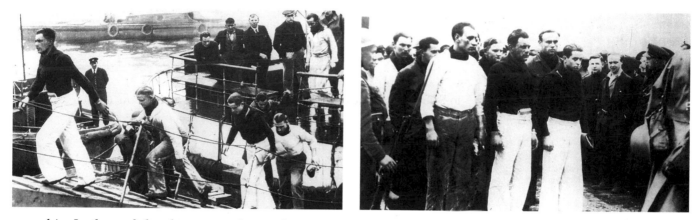

The *Bismarck* survivors landed in Scotland and were taken to London for interrogation before being sent to a series of POW camps where they spent the remainder of the war. Franz Halke stands at the front left of the group shown above.

own ship. In the end the charge was dropped and he remained aboard the *Dorsetshire* during her mission to the Pacific when she helped escort the final British convoy to leave Singapore before the Japanese invasion. He was then ordered back to England and assigned to the submarine service. Seven days after his departure, the *Dorsetshire* was sunk by Japanese dive bombers.

On June 12, Lieutenant-Commander R.H. Wellings, United States Navy, finally neared Boston on board *Rodney*. After the battle he had returned briefly to London where he found himself a minor celebrity: Sir Dudley Pound himself had listened raptly to Wellings' account of the battle. Then he made the journey north to Greenock, Scotland, and boarded the *Rodney* once again. This time the crossing was uneventful but far from boring. He had spent much of it interviewing the *Rodney's* officers, writing notes and reconstructing the battle for his report to Washington. Now as he saw the familiar landmarks of Boston Harbor—Boston Lightship, Graves Light and Boston Lighthouse—he became achingly homesick. He knew every buoy and landmark of these waters that he had sailed since he was a boy. After *Rodney* had snugly berthed that night, he "was not surprised to see Mrs. Wellings looking radiant and beautiful on the pier at the foot of the bow." The next day he, his wife and three-year-old daughter enjoyed tea with the officers of the *Rodney*. The day after that he took his leave of Captain Dalrymple-Hamilton and walked down the gangway of the famous warship for the last time. But like every man who lived to tell the tale, he would never forget the great events he had witnessed.

CHAPTER EIGHT

The Hunt Resumes (1989)

Cadiz, Spain—May 25, 1989

(Above left) The Star Hercules at the wharf in Cadiz harbor.

(Left) The broad afterdeck of the Star Hercules housing the village of vans we nicknamed Venice.

Our 1989 *Bismarck* expedition set sail from Cadiz in the late afternoon and headed west along the southern edge of Portugal. In 1492 Columbus had departed from the Bay of Cadiz as he set out on his great voyage of discovery. Most people thought the Italian explorer was sailing off the edge of the earth. Columbus believed he was sailing to China—instead he found the New World. Such is the uncertainty of an explorer's life. Last year we had hunted for the *Bismarck* and found an old sailing ship.

This year uncertainty was compounded with exhaustion. I had just come off one of the most intense and satisfying experiences of my life—the JASON Project. For two weeks at the beginning of May we had broadcast eighty-four live television shows from the Mediterranean Sea to school children in museums all over North America. Over 220,000 young people had joined us as we explored an underwater volcano and the remains of a fourth-century Roman wreck. It was hands-on science, an electronic field trip to the bottom of the sea that I believed would kindle interest among young people in science as a career. It was also the culmination of my dream of "telepresence," the video technology that allows a scientist on board a ship or in a lab thousands of miles away to be as close to the action as if he or she were inside a submarine poking along the ocean floor.

For the JASON Project we had turned the ship we had rented this year, the *Star Hercules*, into a sophisticated television command center. Based in Aberdeen, Scotland, and serving as a support ship for North Sea oil rigs, it was well suited to this purpose. Its long, broad afterdeck—ordinarily loaded with drill pipe—was now crowded with so many shipping containers that it resembled a small town with a main drag and back streets (we had nicknamed the town Venice, since the streets were often awash with seawater). The superstructure of the *Star Hercules*—housing the bridge areas, the mess and common rooms—would ordinarily be the center of shipboard life (sleeping quarters were mostly below the main deck level). But for the JASON Project the center of gravity had shifted to these long rectangular containers, which we refer to as vans. The vans had been converted into workshops, a television transmission station and a television studio that doubled as the expedition headquarters. From this control van our engineers and technicians had operated the remotely controlled underwater robots while performing for the television cameras. The ship had been bursting at the seams with talent and energy. Scientists, television and movie people, high school students and professional seamen had mixed together and become a team that had performed superbly under pressure. It was difficult to imagine anything topping the experience we had just had.

Now most of the vans were empty or being used for storage, and by comparison the ship seemed deserted. Venice was like a ghost town. The weather was fine, but I couldn't shake my feelings of pessimism. Last year I'd been certain we would find the *Bismarck*, and we hadn't. Now my confidence was at low ebb. I was beginning to think that my *Titanic* luck had run out. Perhaps it was simply that I was exhausted—drained by our two-week Mediterranean high.

(Below) The super-structure and bridge of the *Star Hercules* as seen from a position near the stern. The winch traction unit is in the foreground.

(Bottom) Hagen and I wonder if our luck will be better this year.

Black thoughts filled my head. I worried about Todd. After a year of college, would he have outgrown the immaturity and unreliability that had characterized his behavior on our 1988 cruise? When he had turned up in Cadiz sporting long hair, I had immediately dragged him out on deck and given him a good navy trim. I could cut his hair, but could he cut his behavior to man-size? At least Hagen Schempf was also back. If anyone could handle Todd, he could. I worried about *Argo*. Would the old warhorse, neglected and unused for a year while we concentrated on the high-tech JASON robot, still be able to perform? It was ironic to be going back to *Argo* (JASON's fiber-optic cable wasn't long enough for a search at the *Bismarck*'s depth)—a little like stepping back to a bygone era, like using a horse and buggy instead of a motor car.

In my thinking, *Argo* was already a thing of the past—almost obsolete. It had been through many campaigns and proved reliable—its coaxial cable was still strong—but the vehicle itself was battered and bruised by innumerable launches and recoveries and countless hours spent trundling just above the ocean floor. Before the expedition we had taken it apart for a proper tune-up and overhaul. But there had been no opportunity to test its systems at ocean depth. Would the pressure seals we had opened and resealed now leak, allowing seawater into the delicate equipment? Had we successfully repaired the damage *Argo* suffered during a terrible storm in April as we crossed the Bay of Biscay? Would the three video cameras, the electronic still camera, the 35-mm color still camera and the side-looking sonars perform?

At least our team was solid. There was a lot of expertise assembled here—a core of veterans and a group of talented newcomers. As usual I had drawn on a number of sources for my personnel. The bulk came from the Deep Submergence Laboratory at Woods Hole, technical specialists who understood every aspect of *Argo*'s operation and were well accustomed to the rigors of a mid-ocean search. The U.S. Navy, which was helping fund the trip, had lent us four people with many hours' experience at sea. And there were freelancers such as Frank Smith, who was back on winch duty this year. The British captain and officers of the *Star Hercules* seemed as excited about joining the *Bismarck* chase as had last year's officers. They had even asked to have a set of monitors rigged on the bridge so they could see everything we could in the van. Only the crew, Cape Verdians from the former Portuguese islands off the coast of Africa, seemed untouched by the *Bismarck*. They didn't speak very much English and seemed to have no idea what our expedition was about.

However, my dark mood turned darker before our first day at sea was over, when Frank Smith hurt himself badly. While he was building a new battery box for the bottom of *Argo*, Frank ground his right index finger down to the bone. Captain Derek Latter bandaged the cut, put it in a splint, gave Frank a good dose of penicillin and put him to bed. But one of the anchors of the deck crew was temporarily out of action.

Jack Maurer, one of the watch leaders, urged me to make for a port in northern Spain so Frank could receive medical attention. Jack was an ex-navy captain who had done a superb job of organizing this year's cruise. He was accustomed to being responsible for a whole ship's crew, and I understood his concern. I also knew we had funding for only about ten

days to find the *Bismarck*, so every day lost meant that our chances of locating and filming the wreck were seriously diminished.

Frank was in pretty bad shape, but was typically downplaying the seriousness of his injury. "I'll be back on the job tomorrow," he told me stoically. I wasn't so sure. Then I talked to Captain Latter, who assured me that Frank was in no mortal danger. He would be in pain for a few days, but then he should be fine. I decided against a time-consuming detour. Jack Maurer accepted my decision gracefully, but I knew he thought I was wrong. It must have been hard for him to adjust to a subordinate role after all those years in command.

Fortunately the crisis soon passed. True to his word, Frank was back on duty the following day, his right index finger sticking awkwardly skyward as he worked. Whenever I passed him I couldn't resist pointing my index finger up in the air and saying, "Good idea, Frank. Good idea."

To outward appearances our expedition was off to a fine start, blessed by fine sunny weather that lasted the three long days it took to steam to the search area. This year people were sunbathing on the deck instead of lying in their bunks with a green tinge to their complexions swearing they'd never eat another clam as long as they lived. The trailer park Venice provided places to hide and spaces to congregate. A favorite sunbathing spot was the roof of the van that overlooked the town square with its "swimming pool." The pool had been used to hold amphoras before preservation during the JASON Project. Now it served as an actual swimming pool—just big enough for a couple of people to cool off at one

(Above) Tony Chiu and I watch from the raised platform at the stern as *Argo* is hoisted from the fantail up toward the A-frame.

(Below) Frank Smith uses a welding torch to repair damage to one of *Argo*'s launching winches.

time—and the square a natural social center. Usually somebody had a portable stereo tape player blasting, and Frank had built a barbecue for our evening cookouts. But most of this socializing would end as soon as our search began and the team became fragmented into watches.

As we approached the search area I could feel the team beginning to come together. The night before our arrival, the National Geographic film crew (on board to make a documentary film about the expedition) stayed up late building an elaborate model of the *Bismarck*. They worked in the mess hall, so anyone who happened by could help for a while. Many people did, including several of the British officers. Of these the most enthusiastic about our project seemed to be chief second engineer Rick Latham, a sandy-haired Scot in his late thirties who had served in the Royal Navy and was also an amateur historian and poet. Rick had already immortalized our JASON expedition in verse. Now he had begun a poetic record of our *Bismarck* quest: *"The JASON Project's over now/ Cadiz was port of call./ We changed our team for* Bismarck *Boys/ and welcomed one and all.// We won't forget the JASON*

(Above left) Frank Smith tends the barbecue at a cookout in Venice's town square.

(Above right) Rick Latham (left) and Hagen Schempf.

Squad/ who searched the clear blue 'Med.'/ The trailer park seems empty now/ 'and bigger!' Hagen said.// But, JASON's way behind us now./ All artifacts ashore./ We now go big ship hunting on/ a deeper ocean floor."

By the early hours of the morning the model was finished, except for one piece that connected the motor to the rudders, which was nowhere to be found. (Even on the model the rudders turned out to be the Achilles heel!) But Captain Latter came to the rescue, fashioning a replacement piece himself. Then the model was painted down to the last detail. When it was finished, it looked as good as the *Bismarck* had on the day of her commissioning in Hamburg harbor. We placed the model in the van on the ledge below the long bank of TV monitors we would soon be staring at. It would serve as a talisman and as a reminder of what we were looking for.

We arrived on site on the morning of May 29 and immediately set about the time-consuming task of launching transponders and surveying our initial transponder net. The deck crew worked steadily, and we were done after midnight, in time to lock in our grid using the earth orbiting satellite known as GPS, or Global Positioning System, which would be in position between 3 A.M. and 8 A.M. This daily "window" was the only time we could mesh the transponder net with the exact longitude and latitude of our present position, so that when we found the ship we'd know its exact coordinates.

Somewhere down below, in the relentless dark and the cold, lay the wreck of the *Bismarck*. Was she in one piece or scattered across the ocean floor? I have looked at quite a few wrecks and I have seen the complete range.

(Left) Tom Crook
measures cable
preparatory to a
transponder launch.
The pollywog is
lashed to the deck
in the foreground.

(Inset) Tom Crook
tests a transponder
before launching.

Some look like perfectly preserved time capsules, others like piles of junk. Given the pummeling she took, it seemed unlikely the *Bismarck* would much resemble her former glory. But by all eyewitness accounts she had left the surface in one piece. Was the hull still intact when it hit the ocean floor? Now that we were about to go into action, my sense of letdown was lifting, and my thoughts were turning increasingly to the battle ahead.

The weather was still calm at 7 P.M. when the bright yellow A-frame hoisted *Argo* out over the stern, and we watched as the vehicle slipped beneath the gentle seas. The sun had set by the time *Argo* had descended the five kilometers (three miles) to a position a few meters above the sea floor. Then, as we went through a routine check of all *Argo*'s systems, we discovered that two of the three cameras weren't working. My mood crashed again as *Argo* began the long slow climb back to the surface. Bill Lange, the czar of video who had been around since before *Argo* was built, and Jim Saint, who had worked on the original design of the vehicle's telemetry, would be up most of the night trying to find and fix the problem. Was this a foretaste of technical problems to come?

If *Argo* didn't let me down, there was no reason to miss the *Bismarck* this year. Unlike the *Starella*, the *Star Hercules* was a

Skip Gleason and the deck crew begin an *Argo* launch.

modern ship in excellent shape. The winch was brand new and in tip-top condition. The sleeping quarters were comfortable. There was even air-conditioning (although this had broken down in the Mediterranean when we really needed it). Most important of all, the *Star Hercules* was equipped with a dynamic positioning capability. When it was in DP mode, a computer took over the helm, controlling the ship's powerful bow and stern thrusters and allowing it to hover over a wreck site even in difficult winds and seas. This would make it much easier to saturate our coverage of any area we found interesting. And if we found the wreck, it would be possible to investigate it in minute detail.

But our experience in 1988 had reminded me once again how big the ocean is and how seemingly insurmountable the odds of a tiny robot vehicle finding any shipwreck far from land. I've often compared this process to looking for a needle in a haystack at night in a blizzard with nothing more than a flashlight. Now it appeared that my flashlight— *Argo*—was faulty. The best ship in the world was useless if *Argo*'s three video cameras went blind.

Last year we had covered less than a quarter of the 200-square-mile search area I had laid out based on the three sinking positions left by the British. Because I had been spooked by the mountain and transfixed by the impact crater that turned out to be the wreck of a nineteenth-century sailing ship, I had searched only the area near one of these three positions—the one calculated by the navigator of HMS *Rodney*. This year we would be looking entirely in the mountainous terrain that had seemed so scary. Where there was one mountain there were bound to be others, and like mountains on land, undersea mountains have ridges and gullies, sudden changes in altitude. In such conditions sonar is far less effective than video: every rock outcrop shows up as a target, and the huge sonar shadows can hide a multitude of secrets. So it would be a visual search this year, and that meant hands-on high-quality flying all the way. Todd and the two buddies who'd joined him this year, Billy Yunck and Kirk Gustafson, would have their hands full. They had gotten to know each other from teenage summers spent in Montana and had already been dubbed the Montana Mafia by the crew.

My 1989 strategy was simple: to mow the lawn in a series of east/west lines spaced roughly a mile apart. In a visual search you are looking for a fragment of a debris trail. The tiniest piece of debris can lead you to a wreck. The sailing ship we had found in 1988 had left a debris trail a mile long, so I reasoned that a much bigger ship such as the *Bismarck* would leave one at least that length. And since the debris field from the sailing ship we had found last year ran north/south, I assumed the *Bismarck* debris would also be oriented in this direction. A visual search, with its wider-spaced lines, meant we would be able to cover ground more quickly than we had with our 1988 sonar search.

The next morning, May 30, the wind had freshened to 25 knots, but we launched *Argo* without incident and by 9 A.M. the vehicle was back on the bottom. This time the cameras seemed to be working well, but there was interference on the sonar coming from some part of the system which interfered with the return. When this noise was loud we couldn't tell what we were looking at, making the sonar useless. We would just have to live with it for now and try to fix it later.

Our starting point was inside the 1988 search area, just north of the *Rodney*'s position. For insurance, my 1989 coverage would overlap the area searched the previous year. I had plotted my first search line to take us between the *Dorsetshire*'s position to the north and the *King George V*'s to the south. My personal favorite of the two was the *Dorsetshire*'s fix. After all, it had been the last ship on the scene when the *Bismarck* went down.

Inside the control run it was all business as we drove east toward the mountain, which according to our sonar soundings rose at a steep gradient roughly 1,000 meters (3,000 feet) from the abyssal plain.

As the slope neared, we all tensed a little, wondering just how precipitous it would be. When we hit the incline, Kirk Gustafson, at *Argo*'s controls, responded instantly as he eased back on the joystick and brought *Argo* up—not too fast, but fast enough to keep us well above the bottom. Flying *Argo* is a little like handling a twenty-pound fish on a five-pound test line—if *Argo* hangs up on something or you reel it in too fast, the cable breaks. But Kirk didn't seem to be having any trouble keeping up with the change in altitude, and the bottom continued smooth and sediment covered, revealing none of the dangerous volcanic outcrops I'd feared.

Martin Bowen winches *Argo* out over the stern (top) as another lowering (above) begins.

The plastic model (top) shows how the shapely *Bismarck*'s lines contrast to those of our modern-day workhorse the *Star Hercules* (bottom).

But it remained to be seen how hazardous this new terrain would prove to be. Although it had grown into a whole mountain range in my mind, it was in reality one isolated seamount, an extinct underwater volcano approximately sixteen kilometers (ten miles) across at the base, and surrounded by the flat Porcupine Abyssal Plain. It was big enough to occupy most of the area still to be searched.

Kirk continued to gently ease back on the joystick as the altitude increased. Now we were in newfound land—ours were undoubtedly the first human eyes to look on this piece of the earth's surface. For a moment I ceased being a seeker after lost ships and reverted to my scientific identity, marine geologist. I watched with fascination as we passed over black pillow lavas and rocky outcrops thrust through the sediment, evidence that the ocean floor here had once breathed fire. But for *Argo* the scenery was not dangerous, still primarily bottom mud. I heaved yet another sigh of relief. There was no chance that the *Bismarck* wreckage would get lost against bare black volcanic rock. Against the pale sediment a *Bismarck* gun barrel would stand out clearly.

Through the morning we tracked east, exploring, as we did so, the northern slope of the dead volcano. At our current course and speed, we'd be just south of the *Dorsetshire* position by late afternoon. At about 4 P.M., approximately 2,000 meters (6,000 feet) southwest of the *Dorsetshire* fix, we spotted a piece of man-made debris. A few minutes later we saw another. Todd, who had just assumed his position as *Argo* flyer, eagerly declared that the wreck was close by—shades of 1988. But I wasn't about to get excited yet; the pieces were isolated, not part of a pattern suggestive of a wreck. I had been burned last year by much more solid evidence than this. Nonetheless I decided to investigate. Last year the debris field we had found had run from north to south: the heaviest pieces were inside the crater and the debris got steadily lighter as you moved north. If this new debris was associated with something worth knowing about, there should be heavier material to the south. I ordered a course change in that direction, temporarily abandoning our east/west line.

As we moved south we picked up further occasional bits of debris, but nothing that established a pattern. Around 6 P.M. we encountered three anonymous black objects in close proximity—then nothing. Whatever we had discovered, it gave no indication of being part of a wreck or of being connected in any way to the *Bismarck*. Todd was obviously disappointed, and Hagen teased him about his earlier overconfidence. I could already see their friendship blossoming this year. And so far, Todd had been the model team member.

Lacking evidence that suggested otherwise, I was forced to conclude that the debris was random jetsam from the countless vessels that have plied this busy shipping lane for centuries. But now that we had cut our first line short, I decided to continue south and begin a truncated parallel line back toward the west. We could fill in the rest of our initial line later. So as night fell we found ourselves tracking westward, back toward our 1988 search area. I had a feeling we were in for a long haul.

At 8 P.M. Jack Maurer's watch came on for its second duty of the day. Already the novelty of our expedition was beginning to wear off, and the team was beginning to sink into the repetitious routine I knew so well.

In a round-the-clock ocean search the three watches inevitably assume distinct personalities. I'm sure it has something to do with the times of day each watch covers, but mostly it's the internal chemistry, the mix of people. Often the watch leader sets the tone, but not always.

Not surprisingly, Jack Maurer's eight-to-twelve watch was the quiet, civilized one. The graveyard shift, led by Ron Bowlin, a career navy man, was much looser. Any watch with Bill Lange as *Argo* engineer was bound to be lively. Bill and several others on the watch had read the books featuring Dirk Pitt, the hard-boiled ocean adventurer of Clive Cussler's bestselling novels, including *Raise the Titanic!* Now they took great delight in imagining new and ever more farfetched adventures for their hero. This activity was fueled in part by the presence on board of a professional writer named Tony Chiu. Tony and I were collaborating on a novel based on my own experiences of deep sea exploration. Whenever Tony dropped into the van during this watch, Bill and his colleagues would have new and outrageous plot twists to suggest. With complete disrespect, they had taken to comparing me to Dirk Pitt and to describing our 1989 *Bismarck* expedition as "Dirk Pitt's latest adventure."

I had moved Hagen Schempf and Todd to the four-to-eight shift this year, with Hagen, the only graduate student on board, as watch leader. He was the van comedian, and Todd was his inevitable straight man (he could always be relied on to rise to the bait). The result was a constant stream of banter and backchat that kept the others amused. Things could get downright uproarious when Rick Latham, poet laureate of the *Star Hercules*, dropped in for a visit, which he did often.

On May 31, we tracked east, just north of our original line. As we approached the vicinity of the *Dorsetshire* position, we again picked up isolated pieces of debris, but nothing systematic—no real scent. I wondered once more if there was any way the debris we had been seeing was connected with the *Bismarck* wreck. I turned south, as I had yesterday, breaking short my line, to see if I could pick up a debris trail. Again nothing. Maybe, I thought, this was random debris from the battle, during which the ship had continued to steam in a northerly direction. If so, the wreck could be well to the north of the original search area I'd laid out. The ocean began to seem bigger still.

As day followed day, and endless miles of mud rolled past *Argo's* camera lenses, my team was beginning to show signs of cabin fever. Each isolated piece of man-made debris assumed disproportionate significance. Anything other than mud seemed electrifying. The entries from the video log for June 1 could have been written on any day during our entire first week on site: "12:21—fish; 13:03—octopod; 14:42—rock (black)." And so it went. The mood on board became quiet and withdrawn. Everyone was waiting for something—anything—to happen.

The food seemed to get worse and things began to run out. We'd seen our last lettuce in May. Then there was no more milk. The orange juice went next, replaced by an unsavory purple concoction referred to as bug juice. Potatoes, however, remained in abundant supply. Greasy French fries accompanied almost every meal, usually along with canned vegetables.

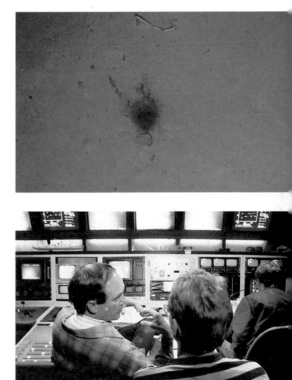

(Above) Hagen Schempf (center) and I discuss some of the isolated pieces of debris (top) that we have begun seeing on the screens in the control van.

The chef was Cape Verdian, but the food contained no trace of the exotic. I think he was doing his best to cook American, but he wasn't succeeding. However, the names of the dishes were always a treat. My favorite was lasagna *au gratin* (fortunately not served with French fries on the side). The Brits didn't seem to notice much, but my troops were beginning to complain.

People soon grew pretty tired of watching *The Terminator* on the VCR, or *Zulu* (a movie about British redcoats valiantly fighting an overwhelmingly superior force of black South Africans). And the main shipboard leisure pastime—the board game Trivial Pursuit—was beginning to seem like the perfect description of our expedition. A spy satellite following our

Hagen and I ponder our next move as time runs out and still there is no sign of the *Bismarck* wreck. In the background is the red-and-white Explorer's Club flag I brought along on the expedition.

behavior would surely have thought us crazy—what with debris-inspired detours and hunches that had played us false, our lines looked anything but systematic. On a time-lapse photograph they would have resembled the flight of a wounded bumblebee in search of a lost flower. In these circumstances, Trivial Pursuit seemed a worthy activity.

At least Tony Chiu and I were making progress on our novel. The plot revolved around a lost Israeli submarine that was carrying secret weapons from Russia in the wake of the Six Days War. Although Dirk Pitt did not make an appearance, there was a dashing oceanographer at the center of the story, and a beautiful female navy lieutenant. As the real-life chase became more frustrating, the novel occupied more of my attention. Perhaps by inviting Tony along I was unconsciously giving myself a fallback position, preparing for failure. Even if we didn't find the *Bismarck*, I would have something to show for the trip.

As midnight neared on Sunday June 4, six and a half days after we had begun our first search line, we had covered 80 percent of the search area—all but the most southern section—and still we had found nothing that led us anywhere. Now I stood at the chart table and considered my options. Although the four-to-eight shift had long ago left the van, Hagen was there with me. As our voyage progressed, I increasingly turned to the younger man as a sounding board.

Together we stared at the record of the invisible tracks *Argo* had made across the bottom. I wondered out loud whether the wreck could have slipped between our lines. We had covered the ground pretty well, assuming the debris field really was oriented north/south and really was a mile or more long. But what if last year's sailing ship had left us a false scent? Should we go back and fill in halfway between the lines we had run, or head south? Hagen and I debated. Going north meant expanding our transponder net—and that took time, time that was beginning to run out. Our existing net would allow us to run one more solid line to the south, thus filling in the area we had initially planned to search. Although I didn't really believe the wreck could be down that way—the debris near the *Dorsetshire* position still pointed my thoughts north—it was really the only logical thing to do, finish what we had started.

Around noon the next day, June 5, we launched *Argo* in sunshine and moderate seas. As we sailed eastward we encountered the southern slope of the volcano: rough terrain but similar to what we had encountered before. The hours slipped by. I spent some time working on the novel with Tony. When I dropped back into the van it was as though time had stood still: *Argo*'s cameras showed the same scenery. Only the monitor showing the navigation track indicated that we had indeed made steady progress to the east.

When Todd's watch ended that evening, he and I went outside and walked aft to the raised platform that looks a little like a miniature fire tower at the stern of the *Star Hercules*, just forward of the A-frame. It was a temporary structure built as a camera platform for the JASON Project, providing a good angle for filming launches and recoveries and a panoramic view of the trailer park. It was also a perfect place to stand and talk, or watch the sunset. The streets of Venice were quiet and, except for a few other sunset watchers, the deck was empty. I told Todd about my latest idea for the novel, a plot twist that would tie up all the loose ends and simultaneously solve the Arab-Israeli problem (no one can accuse me of thinking small). He listened attentively. All his life he'd been listening to me talk about my adventures, my dreams, my schemes, my victories and defeats. But now I listened to him. He told me about his year at college—he had switched halfway through from Northeastern to the University of Colorado. He talked about his girlfriend who had spent the previous Christmas with us. He was in love. The year had been full of ups and downs, but he was brimming with life, thinking about the future. Then we talked about the *Bismarck*. Todd had read the books, he knew all about the ship. His watch was going to find it—he was certain.

A quiet moment on the stern observation tower.

I stayed awhile after Todd had gone, pondering the past and future. How many more expeditions like this one would there be for me? What sort of world was I leaving to my sons and their children? The evening air was still warm as I headed forward, threading my way through Venice's dry streets. On my way, I looked into the van to see how the eight-to-twelve watch was doing. The room was quiet. Jack Maurer was conferring with the navigator Cathy Offinger, who flashed me a smile. Al Uchupi called me over for a moment to look at some video of an interesting geologic feature spotted earlier. At the *Argo* station Kirk sat immobile as a statue, one hand resting on the joystick, his eyes fixed on the video screen, while part of his mind was undoubtedly somewhere else—maybe skiing in deep powder down a Montana mountain. This may not be the fun watch, I thought idly as I stepped back into the tangy night air, but if the wreck is down there, they're not going to miss it.

When I got to the mess hall, I sat down, poured myself a glass of red wine, popped a handful of potato chips in my mouth and settled in for a couple of hours of Trivial Pursuit. Dice rolled, counters moved along the board and members of the National Geographic crew kibbitzed from the sidelines. By this point in the cruise they must have been wondering if, for the second year in a row, they would be going home without a movie. In a matter of minutes the battleship *Bismarck* couldn't have been farther from my thoughts.

(Left) I point out some wreckage on the video screen a few minutes after the discovery of the first debris. In the foreground is Cathy Offinger; Jack Maurer sits beside me. At the end is Kirk Gustafson at *Argo*'s controls.

CHAPTER NINE

Bingo!

Eastern Atlantic Ocean—
June 5, 1989

Except for the four of us playing Trivial Pursuit—and our tiny audience in the next booth—the only bodies in the mess hall of the *Star Hercules* were a few people about to go on duty for the midnight-to-four watch. They were grabbing "mid rats"—midnight rations—before heading to the van. My partner Tony Chiu and I were sitting in a banquette with our backs to the mess hall entrance; our opponents were across from us. As I pondered the answer to the next question, I heard Al Uchupi's voice over my shoulder.

"Bob, we've encountered some debris I think you should have a look at." Uchupi's tone was matter-of-fact. He might have been discussing the weather or an article he had just read on the geomorphology of deep-ocean sediments. But Al isn't one to cry wolf.

I was out of my seat like a catapult, vaulting over the banquette in one motion as potato chips and Trivial Pursuit pieces scattered in every direction. This was one game we weren't going to finish. I ran full tilt for the control van, leaving Uchupi and the others far behind in my wake.

When I reached the van, a clump of small black objects was just coming into view. Although to an untutored eye they might have looked like nothing more than dark smudges on the sediment, there was no doubt that they were pieces of man-made material.

A scene of quiet celebration after the discovery of the first debris. Will this debris trail lead us to the *Bismarck* wreck? Is it associated with the *Bismarck* at all?

Jim Saint was already rewinding the video so I could have a look at what they had seen. At 23:52, Cathy Offinger had noted in the navigation log, "Debris." I stared at the hazy black-and-white images on the TV monitor. Apart from a small piece of pipe, the objects were nondescript, but they kept coming. Uchupi had, of course, been right. This discovery was something quite different from the isolated man-made objects we had seen up until now. This was a continuous pattern, but was it *Bismarck* debris? I thought about the sailing ship from last year. I didn't want to make the same mistake. I looked up at the real-time video image. We were passing over another small piece.

"Looks like we've got something this time," commented Jack Maurer.

"Yeah, absolutely no doubt about it," I replied. "But what? If it's *Bismarck*, we've got two choices. Either this stuff was shot off during the battle or this is part of the debris field."

"We're not picking up any sonar contacts on the sidescan," reported sonar operator Mel Lee.

"What's that?" I asked as a larger piece loomed onto the video screen. "Jim, zoom in on that. Let's take a closer look. Whatever it is, it's got a shadow. Definitely man-made."

When I'd arrived in the van it was already crowded. A watch change was in progress as the midnight-to-four shift prepared to take over. Now the film crew rolled in with cameras and sound gear and started to set up. More people straggled in—the word had obviously spread rapidly through the ship. Soon the van was crowded almost to bursting point.

Usually, when a new shift takes over, the previous watch disappears fairly quickly, but this time almost everyone hung around, wanting to be in on the big moment when we found the wreck. The mood, while serious and businesslike, was also festive. The monotony of our fruitless search had finally been broken.

With the *Star Hercules* at dead slow, we kept going east and continued to pick up debris. It was intermittent—patches of blank bottom followed suddenly by a tiny piece, or a clump, or a large square object, or something that looked like a piece of pipe. Unlike the false scents we had followed near the *Dorsetshire* position, this one remained strong. I was more and more sure that we had found a genuine debris field associated with a wreck, not just a few pieces shot off during a running battle.

After about twenty minutes or so the bottomscape abruptly changed, becoming mottled and patchy. As we moved over this area the debris started to thin out. Were these two facts related? I was puzzled, but I didn't have long to ponder because suddenly the underwater landscape changed yet again, this time to very disturbed bottom, which looked as though rocks and sediment had been put through a blender. Could this be part of an impact crater? If so, it had been one hell of an impact. We kept going slowly eastward and soon were again passing over the strange, patchy bottom. By now we seemed to have run out of debris. My puzzlement deepened.

Then we were back in all-too-familiar terrain—flat, featureless mud. So we looped south and headed west, the pattern repeating itself in reverse. Finally the pieces of the jigsaw puzzle began to fit together. The deeply disturbed bottom was the path of an underwater landslide, an avalanche of sediment. This landslide was also responsible for the patchy areas on either side; as it had flowed downhill it had left a trough into which the sediment on either side had partially drained, the way river banks erode after a flash flood. But what had caused the landslide? I was pretty sure I knew the answer.

First I needed to learn more about the debris field we had discovered. Which way did the debris point? Somewhere near the heaviest debris a wreck undoubtedly lay. So, for the next several hours we zigzagged slowly north. As we did so the pieces of debris became heavier. In an exact reverse of the sailing ship we had found last year, the trail pointed north.

By the time the sun rose the crowd of spectators in the van had dwindled down to a hardy few. Unlike the *Titanic*, the first debris hadn't led us immediately to a wreck, and we had yet to find anything we could definitely identify as the *Bismarck*. But we now had a reasonably good fix on the axis of the main debris field and a fairly good sense of the axis of the landslide. The debris seemed to run from south to north with a slight tilt to the east. The landslide was oriented from southeast to northwest. If, as I now believed, the *Bismarck* had caused the landslide, then the place to look for the ship was at the intersection of the landslide axis and the axis of the debris. I plotted this position on my chart. It was north and a little to the east of our first debris sighting. With mounting excitement I ordered a course for this area.

It was just after 9 A.M. and Jack Maurer's discovery watch was back on duty—with considerably less sleep than usual—when we approached the area where I had calculated the wreck should be. I was feeling cocky;

I ponder the cause of the avalanche of sediment we are seeing on the ocean floor.

(Above) The twelve-to-four watch. In the foreground is *Argo* flyer Billy Yunck. Behind me are watch leader Ron Bowlin and navigator Tom Crook.

(Below) The first chilling image of a boot appears on our video screens.

(Opposite) This scale diagram shows the depth of the area we were searching in relation to the size of the Empire State Building and Eiffel Tower. This also gives a good idea of the massive size of the underwater volcano that dominated our 1989 search area.

I was sure the *Bismarck* was within my grasp.

"We're entering the avalanche area now," I remarked as churned-up bottom again appeared on the screen. "Now keep your eyes peeled. I'm just worried about burial." This was my nightmare, that we would find the main wreck but not be able to see it because it was hidden in the sediment.

"Heading o-four-o," called out navigator Cathy Offinger.

"Roger that," I replied.

"I'm getting a forward sonar contact," sang out Mel Lee.

"Go down, Kirk. There's something right in the middle. Go down."

"Going down," Kirk responded as he pushed gently forward on the joystick.

"Stop! Stop!" I was almost shouting. I didn't want Kirk to crash.

"Roger," Kirk replied quietly. He'd already anticipated my command.

"Down look, down look. Thar she blows! Give us a fix, Cathy." *Argo's* downlooking video camera was staring at a major piece of wreckage.

"Position is nine-one-three-eight east, minus one hundred south," Cathy called out.

"Roger that," I replied. "We got it, Al. I don't know how much we got, but we got it."

And so I believed. As we continued over the area, we saw definite

evidence of an impact crater, glimpsed some major wreckage, including a big piece of superstructure and a section of ladder. This was definitely not a sailing ship—it was something much bigger—but we still lacked conclusive evidence that it had anything to do with the *Bismarck*.

We spent the rest of the morning in a leisurely loop back toward the target, in the process exploring areas of the landslide to the north and west. Well to the south we picked up more debris. Just before noon we came upon a lonely boot lying on the disturbed sediment. The van went silent until this chilling image faded from view, a ghost from long ago. After almost fifty years there would be no human remains down here, but that boot was awfully spooky. Had it belonged to a young German sailor Todd's age, or younger?

At noon, as we again approached the target area, we passed over a sizable hunk of wreckage, then the edge of the impact crater. As soon as the watch had changed and Ron Bowlin's gang had assumed their positions, I asked the bridge to switch us to DP mode, dynamic positioning, a process that takes about half an hour. This would allow us to cover the area at a snail's pace. If the wreck was in here, we would find it.

Back and forth we went, tentatively identifying one large piece as perhaps a piece of the bow or the stern. A long trenchlike feature was wishfully identified in the log as "Axis of ship." But after four hours of saturation coverage I was forced to admit defeat. We had discovered a lot more wreckage, many minor pieces of debris and plenty of evidence that something big had hit here. But if the impact crater had been caused by the main hull of the *Bismarck*, the wreck was no longer to be seen.

Al Uchupi was convinced my burial fantasy was unfounded. The sediment wasn't thick enough to hide something that big. So if the ship had launched the landslide, then it must have slid down the slope with it. But how far?

As I contemplated my next move I became aware of how tired I was. When we discovered the first debris I had already been up for twelve hours. Now I had been awake for close to twenty-four hours and the wreck didn't seem any closer. My body ached with fatigue, but there was no way I would sleep until we found something conclusive. I opened another Coke and plotted a course down the middle of the landslide.

At times like this there are usually as many theories about where the wreck is as there are potential theorists. Every sonar target becomes the ship, every piece of disturbed bottom becomes the primary impact crater. I'm used to this; everyone loves to second-guess the man in command. Besides, I welcome advice, as long as it doesn't lead to mutiny. There was no danger of that now, because we all felt we were close, that it was just a matter of time before the *Bismarck* would fall. Al Uchupi and others were arguing that the slide must have carried the ship right out onto the abyssal plain to the southeast, that I should be looking down there. I wasn't so sure, but the theory seemed worth checking out. Once we had gone down the landslide we would continue out onto the plain.

As we slalomed down the avalanche, I marveled at the power unleashed by whatever had caused this underwater mudslide.

Star Hercules

1,052 ft.
(320.7m.)

1,250 ft.
(381.8m.)

Argo

15,500 ft.
(4700m.)

We sighted more debris, but nothing remotely as impressive as what we had found in the morning—until we hit the field of boots.

We were maybe halfway down the avalanche when suddenly there were boots everywhere. I couldn't help thinking it was like a parade ground. Most of the boots were scattered randomly, but one pair looked as if someone had been wearing them recently, and seemed to have trousers still attached—surely an optical illusion, probably just the shadow from *Argo*'s lights. But the sight sent shivers up and down my spine. How long had the wearers of all these boots waited for rescue that didn't come? Or had they been trapped inside the sinking ship, spilling out as it descended to become food for bottom fish? So many boots, so many young men.

Our ride down the landslide continued. The farther south we went, the more it felt as though we were losing the scent. We had run out of the landslide—roughly two kilometers long, we estimated—and were out on the abyssal plain, when Jack Maurer's shift came back on duty. That meant it was eight o'clock. I must have missed supper, I thought groggily, as I downed another Coke. I had been without sleep for almost a day and a half, but I hung in as we plodded on. The plain proved empty.

Jack Maurer and I look at a sonar print-out while discussing whether or not to lower *Argo* back down to viewing altitude.

As we turned north, back toward the landslide, I considered how on each expedition there was always a lucky watch. This year the luck seemed to be with Jack Maurer and his crew. They had made the first discovery and had been on duty when we searched the impact crater that morning. Maybe they would be the ones to find the ship. I hoped they did it soon, as I didn't think I could stay awake much longer.

We tracked slowly northward with *Argo* at an altitude of 25 meters (80 feet), high enough for its sonars to scan roughly 250 meters (800 feet) to either side. I was interested in finding something big, something that would cause the sonar tracer to burn a hole in the paper. It was getting close to 10 P.M. My endurance test was approaching the thirty-six-hour mark. Really, I told myself, I've got to get some rest.

"Go down to ten meters," I said. "Let's see what the bottom is like here."

"That looks like a skid mark," commented Al as the sediment came into view. We were back in the landslide. Skidmarks, obvious gouges in the bottom mud, usually meant a sizable chunk of debris was nearby, which had skidded when it hit.

"Oh, wow, look at that!" sang out Kirk, flying *Argo*.

All eyes stared at the murky image that was creeping slowly into the frame of the video monitor. It looked like a huge gear, a great round object with ser-

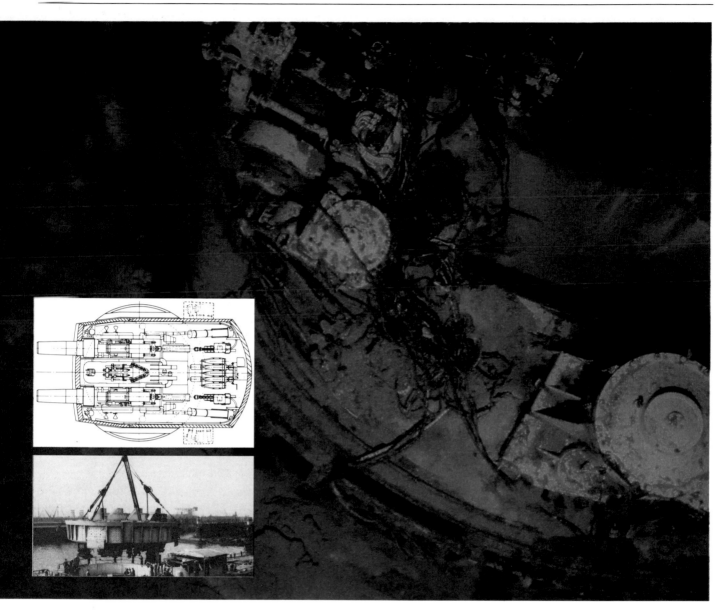

rated teeth ringing the inner rim.

"Bingo!" Kirk shouted, unconsciously echoing an identical exclamation at the discovery of the *Titanic* boiler in 1985.

"I think we've found ourselves a turret," I announced happily. "All right. Let's get the scale. Where's a ruler?

Somebody found me a plastic ruler. I used it to work out the ratios and formulate the equation to calculate the true size of the image on the television screen.

"Twenty-five is to 14 as 9 times 1.6 is to X."

"Exact science," joked Mel Lee.

"So X equals 8 meters. That's a main turret."

"They didn't have those on nineteenth-century sailing ships," remarked Cathy, with tongue firmly in cheek.

I looked at the freeze-frame image Jim Saint had put up on one of the monitors. Those serrated teeth would have meshed with the gears of the turret's turning mechanism. At last we had our definitive image, our

(Above) Upside-down on the ocean floor, one of the *Bismarck*'s four big gun turrets exposes its internal mechanisms that are similar to those shown in the turret blueprint (inset top) and in the photograph (below). (Inset bottom) A gun platform is lowered into an open barbette.

Bismarck fingerprint.

Surely now it would be only a matter of hours before we found the ship. I had thought this once already and been dead wrong, but I could stay awake no longer. I left instructions to continue searching in the area and headed for my cabin where I crashed into my narrow bunk. But strangely, sleep didn't come so easily. From my bed I could just see the video monitors I had had set up in my cabin that showed me exactly what they were seeing in the control van. This innovation allowed me to be in on the action even when I was away from the van. I didn't want to repeat my *Titanic* experience, when the big discovery had happened while I was sitting in my cabin reading a book.

This was a wreck site like none I had ever encountered. First the debris trail led to a dead end. Then the landslide seemed to be empty. I've often compared an underwater search to the game of Clue I played as a child. In it you take pieces of data and test them against a logic tree, a hypothesis. When one hypothesis fails you plant another tree. This game of Clue would have been a stretch for Sherlock Holmes or Hercule Poirot. There were so many clues and they led off in so many different directions. Yet again I ran over some of the possibilities.

Hagen strains at the winch during a difficult night recovery of *Argo*.

Perhaps the avalanche had been caused by turrets or other heavy wreckage, not the ship herself. I remembered how the *Titanic* bow had planed away while the stern sank straight down. Had the *Bismarck*, which according to all eyewitness reports left the surface in one piece, planed off from the sinking site while turrets and other heavy material fell off at the surface and plunged straight down? If so, the main wreck might have nothing to do with the landslide, contrary to my original assumption. The *Titanic*'s bow had planed away at an angle of twelve degrees, so that after falling 4 kilometers (2.5 miles) from the surface it was 600 meters (1,970 feet) from the stern. But here the ocean floor was 4.8 kilometers (3 miles) down. So the main wreck of the *Bismarck* might be as much as 1,000 meters (3,280 feet) away from the impact position of the turret (slightly uphill from where we had found it). As these thoughts churned in my head, I fell into a restless sleep.

The next morning when I returned to the van, it was obvious that the night watches had become mesmerized with the turret. They had kept circling back over its position. Hagen was convinced the turret was actually a barbette, the mount on which a turret sat, and that the barbette was still attached to the hull. The ship was right here, buried beneath the mud. I reminded him that Al Uchupi had dismissed this as impossible.

Clearly it was useless to continue this haphazard searching. It was time to systematically eliminate all possibilities, to map the limits of the debris in every direction. It was simply a matter of time before we ran into the wreck. I stared at the model of the *Bismarck* resting silently on the ledge below the bank of television monitors. Soon I would be looking at the real thing.

All day on June 7 we explored the perimeter of the debris field and landslide areas. By mid-afternoon we had closure to the south. Then we ran a northwest line paralleling the eastern edge of the landslide. About halfway up we ran over a small patch of debris less than 200 meters (660 feet) wide. Was this part of a second debris field? It seemed unrelated to the main debris area to the west of the landslide. Perhaps this patch would lead us to the main wreck, but it didn't seem likely. At any rate, we would return to check it out later. Meanwhile we continued north and crossed the north end of the landslide, eliminating that area from contention, then looped south and began to explore the upper part of the main debris trail. We found some big pieces of wreckage, including a chunk of superstructure complete with portholes. We worked our way west in a great zigzag until we had run out of debris. The only remaining *terra incognita* was the area to the east of the tiny debris patch we had gone over during the afternoon, situated on the eastern edge of the landslide.

It was just after midnight on June 8 and the tenth day of our search had begun as we headed back east. Finding the wreck in this debris field was turning out to be as time-consuming as discovering the first debris. Soon we saw the familiar scarp indicating the western edge of the landslide, and then came the mixed-up bottom of the slide itself.

From the couch in my cabin I could watch a set of monitors that showed me everything the duty watch was seeing in the control van.

"Large sonar target 200 meters to starboard," announced the sonar operator.

It was probably geology, I thought, but worth investigating. We looped around to take a look, crossing over a corner of the small eastern debris field in the process. With *Argo* at the end of a three-mile cable, turning is not done quickly.

The wind had been picking up and we were having trouble keeping the ship on course as we headed for the sonar target. Instead of passing over it, we were blown east, missing it by about 100 meters. Again the sonar tracer began to burn a dark-brown image onto the pale paper. It was the same target—probably a scarp, I reassured myself again.

It was 3 A.M. and I was exhausted. Before heading for my bunk, I left instructions that two passes were to be made to the east of the landslide. These would close off the second small debris field and should finally settle the question of whether the wreck could conceivably be in that direction. This time when I collapsed into my bunk I fell instantly asleep.

Six hours later I snapped awake. It was after 9 A.M. and I was still tired. Maybe I would take it easy just a bit longer. I slipped on some clothes and flopped down on the couch, from which I had a good view of the monitors in my cabin. The navigation plot indicated that we had just entered the landslide area and were heading south-southeast toward that sonar target we had missed before I'd gone to bed.

Clearly we hadn't found anything while I was asleep—or my beauty rest would have been cut short. It appeared that we now had our quarry surrounded, boxed in on all four sides. The wreck had to be inside our encircling search lines, in the landslide or the debris field. It was now a question of running a series of tight lines back and forth across the area until we found it. But I was losing heart and running out of time. In three days I would have to head home.

I turned my gaze to the *Argo* monitor. It was the eight-to-twelve

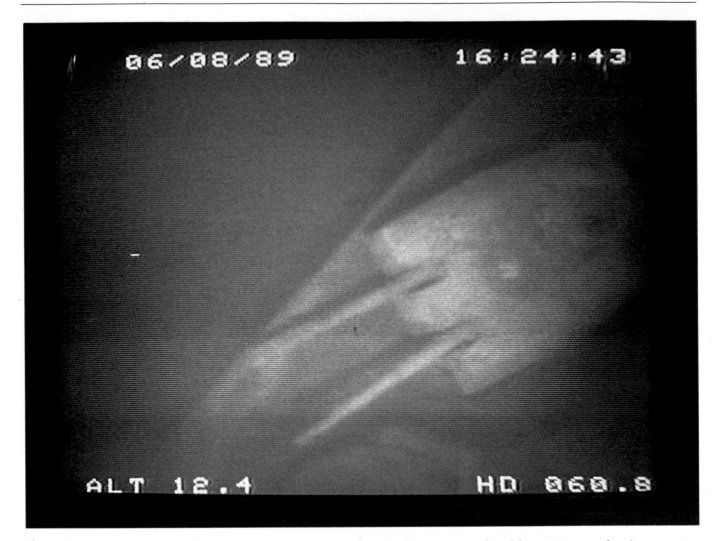

06/08/89   16:24:43

ALT 12.4   HD 060.8

Our first look at the *Bismarck*: the twin barrels of a gun turret still look dangerous and ready to return fire.

watch, so Kirk would be flying. I visualized him sitting at the *Argo* station, his eyes fixed on the monitor and its altitude reading. The landslide, with its frequent scarps and scattered debris, was challenging terrain. I watched to see how Kirk was doing. To me, watching a good flyer is like watching a good hockey or basketball player. Now I lay back on my couch and watched with pleasure as Kirk adroitly glided the vehicle over the rugged landscape.

When a big white scarp loomed into the view of *Argo*'s forward-looking camera, I was almost chuckling as I watched Kirk react in a split second and begin reeling in cable. If I had been standing in the van I would have been yelling at him, "Come up, come up!" But he couldn't hear me from my cabin. I felt detached from the consequences. I could see it was going to be close, but it looked like Kirk would make it.

Then I saw the gun—no, two gun barrels—jutting from a turret. The scarp was the goddamned *Bismarck*!

"We've got it!" I yelled, so loud that I was heard two corridors away.

Like a shot I was out of my cabin, my fatigue completely forgotten. We had found the ship.

Inside the control van, the eight-to-twelve watch had also been fooled. Things were quiet as usual. Kirk Gustafson was listening to music on his Walkman, and Jack Maurer and Cathy Offinger were chatting quietly when Mel Lee started getting a hard return on the forward sonar.

"Target 150 meters dead ahead," Mel commented. "We're really burning paper."

Al was staring at the chart, pondering the landslide. He figured we were coming in on its western edge. "It's a scarp," he called out matter-of-factly.

"That's no scarp," Cathy burst out, as the gun barrels came into view. In the navigation log she wrote in big block letters, "GOT IT."

In a matter of moments, *Argo* had passed over the hull of the *Bismarck*. Kirk winched in frantically as the vehicle rose up over the steep superstructure of the ship. Anyone watching a video screen caught glimpses of guns, gaping holes, mangled metal. A snapshot of history and then it was gone—almost as if it had never been there.

Then I burst into the van.

"Well, I guess you slept through it again." Jack Maurer taunted me with the memory of how I had missed the *Titanic* discovery.

"No way, Jack," I responded. "I saw it all in my cabin."

As Jim Saint replayed the discovery sequence, I couldn't contain my pleasure. "Look at that baby!" I exclaimed. "We've got it! All right!"

Word spread rapidly through the *Star Hercules*, and soon the van was packed. Todd and Hagen were among the first to arrive.

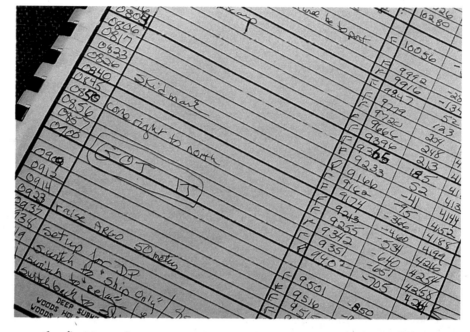

(Below) A page from the navigation log shows Cathy Offinger's triumphant notation at the moment of discovery: "GOT IT."

"How much did we miss it by, Dad?" Todd asked as we watched the video one more time.

"About a hundred meters," I told him. I had checked the track lines and seen just how close we had come on our previous sweeps down the landslide. We had barely missed the main wreck several times, but the sonar had either been down or, as had happened late in the night before, the wind had blown us off course. Without reliable sonar and without a logical debris field pattern, one hundred meters might as well be one thousand. I could see Todd's disappointment, mixed with pride and elation. After all, we had finally found the ship.

I congratulate the discovery watch leader, Jack Maurer.

Whatever happened now, our second *Bismarck* expedition was a success. It was as if a huge pressure had been suddenly released. And with the release came a flood of thoughts as the *Bismarck* story came pouring into my head. As I stared at those mute guns and the blasted superstructure, the awful last hours of the *Bismarck* were suddenly real, immediate, not buried inside dry history books filled with impersonal print. Men had lived on this ship, fought bravely for her during her hopeless final battle, and died.

CHAPTER TEN

Exploring the Bismarck

*Eastern Atlantic Ocean—
June 8, 1989*

It seemed that somebody up there wasn't too happy about our discovery. Throughout our long and frustrating search the weather had been almost perfect. Now it was turning downright nasty. The wind was picking up by the minute, the seas were rising. I couldn't escape the thought that *Bismarck* weather was brewing just as *our* last battle was looming.

It was time to take our first detailed look at the wreck of the ship that had lain unseen for almost fifty years. Not surprisingly, the control van was crowded with almost every off-duty body. I knew that on the bridge of the *Star Hercules* there would be an unusual number of officers hanging around, sharing in the drama. Even the Cape Verdians were curious. We all knew we were not just reliving history, we were making it. This was a hell of a lot more interesting than rerunning *Zulu* or *The Terminator* on the ship's VCR.

As we switched the ship over to DP mode and prepared for battle, the twelve-to-four watch came on duty. I received congratulations from Bill Lange and the gang. "This is definitely Dirk Pitt's most amazing adventure," Bill teased.

Just before the new watch took over, I noticed Lange staring at a note that had been tacked up on one of the equipment racks. I asked him what it was.

"News," he answered laconically and then went back to reading. "They're killing students in China," he finally added.

I walked over and read the bulletin. It was a handwritten note in point form, probably from the captain, summarizing recent news events. It mentioned a plane crash, a bad day on the Hong Kong stock market and then, "It is estimated that more than 7,000 people have been killed by

(Opposite) *Argo* explores along the port rail amidships in Ken Marschall's haunting recreation of our exploration of the wreck.

(Above, top to bottom) *Argo* hits the water and begins its descent to the wreck.

government troops in Tienanmen Square in Beijing."

For two weeks our lives had revolved around an 800-foot-long piece of metal on the bottom of the ocean. Our communication with the outside was sketchy at best. The real world seems so distant when you're at sea. The news of these troubles in China came as a jolt. The *Bismarck* was not the only thing in the world, after all.

But right now it had to be my major concern. We'd raised *Argo* to 50 meters (140 feet), and shortly before 1 P.M. brought it directly over the spot where our navigation now told us the wreck lay. About 30 meters (85 feet) from the bottom a ghostly gray form materialized in the murky distance.

I give instructions to Billy Yunck as he flys *Argo* over the *Bismarck*.

"Go slow, Billy," I ordered, and Billy Yunck immediately eased up on the joystick.

Gradually the details of the picture came into focus. We could see guns and superstructure.

We came down just aft of the bridge on the starboard rail, almost exactly at the point where the discovery run had crossed over the ship. But this time we could dawdle as much as we wished. The *Star Hercules* was in dynamic positioning mode, and its computer responded to every minute key command from the navigator, instantly transmitting precise instructions to the bow and stern thrusters. We could almost turn on a dime if we wanted. But we couldn't do anything about the swell, which was causing the ship to heave up and down and the cameras to zoom in and out toward the wreck in a seesawing action.

"Come up, Billy," I ordered, and Billy Yunck, who was having the fly of his life, promptly pulled back on the joystick. The 5.9-inch (150-mm) guns of the starboard middle turret loomed perilously close, but *Argo* pulled up in time.

"Zoom down. Zoom down. Wide down," I instructed the *Argo* engineer, Bill Lange, who was working just as hard as the flyer. "Okay, fire. Shoot the hell out of that baby." The bigger turret was remarkably preserved. The armor was intact and both guns were there, but one barrel was at maximum depression while the other was slightly elevated.

During our search mode the engineer has it easy until something worth photographing appears on the monitors. Now Bill was having to switch constantly between three video channels as I called for different cameras, while taking color still pictures of everything worth documenting. But with only seven hundred shots in his 35-mm camera cartridge, he had to be careful not to get carried away. Someone had put Johnny Horton's song, "Sink the Bismarck!" on the van stereo, and the singer's booming voice provided an ironic counterpoint to the images passing before us.

"Go left. Okay. Zoom down." We were now looking at a second set of guns, just forward of the 5.9-inch turret. This was the starboard 4.1-inch (105-mm) antiaircraft gun position, and it showed much more damage. Both guns were pointing crazily skyward like staghorns—these were the first guns *Argo*'s video eyes had seen.

With each passing minute we were getting a better sense of the state of the wreck, but it was difficult to visualize the whole. I looked at the plastic model that had been so painstakingly constructed by the National Geographic crew during our voyage out from Cadiz.

"Does somebody have an X-acto blade?" I asked. A small knife was handed to me, and I could see the look of horror on the faces of the camera crew as I began to hack off pieces of the model's superstructure. But no one complained; after all it would make good footage. I continued to dismember the model as our investigation continued.

As we moved sideways toward the middle of the ship, we had to step up onto another deck level. Just forward of us was the cylindrical base of the starboard director for the secondary armament. It was an empty hole. With a shock, I realized that the deck we were on was the base of the forward superstructure tower. Observers during the battle had agreed this part of the ship took the most punishment, but now it was completely gone, and with it the foretop main fire control tower where the *Bismarck*'s first gunnery officer had directed the heavy guns.

We moved forward and stepped up another deck. A solid-looking structure—it looked like a pillbox—came into view. The forward conning tower was still there! This was the reinforced part of the captain's bridge

(Above) I begin to dismember our model to match the wreck as Peter Schnall of National Geographic Televi- sion records the moment.

(Below) An antiair- craft gun mount with one of its barrels missing.

where Lindemann and Lütjens would have directed the final battle. It was a good thing we hadn't run into the ship here, where it was highest, or Kirk would have almost certainly crashed.

I was surprised at the condition of the conning tower: its heavy armor still looked capable of warding off enemy fire, let alone *Argo*. We know many people died here, yet the roof showed no evidence of shell damage. I wondered how long the admiral had lived. Had he perhaps shot himself when he knew the ship was sinking? German navy men had a powerful sense of honor. I could almost imagine the fatalistic Lütjens savoring the chance to die with his ship in battle.

And how had Captain Lindemann survived as long as he apparently did, long enough to go down with his ship? Perhaps with his ship unsteerable, his big forward guns knocked out and the fate of the battle out of his hands, he had left the bridge to rally his troops. It would be typical of him to want to boost his men's morale even when all was lost. Lütjens would never have considered such a breach of protocol; he would have stayed at his post, stoically awaiting the end.

An overhead view of an antiaircraft gun located on the starboard side below the aft fire control station.

Forward of the conning tower the two-tiered open bridge was still visible, its walls wrecked by shellfire and its movable wings (these would have been folded back during the battle) apparently gone. But it was still possible to imagine standing on its deck and watching the great ship steam into harbor. The big binoculars that Josef Statz had seen during the waning moments of the last battle were long gone, however, and the conning tower area was riddled with shell holes (we later counted more than fifty).

Stepping down from the bridge, we glimpsed the port 5.9-inch mount, its roof plate gone but both of its barrels in place. Then we moved forward over the gaping mouth of turret Bruno—the base, called a barbette, remained. This great round hole lined with gear teeth, and with the ribs of its structure receding down into blackness, looked like it was about to swallow *Argo* whole. Down on the port side of the barbette there was dramatic evidence of a shell hit that had exploded at its top edge, undoubtedly one of the early hits that had put the forward guns out of action. I sliced turret Bruno off the model and we moved forward to turret Anton, which was another gaping chasm.

Just forward of Anton we crossed the breakwater—it looked undamaged—and moved out along the forward deck. The starboard anchor capstan was still there, and a length of anchor chain ran from it forward and diagonally toward the starboard side. We followed this until it disappeared down a jagged shell hole—this looked like a hit from one of the *Rodney*'s big 16-inch guns. Most of the decking, however, was in

The gear teeth of an open turret barbette today (above) and the barbettes as they looked during construction (below).

amazingly good condition—apparently untouched by the woodboring worms that had devoured most of the pine decks on the *Titanic*. Only teak had survived on the *Titanic*; we are now certain that teak decking was used on the *Bismarck*. As we moved toward the bow I noticed dark patches discoloring the decking, and wondered what they could be. Perhaps the wood was deteriorating faster here than elsewhere for some reason.

We traveled on and were soon very close to the bow. Would it still have that jaunty flare, or would it be crushed and buckled by the impact with the bottom? The starboard anchor chain rubbing plate and hawse pipe were both undamaged, and a piece of starboard railing just forward of this was still standing. Then we saw the tip of the bow, or what was left of it. A crescent-shaped chunk had been carried away, giving it something of a snub nose. Given the massiveness of the ship's construction at this point, the damage could only have been caused by a direct hit from a heavy-caliber shell.

Now we worked our way ever so slowly back toward the stern along the port side of the ship. The railing on this side was completely gone—

some of it may have been portable, removed before a battle—but the big mooring bollards were still firmly in place, and very little shell damage could be seen on the horizontal surfaces. So far, the ship was a strange mixture of destruction and preservation. Almost all the superstructure had been blasted away, but we'd seen no sign of structural failure in the hull itself.

By the time Todd and Hagen's four-to-eight watch had come on duty, we were ready to begin our painstaking investigation of the stern half of the ship, the area aft of the forward superstructure. This was where most of the survivors had gathered before leaving the ship. The surface weather had been deteriorating steadily, and the resultant heaving of *Argo* made Todd's job even more difficult. Watching the video began to make me feel slightly sick to my stomach as the image yawed back and forth. I began to worry that we wouldn't be able to recover *Argo*, that we would run out of film before we could reload the color still camera.

"This must be where the funnel was," I commented as I broke off the model *Bismarck*'s single stack from the base. Below us were the large rectangular openings of the uptake pipes from inside the funnel, through which smoke, fumes and excess heat from the boilers had escaped the ship. As we inched aft, we came over the airplane deck (technically the Aufbaudeck). There was the catapult that had failed to launch even one of the Arado reconnaissance aircraft during all of Exercise Rhine. I ripped the planes off the model. We followed the track to the port side. There, just as eyewitnesses had said, was the huge hole left by a tremendous blast when a 16-inch shell from *Rodney* ignited the ready service ammunition magazine.

The two single-plane side hangars were missing, but the twin hangar was still standing just aft of the catapult. On its roof the remnants of the *Bismarck*'s main mast jutted upward, a stub of metal pipe. The battle standard had perished long ago—as had the captain's and the admiral's launches, which I removed from the model. We were now passing over the area of the after superstructure. The two searchlight platforms were gone, but their big cylindrical bases were there, and between them the similar-looking base of the searchlight director.

Now the roof of the after fire control station gradually came into our sights—the exact place where the baron had huddled with Heinz Jucknat, Adolf Eich, Franz Halke and other survivors waiting for the British to cease their merciless fire, waiting for the order to abandon ship. The station was intact, just as he had described it—except for the roller path and hole in the roof where the rangefinder cupola had sat before it was knocked off by a 14-inch shell from the *King George V*, leaving the baron unable to direct the fire of the after turrets. We could see no damage to the rest of the roof or the sides. It was amazing that it had survived the battle so well, since it was not a heavily armored structure.

As we continued sternward I wondered if all four turrets would be gone. We had only found one of them during our hunt. Here was Caesar, another gaping hole, but one of the ship's boat and airplane cranes had fallen over it (we now believe it to be the starboard crane). The sight reminded me a little of the way the mast of the *Titanic* had fallen back

I yank the mainmast off the model, which is beginning to look as though it has been through a battle.

All that remains of the stump of the mainmast.

against the bridge. But how did it get here, more than 50 meters (140 feet) from its original position just aft of the funnel? The pieces of wire still attached to it might hold the clue. Perhaps the crane had come off during the battle, but remained moored to the deck by wiring that had broken off with the impact.

Turret Dora was also an empty mouth. So all four turrets had left the ship, most likely when it rolled over at the surface. To the starboard of Dora was another big shell hole, probably the one into which many survivors fell as they fled the choking smoke and fires inside the ship.

As we moved out onto the stern deck, we could see that the wooden planking here was also in good shape. We continued slowly aft. What were those dark markings on the wooden deck? They reminded me of the

discolored patches we'd seen near the bow, but this time they were more distinct. We could see straight edges—undoubtedly paint. A chill ran down my neck. We were looking at the swastika—painted over after the ship left Norway. Time and seawater had uncovered it. I glanced over at Hagen, wondering what he was thinking.

The roof of the after fire control station where Burkard von Müllenheim-Rechberg directed the *Bismarck*'s final four salvos. The circular section is where the range finder telescope sat. The diagram (top) shows its location.

Suddenly the swastika sheared away as if chopped by a guillotine. Part of the stern was missing! Compared to the nick in the bow, this was a major structural failure. As we moved off the stern we glimpsed rubble down below, but there was no sign of the vanished chunk of hull. This was the *Bismarck*'s Achilles heel: was the damage related to the torpedo hit that crippled the rudders? Or had it happened on impact? My mind went back to the big chunk of wreckage we had seen in the area where I'd first looked for the main wreck, the area I believed the ship had hit before starting the landslide. In our overeagerness we had tentatively labeled it "bow or stern." Perhaps it was the missing piece left behind while the rest of the hull skied down the slope to its current resting place. I took out the knife and sawed a neat chunk off the stern of the model.

For almost five hours we beetled our way along the deck of the ravaged ship, awed by the devastation yet marveling at how much remained, how powerful and proud she still looked. At one point we found a 4.1-inch antiaircraft gun pointing crazily skyward as if trying to shoot down one of those pesky slow-moving Swordfish, but its attitude was anything but warlike. The barrel was decorated with a frilly sea anemone like a flower placed inside it by a peacenik. It was an image I would

(Above) When *Argo* broke the surface after our first detailed look at the wreck, it was tangled in polypropylene fishing line.

(Above right) Martin Bowen (left) Todd, and Casey Agee work to free the line from the frame.

take with me always.

By the time I gave the order to recover *Argo*, after six hours of exploration, the *Bismarck* model looked drastically different. All the secondary turrets were still there and many of the antiaircraft gun mounts were still in place, although some of the barrels were missing. We saw no sign of the two 4.1-inch mounts on either side of the funnel (Alois Haberditz's battle station was gone, and there were no guns left near the heavily damaged bridge area). However, along with the main armament, almost all of the ship's superstructure was missing (we had seen a great deal of it in our searches of the debris field). Nonetheless, if you put the turrets back on, the ship would have looked amazingly like she did in her heyday. The *Bismarck* was indeed a wreck, but a dangerous-looking one—still sleek, still armed and lethal, still confident of her power.

When *Argo* broke the surface, darkness was approaching and rain lashed the fantail. Skip Gleason stood in the hero bucket, while Frank Smith and the other members of the deck crew worked with him to bring the sled swiftly home. (The hero bucket is a metal cage suspended off the stern that allows someone to work closer to the water during recovery in high seas without being swept overboard. The water commonly comes up to your waist.) This was the most dangerous *Argo* recovery of the expedition, and it required all the skill and experience of my team. Skip reached out with the extendable pole and clipped a line onto the frame. Then the stern of the *Star Hercules* rose on a big swell; *Argo* came clear of the water and began to swing like a two-ton wrecking ball. Just in time, Todd—as always in the thick of the action—got another line onto it, and the beast was tamed. Soon it rested on the deck dripping seawater.

Immediately I noticed that *Argo's* battered frame was tangled with a polypropylene line; it was blue, probably from a fishing net—garbage in the middle of the ocean. We used to think the oceans were too big to be affected by pollution, but now we know differently. That's why ocean scientists are among the most vocal of environmentalists. They know just how fast we are poisoning our planet.

Once the line was freed, I gave it to Cathy Offinger—I didn't want people scavenging pieces for souvenirs. "Maybe we can use this in some way," I suggested. "Perhaps as part of some sort of memorial for the ship." I knew that Cathy would come up with something.

By now we had explored the ship quite thoroughly. Our next goal was to get color video. National Geographic wanted it for their film, and I wanted to show the world what the ship really looked like. (I wouldn't know until after the cruise whether *Argo's* color still camera had provided us with color pictures of the wreck and the debris field.) The problem was that *Argo* had never been outfitted with color video cameras; the system we'd rigged up and brought along was thus being tested under very difficult conditions. Furthermore, since our coaxial cable didn't permit us to send real-time color images from the ocean floor, we would only know if we had color video once *Argo* was back on board.

To add to my anxiety, *Argo* now seemed to be on its last legs. Throughout the cruise the sonar had worked erratically, and the cameras and altimeter had malfunctioned on several occasions. We had recently discovered that a short circuit caused by water leaking into the sonar system was at the root of the problem, and we had no way of fixing it on board—a new pressure seal was needed. In addition, the trouble in the one system seemed to be spreading to others. It was possible *Argo's* telemetry would soon stop working. And now we were asking the old guy to do something he had never done. Frankly, I wasn't optimistic. Nonetheless, that night Bill Lange and Jim Saint stayed up late to rig the new cameras and prepare *Argo* for a morning launch.

Friday June 9 began promisingly. Although the wind and waves were still high, warm sunshine bathed the deck as we launched *Argo*. But almost two hours later, with the bottom rapidly approaching, the video monitors went blank. We had lost our electronic link with the vehicle and were totally blind. I imagined the worst as I ordered recovery and the clock ticked away. Sunday would be our last day on site, and the prospect of getting color video was receding by the minute.

The technicians eventually found the problem—a fuse had blown in one of the sled's computers—and it was quickly replaced and tested. Two hours later, clouds were closing in and the weather was again looking ominous as *Argo* entered the water at 4:30 P.M. At 6:34 the bottom came into view; seven minutes later we were over the wreck.

Cathy Offinger cleans the soot off a survival suit after a minor fire in the storage van.

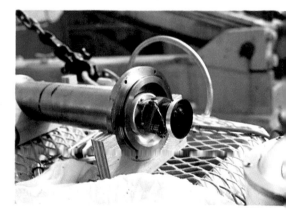

The lens of one of the color cameras we installed on *Argo* in a vain effort to get color video footage of the wreck.

Determined to get the best color video possible, I turned myself into a kamikaze pilot, taking risks with *Argo* that I had never dared before. As we worked, the weather continued to worsen, testing the *Star Hercules'* bow and stern thrusters to the limit and stretching our flyers to the breaking point. On one occasion I ordered the sled lowered inside one of the turret holes—into the mouth of the monster—but all we could see was darkness. This was not a *Titanic*-style grand staircase interior of the ship. Later I brought the forward-looking camera close enough to some of the remaining secondary armament and alongside part of the hull where we could see evidence of hits from the British secondary guns. In some cases the shells had splattered like bugs on a windshield, seeming to leave the armor intact, but the 145 mm thick splinter belt in the area just aft of where we first crossed the ship showed considerable evidence of shell penetration. From our investigations so far, it seemed that damage to the ship was much worse on the port side, which made sense since this was the side that had faced most of the fire from the *Rodney* and the *King George V.* Surely there would be much more damage below the mud line, just as most evidence of the iceberg damage to the *Titanic* had been hidden from our view. We could see, however, that the ship was buried more deeply at the stern than at the bow, which tended to support my theory that it had hit stern first. Just after midnight we decided to call it a day, and *Argo* began another long, slow climb to the surface. If the color video cameras had worked, the results ought to be spectacular.

The rope cross memorial made by Rick Latham.

While some of us slept and the weather stayed awful, another storm was brewing—this one of the human kind. Until we found the ship, most people on board—really with the exception of the British members of the ship's crew—had treated our mission rather casually. Bob Ballard was going after another wreck—if we found it that would be great. But once we discovered the first boot on the sea floor, there was a distinct change in tone. Beforehand some people had made lighthearted remarks about the events of May 1941, made jokes about Nazis—that sort of thing. With the boots the irreverence had disappeared. And when we found the wreck itself, those boots suddenly began to belong to real people, people we had read about, felt we knew, and who had died on that ship. This was no longer a laughing matter. I remembered how powerful an experience it had been finding the *Titanic*.

The mood turned serious—not somber, but respectful. People kept their feelings to themselves, but I could tell that almost everyone was affected. It got to different people in different ways. Jack Maurer, the veteran ex-navy captain who was outwardly always the picture of self-control, later told me that there were times he simply had to leave the van to be by himself. I sensed the change especially in Hagen. As the "token German" on board he had taken his share of ribbing. Fortunately he had taken it all in stride, even though his attitude toward the *Bismarck* was already different from the year before. Meeting the baron had made the ship real to him, had convinced him to come back in 1989 even though our expedition had nothing to do with his thesis on deep-submersible robotic arms. Now his smart-aleck side disappeared completely. It was as if he was rediscovering some part of his identity that he had denied or forgotten or simply hadn't realized existed. After all, he had spent most of his life abroad and belonged to a generation of Germans whose parents had been too young to fight in the war.

It seemed natural that Hagen should be the one to take charge of whatever kind of memorial we organized for the *Bismarck*. And when I called him into my cabin to discuss it, he readily agreed. Neither he nor I realized what emotions we were about to stir up.

Unknown to either of us, Cathy Offinger had given the polypropylene fishing line we had raised from the wreck to the *Star Hercules'* second engineer, Rick Latham. Ever the enthusiast, Rick had suggested we use it to make a memorial cross. As the ship's resident bard, he seemed the perfect man for the job. His epic poem about our expedition was nearing completion—and we had given him plenty to write about. Now he was to play a role in the story. He welded two pieces of metal together to form a simple cross, then he wrapped it carefully with netting so it looked like rope. It was a nifty job, and Hagen was delighted. Perhaps we could rig *Argo* with a solenoid—an electromagnet—Hagen suggested, and arrange to drop the cross on the deck of the ship during the next lowering.

It seemed like a great idea until he began discussing his plans with other members of the crew. A Christian cross on a Nazi ship? Visions of the cross resting on the swastika suddenly turned our innocent tribute into an apparent memorial for Nazi Germany. Many on board were rightfully offended by the idea. But one former U.S. serviceman was unforgivably abusive, saying any memorial to the *Bismarck* would be like honoring Satan. Suddenly Hagen found himself in the middle of a broiling debate.

Hagen is a born diplomat, however, and he kept his cool, consulted widely and came up with a plan that satisfied almost everybody—including Rick Latham, who wasn't in the least offended that his handiwork had been rejected. In fact it was Rick who planted in Hagen's head the idea for a naval memorial that transcended a single ship or wreck. Instead of placing an object on the ship, we would have a simple service in honor of the crews of both the *Hood* and the *Bismarck*, to commemorate the wasteful loss of life and the futility of war. Instead of a cross, a simple rope wreath would be tossed into the water in memory of those who had died. The ceremony would take place away from the wreck site so there was no chance the wreath would land on the ship. Quickly the human storm abated.

But the meteorological tempest tossing our vessel did not. All day on June 10 we waited out the weather. But the barometer kept falling—in all my years at sea I've never seen the pressure so low. My spirits weren't far behind: the color video cameras had proved a bust on our first try, hopelessly out of focus, even though they had worked fine on the surface. I ranted and raved at Bill Lange and Jim Saint, who gamely went back to work. But if we couldn't get *Argo* back in the water, we would never know if their adjustments had succeeded.

It was a strange feeling to be in the middle of a battle but unable to do anything. There was a sense of suspended animation, of being stopped in mid-sentence. Instead of being the center of the action, the control van became a backwater. Watches were suspended; people slept or read or ate

Canuto Santos Silva works on the rope wreath.

The completed wreath awaits duty at the memorial service.

into their dwindling hoard of snacks. They played games or sat and talked in a quiet corner. Trivial Pursuit made a brief comeback. I spent the morning working with Tony Chiu on the novel—by now we had almost outlined the whole plot. Sometime in the afternoon, having nothing better to do, I dropped by the van, expecting to find it empty.

To my surprise I found Todd engrossed in conversation with Cathy Offinger. I knew I was an interloper, but I was curious. Cathy had known Todd since he was six, and she had babysat for him and his brother Douglas. She'd always liked him, but I'd had no idea they had become friends. They looked up, greeted me briefly and then returned to their chat. I made a few stabs at joining in, but they weren't interested in talking to me. I got the message and after a few minutes I left, but the scene stayed with me long after. This was a Todd I hadn't seen before.

I later learned from Cathy that she was as surprised and pleased as I

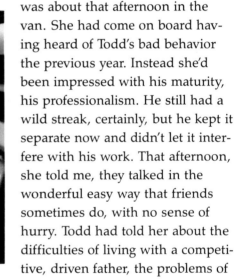

was about that afternoon in the van. She had come on board having heard of Todd's bad behavior the previous year. Instead she'd been impressed with his maturity, his professionalism. He still had a wild streak, certainly, but he kept it separate now and didn't let it interfere with his work. That afternoon, she told me, they talked in the wonderful easy way that friends sometimes do, with no sense of hurry. Todd had told her about the difficulties of living with a competitive, driven father, the problems of

Todd flies *Argo* during our final do-or-die run over the wreck.

being the son of somebody suddenly famous. "How come you're not like your father?" people would ask. He talked about school and girls and gave Cathy advice about how to handle being a single parent (she was recently divorced with a seven-year-old daughter). He talked about his dream of getting a Ph.D. and going into some kind of technical field. This was a different Todd, a son I was only beginning to know as a man.

It wasn't until the afternoon of Sunday June 11, our last day, that the weather broke sufficiently to risk another lowering. What the hell, I thought. If I lose *Argo* now it won't be the end of the world; this may be the last time I use *Argo* for exploration. Let's go for broke. And that is literally what we did.

Just before 6 P.M. we arrived over the wreck and began our final do-or-die run. If my previous lowering on the ship had been kamikaze, this one was crazy kamikaze. Todd couldn't believe how close I was asking him to fly. The spectators in the van looked at me with amazement as *Argo* came within a hair of crashing time and again.

By the time the 8 P.M. watch took over we had gotten some amazing close-ups of the ship. With Kirk Gustafson at the controls, we began working our way for one last time over the stern half of the vessel. Just as we approached turret Dora, the lights suddenly went out.

"Come up, come up!" I shouted uselessly at Kirk, who had already pulled back hard on the joystick. I wondered if we really had lost our intrepid underwater eyes for good.

But if the cable had broken, the electric current indicator would have gone to ground, indicating that all our electricity was flowing into the sea. The needle hadn't moved; *Argo* was wounded but still there. Two hours later, when *Argo* reached the surface, we could see that its lights were bashed up and dangling crazily, but the cameras looked unharmed. Turret Dora had scored its first hit in almost fifty years, I thought wryly.

As it turned out, our final daring attack on the *Bismarck* had been in vain. Once again the color video cameras were out of focus. So if the color stills didn't turn out, I would have no color images of the wreck at all. The National Geographic crew and I consoled ourselves with the rationalization that black-and-white was somehow more appropriate for a battleship.

Although I'd sworn to keep our discovery secret until we had left the area—to keep the location from reaching souvenir hunters—that night while we were still recovering transponders I could wait no longer. But sending out our cryptic telexes turned out to be one last *Bismarck* adventure. The problem was the ship's antiquated telex machine—a genuine anomaly on such a modern vessel involved in such a high-tech enterprise. Every few minutes the teletype would overheat and begin to smoke. While we waited impatiently, Captain Latter would carefully disassemble the machine, remove the offending parts and put them in the freezer. When they'd cooled sufficiently, he put the thing back together and the message could continue. The first to receive the news were Woods Hole, the Quest Group and National Geographic Headquarters in Washington. National Geographic promised to send a message to Baron von Müllenheim-Rechberg, whom we'd invited to come with us, but who had declined because of his wife's ill health.

Early on the morning of Monday June 11, eighteen days after departing Cadiz, we recovered the last of our transponders and set a course for southern England. National Geographic had promised to inform the Ger-

The final recovery: a damaged but intact *Argo* is brought safely home. (The hero bucket is clearly visible extending out from the stern.)

man embassy of the discovery, and the press probably knew already. Soon the word would be out.

Would the return of the *Bismarck* to the light of day be welcomed by the Germans or ignored? Would I be accused back home of glorifying a Nazi warship? Later in the day we received the following message from Germany: "The Baron sends his congratulations to Dr. Ballard and his team for this great discovery." I wondered if other *Bismarck* survivors would also welcome our accomplishment.

At least the controversy on board had completely died down. Captain Latter had willingly agreed to conduct a brief memorial service. So, after lunch the next day as we steamed away from the site of the *Bismarck*'s last stand, the Woods Hole team gathered with the ship's crew and officers, all smartly turned out in their dress uniforms, near the stern of the *Star Hercules* to pay tribute to men who'd died so long ago. The weather was beautiful—bright sun and a peaceful following sea. As the stern of the ship rose and fell gently with the Atlantic swells, the captain spoke the words Hagen had written:

Captain Derek Latter (second from right) conducts the service in memory of all the sailors who went down with the *Bismarck* and the *Hood*. Flanking him are Hagen Schempf (right) and Rick Latham.

"Being gathered here today gives us the opportunity to remember those British and German seamen who lost their lives during the days of this tragic sea battle. We have the opportunity here to put to rest all those souls lost at sea during the battle. May they rest in peace from here on forth. We should look at this ceremony as a moment of remembrance for those people caught up in the turmoil of war, all of them having suffered, many of them dying. Let us hope that this kind of human suffering and sacrifice may never be asked of mankind again."

The captain called for a minute of silence. With only the sound of the wind and the throbbing of the ship's engines as background, I remembered another shipboard service that had taken place forty-eight years earlier, aboard the HMS *Dorsetshire*. I imagined I could hear the plaintive strains of the German sailors' lament, "Ich hatt' einen Kamaraden," as a flag-draped body disappeared. The minute of silence over, we watched as the rope wreath was tossed overboard and sank swiftly out of sight. People drifted away quietly, alone with their thoughts. I knew that few on board had failed to be touched by the ceremony.

There was no wild victory bash as we sailed for shore. Finding the *Bismarck* seemed bittersweet. People tended to gather in small groups, to celebrate quietly. The sadness was two-edged: not only had we uncovered a war grave, but our team was breaking up. Those who had been on board the *Star Hercules* since late April, who had lived through the intensity of our Mediterranean cruise and live broadcasts from an ancient Roman wreck as well as the ups and downs of the *Bismarck* chase, were suddenly aware that this close-knit group was about to disappear. For the crew of the *Star Hercules*, it was back to the monotony of milk runs to oil rigs in the North Sea. For the Woods Hole crowd, it was a return to the routines of shore life.

Todd and his buddies celebrated with high spirits and beer. Now that

A parting shot of the *Bismarck* team as the *Star Hercules* heads for home.

work was done, my son's daredevil streak re-emerged, as I discovered while taking a stroll near the stern. First I saw Todd's buddies Billy and Kirk standing near the hero bucket, each looking like he had just swallowed a goldfish. I knew something was up. When I approached I saw Todd outside the bucket with only his feet locked into the cage as he leaned back out over the ocean, while the swells rose and fell, occasionally drenching him in spray. I yelled and he quickly hauled himself back on board. Suddenly I had reverted to being the stern parent, and he had become just a boy caught in an act of mischief. I didn't realize at the time how much these kinds of risks were part of his life.

As our ship neared port, I spent much of my spare time rehearsing the statement I planned to make to the German people about our discovery of the wreck. Hagen had translated it into German and now was coaching me on the correct pronunciation of the words. Meanwhile the thoughts of most of those on board turned to the future—to seeing friends and loved ones and eating a good meal and sleeping in one's own bed—thoughts not unlike those of the British sailors who'd caught the *Bismarck*, seen her sink, and then turned for home and a brief shore leave before sailing back to the relentless battleground of the Atlantic.

Rick Latham had finished his poem. Its closing lines seem as good a way as any of ending the story of our successful hunt for battleship *Bismarck*: "*So people of the Fatherland/ take pride in what I say. She came, she fought, she died for you and here she lies today ... // ... and all next week, next month, next year. / Forever there she'll be. / The monarch of the ocean floor. / The* Bismarck. *R. I. P.*"

Bismarck

THEN AND NOW

The robot vehicle *Argo* explores the ghostly hull of the *Bismarck*, which still echoes the sleek power shown during her launching in Hamburg fifty years before. As we worked our way carefully from the bow to the stern, we were both amazed at the devastation and impressed by how much of the ship remained.

THE *BISMARCK* TODAY:
A Port side View

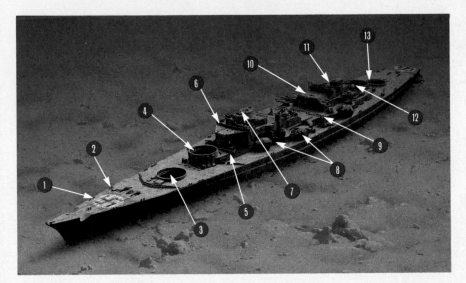

1. Swastika on the bow deck.

2. Starboard anchor chain lying in a shell hole.

3. Barbette for turret Anton.

4. Barbette for turret Bruno.

5. Port side forward 37–mm antiaircraft guns.

6. Blasted remains of the open bridge.

7. Roof of the conning tower.

8. Turrets and 5.9–inch guns of the port side secondary armament.

9. Grid of the catapult ending in a huge shell hole on the port side.

10. Roof of the airplane hangar where launches were once stowed.

11. Roof of the aft fire (gunnery) control station.

12. Barbette for turret Caesar with a section of crane lying across it.

13. Barbette for turret Dora.

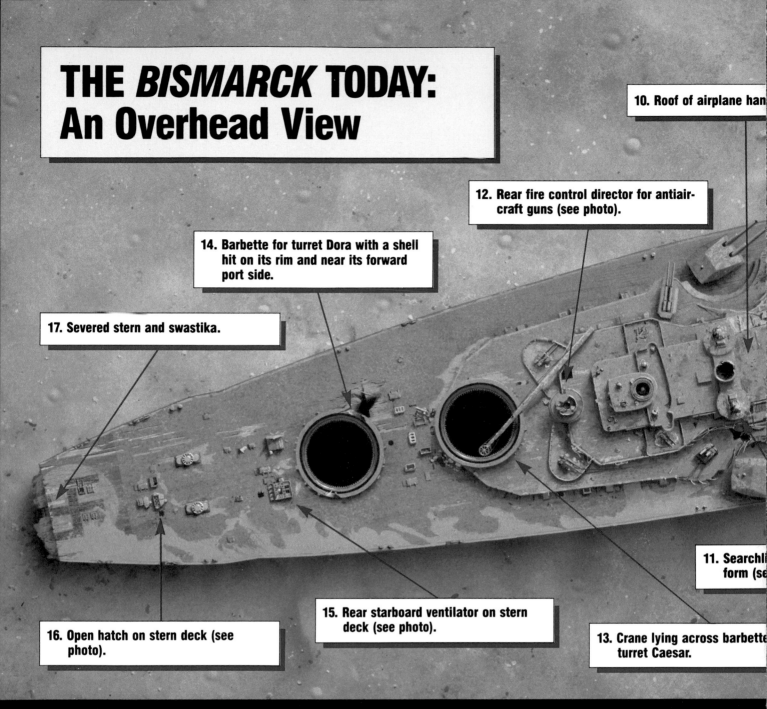

THE *BISMARCK* TODAY: An Overhead View

10. Roof of airplane han

12. Rear fire control director for antiaircraft guns (see photo).

14. Barbette for turret Dora with a shell hit on its rim and near its forward port side.

17. Severed stern and swastika.

11. Searchli form (se

15. Rear starboard ventilator on stern deck (see photo).

16. Open hatch on stern deck (see photo).

13. Crane lying across barbett turret Caesar.

This hatch on the stern deck (left) has lost its cover as shown in the right of the photograph (above). The curving shape to the left is the base of the ventilator also shown (above).

The serrated circular base for the starboard crane, shown (above) in 1940 before the crane was mounted on it, can be seen in the upper right of our 1989 photograph (left).

9. Huge shell hole on port side of catapult.

5. Small port side 37–mm antiaircraft gun (see photo).

...gar (see photo).

...ght on rear starboard plat-
...e photo).

...for

6. Conning tower and damaged open bridge area.

7. Funnel (smokestack) (see photo).

8. Serrated base for starboard crane (see photo).

Considering the heavy shelling this area of the ship received, the tower for the rear antiair-craft fire control director (above) is remarkably intact as seen from above (left).

12

11

The searchlight itself was blown away in battle but two rectangular panels from its base (left) can be matched to those in the photograph (above).

2. Ventilator and hatch on bow deck.

1. Starboard anchor chain and shell hole.

3. Barbette for turret Anton.

4. Barbette for turret Bruno with a shell hit on its rim and near its aft port side.

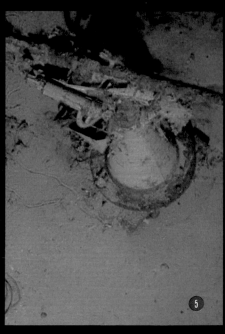

Although stripped of its tarpaulin, the small antiaircraft gun shown (above) stands largely intact in the photograph (left).

The bases of the exhaust pipes for the diesel engines that once encircled the top of the funnel (above) can be seen in the center of the *Argo* photo (left).

One of the V-shaped supports from the boat davits that held the launches to the roof of the airplane hangar (above), now sits askew on the hangar roof (left).

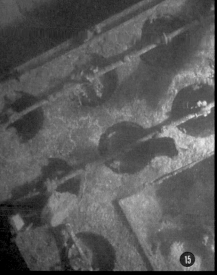

The insides of a ventilator on the starboard deck near turret Dora are illuminated by *Argo*'s lights (left). With its metal cover on, this ventilator would resemble the one shown (above).

(Above) A section of the starboard fore-deck near the anchor capstan shows that the anchor chain is still there. But instead of stretching forward toward the hawse pipe near the bow (see photograph on right), the chain lurches to starboard and disappears down a gaping shell hole, most likely caused by one of Rodney's 16-inch guns.

The Foredeck

This area of the ship is in surprisingly good shape, considering the pounding the Bismarck took during its final

battle. This is a tribute to the accuracy of the British fire, which was concentrated on the forward superstructure and the forward turrets. Unlike the Titanic, where the decking was pine and had been eaten away by wood-boring organisms, the teak decking on the Bismarck is mainly intact.

The Bridge and the Conning Tower

Although the open bridge forward of the conning tower is a shambles, the heavily armored conning tower itself is remarkably intact despite shell damage. Missing is the cupola of the range finder for turrets Anton and Bruno, but the circular mount is still there.

(Above) This photograph of the *Bismarck* when she was still under construction mirrors Ken Marschall's depiction of the bridge area as it is today (left). In the photograph, the mount for the forward range finder has not yet been installed.

(Right) The starboard side of the conning tower with the range finder mount visible.

(Below right) The starboard portion of the forward breakwater.

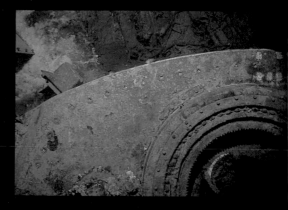

(Left and below) What remains of the port secondary fire control station and how it looked in 1941.

(Opposite left) This 105–mm antiair-craft mount, just below and forward of the control sta-tion, can be seen in its original condi-tion in the center of the photograph (bottom).

(Opposite right) All the secondary ar-mament is still in place, but the port side 150–mm (5.9-inch) turret farthest aft was badly damaged by a shell that tore away the back plate of its top.

The Port Side

Just how devastating the effects of the British barrage were can be seen by comparing this painting of the port side with the photograph (below) of the same area in 1941. The control station for the port secondary armament has been blast-ed away but most of the guns are still there.

The Catapult

Used to launch the Bismarck's *Arado float planes (below) from the ship, the distinctive grid of the catapult is still clearly visible running across the deck amidships.*

(Right) This *Argo* shot of the catapult grid (minus most of its deck cover), matches the area marked by a dotted line in the photo (below). Note the ladder to the small platform in the lower left.

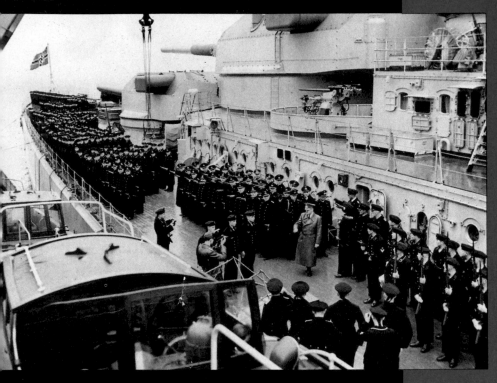

The Starboard Side

The starboard side aft of amidships looks much as it did the day Hitler came on board to inspect his brand-new battle-ship. In the 1941 photograph (above), the Führer has just stepped out of the door behind him and appears to be about to leave the ship. In Ken Marschall's painting (right), Argo illuminates the same area today.

(Left) An overhead view of the open door and the skylights on the deck beside it.

(Below left) The 37–mm antiaircraft gun emplacement on the upper deck remains battered but intact.

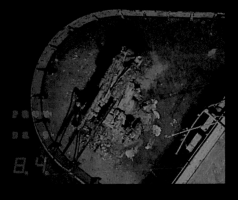

Antiaircraft Guns

The open-air antiaircraft positions were perhaps the most challenging battle stations aboard the Bismarck. The noise and smoke must have been overpowering at times. Airplanes are also far more difficult targets to hit than lumbering enemy battleships, as proved by the fact that during the entire Bismarck sortie not one British plane was shot down.

Right) Marine encrustations add a peaceful plumage to two of *Bismarck's* 105–mm antiaircraft guns, the sternmost of of this caliber located on the starboard side (see diagram). They were probably blasted upward into their present posi- tion during the final battle. Identical guns can be seen in the photograph (above) taken in 1941.

The Crane On Turret Caesar

During the battle or the sinking one of the cranes was ripped from its mount and ended up lying across the mouth of turret Caesar many feet away. We can only assume that part of the crane's rigging became tangled, preventing it from being swept off the ship during the descent.

The photograph (left) shows the port side crane in use. The mosaic of three still pictures (right) shows the barbette of turret Caesar with the crane lying across it.

This picture taken during Hitler's visit to the ship shows him standing at roughly the point on the stern swastika where the hull broke away.

The Stern

Students of battleship design were excited by our discovery of the severed stern. Such a spectacular structural failure is suggestive of a serious weakness in the Bismarck's design.

The section of the missing stern we located in the debris field (above) matches the area outlined in the photograph (right).

(Above) Below the sheared-off stern, jagged debris hangs outward.

(Above) The truncated swastika on the stern deck.

The arrow on the 1941 stern photo

(above) points to a seam in the hull plates, probably the line along which the hull broke.

CHAPTER ELEVEN

Bismarck Conclusions

The wreck of the *Bismarck* proved as elusive as did the battleship during her brief life. Our combined search in 1988 and 1989 lasted three weeks, almost as long as our 1985 hunt for the *Titanic*. This despite the presence of many witnesses to the event and more than one "reliable" estimate of the *Bismarck*'s sinking position. In fact, our search area was somewhat smaller than the quadrant within which the *Titanic* was found but, as in 1985, we only found the *Bismarck* as time was running out, near the end of the last leg of our search. Somehow this seems appropriate. She was, after all, a mighty battleship; she put up a brave fight, and she sank in one piece. Finding the *Bismarck* should not have been easy. In fact, it turned out to be much more difficult than I had dreamed possible.

When I first read the *Bismarck* story I was struck by the number of parallels to the *Titanic*. A new ship, reputed to be the last word in modern technology, goes down on her maiden voyage with enormous loss of life. Many of those on board believe the ship to be invincible, virtually unsinkable. A recent advance in science plays a critical role in both events. The *Titanic* was one of the first ships to use wireless communication; without the SOS that brought the *Carpathia* to the scene, surely everyone on board would have died. The *Bismarck*'s fate would likely have been quite different but for an advance in radar that allowed the shadowing British ships to keep track of her after she broke through the Denmark Strait, a fact that seems to have seriously disheartened Admiral Lütjens and affected his normally sound judgment. When he finally did break contact, he was so reluctant to believe his good fortune that he continued to send out long radio messages—messages that helped the British find him again.

But there the parallels between the two stories end. The *Titanic* was a passenger ship traveling in peacetime. Perhaps her captain was overconfident. Perhaps the iceberg could have been avoided by a more prudent seaman. But the captain and his ship bore no evil intent. In stark contrast, the *Bismarck* was a ship of war, designed to destroy before it could be destroyed. Of course, the eighteen-year-old boys who died on the *Bismarck*—and on the *Hood*—were innocent victims of historical forces of which they were barely conscious and over which they had no control.

Misjudgment and bad luck played a part in the *Titanic* tragedy, but the number of blunders and strokes of pure fortune that punctuate the *Bismarck* saga is quite astonishing, even taking into account the haze of battle and the difficulty of communications at sea during wartime half a century ago. First, there is the incredibly lax security accompanying the opening stages of Exercise Rhine, when the *Bismarck*'s movements were picked up by the British on three separate occasions from three different sources. And what of Vice-Admiral Holland's failure to take full advantage of his attacking force, *Hood* and *Prince of Wales*, maneuvering them in unison to the delight of the German rangefinders? Or the mistaken attack by a fleet of Swordfish on the *Sheffield*, comical in retrospect only because no hits were scored? What about Admiral Wake-Walker's failure in letting the ship slip away in the middle of the Atlantic, or Admiral Lütjens' foolish continuation of radio communication after he had escaped? Worst of all is

At Baron von Müllenheim-Rechberg's house in Bavaria a group of *Bismarck* survivors gather to look at video images of their long-lost ship. (Left to right) The baron; Heinrich Kuhnt; Hans Zimmermann; Otto Höntzsch.

Admiral Tovey's miscalculation of the *Bismarck*'s location based on these radio communications. It seems unbelievable that Tovey and his navigators did not catch their error sooner, especially since their calculation yielded a position that contradicted what Tovey's own instincts told him. By the time they corrected the mistake, the *Bismarck* had virtually escaped. The discovery of the *Bismarck* by a lone Catalina flying boat seems an extraordinary piece of good luck; even more so does the fatal torpedo hit on the rudder from a Swordfish bomber, an archaic piece of aerial technology that made the ultramodern battleship seem a spaceship in comparison.

In the roll call of the deep, the long list of ships that have sunk on the high seas, both the *Titanic* and the *Bismarck* are names to conjure with. Their fame is likely to last because each seems to symbolize something about her era. The sinking of the *Titanic* heralded a loss of technological innocence, of unquestioning faith in the power and perfectability of machines. The *Bismarck*'s sinking portended the end of the age of battleships. Even when she was built she belonged to an obsolete species, but naval strategists had not yet fully comprehended the fact. She was one of the most powerful battleships ever built, but she was the wrong ship at the wrong time. Hitler would have been smarter to order more submarines, and to give his navy an air arm and complete the two aircraft carriers then under construction.

The *Titanic*, which sank on April 15, 1912, with a loss of over 1,500 lives, was 882 feet long and 92 feet wide and lies at a depth of 12,460 feet.

As well, the sinking of the *Bismarck* represented a small but significant turning point in the progress of World War II. It gave an important psychological boost to Britain six months before the United States finally entered the fray, at a time when the Third Reich seemed unstoppable. From this point on, the British held their own in the battle of the Atlantic. Although allied shipping continued to suffer heavy losses from U-boat attacks, Great Britain's maritime lifeline was never again under serious threat.

The *Bismarck*'s sinking was a blow to Hitler's prestige and changed his attitude toward the navy. Previously he had given Admiral Raeder very much a free hand. Now he forbade the head of the Kriegsmarine to send any more ships on sorties into the Atlantic. As Raeder later wrote in his memoirs, after the *Bismarck*, for the Germans "the naval war was given an entirely new face." However, this change in German policy had little effect on the ultimate course of the war at sea. And far more important in the overall scheme of things was the successful invasion of Crete taking place while the *Bismarck* chase was on, a success undoubtedly abetted by the *Bismarck* diversion.

From a strategic point of view, the *Bismarck* episode was not as significant as it seemed at the time. In the months following her sinking, the network of supply ships and tankers sent out to support her and the *Prinz Eugen* were all located and sunk. Never again was Germany able to deploy an effective resupply system for surface raiders. And it is this fact, not Hitler's newfound intransigence, that put an end to the Atlantic raids. *Bismarck* and *Prinz Eugen* were the last major German surface warships to venture into the Atlantic. However, the reason for this, according to naval historian Dan van der Vat, was the breaking of the German naval Enigma code, which was taking place while the *Bismarck* chase was on (the naval code was the last part of Enigma to crack). It was the breaking of this code, combined with more effective anti-submarine tactics and weapons, not the absence of surface raiders, that considerably strengthened the Royal Navy's subsequent success in escorting convoys.

There is no question that the *Bismarck* was a very fine battleship, but just how good was she? Much of her reputation seems to be based on the brief dramatic battle with the *Hood*. But though these were then the two largest warships in service, they were not in the same league. The *Hood* was a battle cruiser, a holdover from an earlier era of naval warfare when high speed could be attained only by sacrificing weighty protection, particularly on her decks, and firepower. As well, the *Hood* was structurally far inferior, having large open compartments in contrast to *Bismarck*'s system of transverse bulkheads and fully waterproof compartments. It should also be remembered that two of the three hits the *Bismarck* suffered during her first engagement resulted in damage that seriously hampered her in the days that followed, slowing her down and reducing her fuel reserves. The myth of her invincibility was shattered in her first battle, even though she sank the most famous British warship of the time.

The *Bismarck*, which sank on May 27, 1941, with a loss of over 2,000 lives, was 823 feet long 118 feet wide and lies at a depth of 15,700 feet.

Perhaps the most balanced analysis of the *Bismarck*'s strengths and weaknesses is found in *Axis and Neutral Battleships in World War II* by William Garzke and Robert Dulin. They argue that the *Bismarck*'s mixed-caliber secondary battery and four main double turrets consumed too much weight, and that these powerful and well-protected ships could have been even more formidable: "Triple turrets with 380-mm guns and a dual purpose battery would have produced greater firepower and also permitted more armor protection. Although superior to their British contemporaries, these German ships [the *Bismark* and *Tirpitz*] were somewhat inferior to comparable American, French, and even Italian ships in many respects. In fact, had Winston Churchill been successful in bringing the French navy's *Richelieu* over to the Allied side in 1940, she would have been a more serious threat to the *Bismarck* in a naval engagement than the newly completed *King George V* and *Prince of Wales*. The severe damage sustained by the *Bismarck* before her sinking on May 27, 1941 indicates a good protection system, but it also attests to good damage control and crew discipline." The accurate gunfire that sealed the fate of the *Hood* was as much the result of her well-trained gunners as their use of stereoscopic range finders, which put shells accurately on target early in an encounter. In sum, although the *Bismarck* was a redoubtable warship, she was not, as has so often been said, "the most powerful battleship yet built."

Nonetheless the state of preservation of the *Bismarck*'s hull confirms that she was very well made indeed. We found very few shell holes in the wooden decking and few signs of shell damage in the horizontal surfaces of the remaining superstructure. Of course, the British guns were firing at close range and minimum depression for most of the final battle. And the few glimpses we caught of the sides of the hull, and in particular of the heavily armored conning tower tell a very different story. The conning tower area looks like Swiss cheese, and British shells did penetrate the splinter belt, located just above the corner belt. However, the inability of the British to sink the ship with gunfire is further testament to the soundness of her construction.

The condition of the wreck should settle once and for all one controversy that has persisted since the day of the ship's sinking. When the *Star Hercules* reached port in England after our discovery, almost the first question posed to me by the British media was, "Did we sink her or was she scuttled?" The German survivors were all adamant that it was the

A port side view of the wreck showing the major hits sustained by the *Bismarck* during her final battle. This side received the heaviest fire from the *Rodney* and *King George V* and thus suffered far heavier damage.

1. Shell hole with anchor chain.

2. Large hole by turret Bruno.

3. Several large shell holes in open bridge.

4. 23 hits show on the side of this gun turret and the back of its plating is gone.

5. Two holes here, and a shell fragment hole in the upper splinter belt.

6. Four shell holes; two in splinter belt and one in main side belt.

7. Largest hole on ship; probably caused by an ammunition magazine explosion.

8. Shell hit near turret Dora.

scuttling charges set off shortly after 10:20 A.M. by Gerhard Junack and his machinery division crew that sank the ship; but many of the British participants continued to claim that the *Dorsetshire*'s torpedoes, the last one fired soon after 10:30 A.M., did the job.

Both Ludovic Kennedy and Burkard von Müllenheim-Rechberg, in their books about the *Bismarck*, record the eyewitness reports that scuttling charges were set off before the ship sank. And as Kennedy points out in the introduction to this book, the British Admiralty's official report gave credence to the scuttling. But no one could know how effective the scuttling was until the ship was discovered.

We found no evidence on the wreck of the implosions that occur when a ship sinks before it is fully flooded. For an example of the two ways a ship can sink, you need only look at the two main pieces of the *Titanic* hull as we found them on the ocean bottom. The bow, which had been opened up by the iceberg and filled with water over the two and half hours between the impact and the final plunge, was virtually intact except for damage sustained when it hit the ocean floor. The stern, which had not been hit and was only partly flooded when the ship broke in two and sank, was totally devastated, a chaos of twisted and torn hull plating. This was because the pressure of the water outside the hull was much greater than that of the air still trapped inside. If the *Bismarck* had sunk before the flooding of all her watertight compartments was virtually complete, this pressure differential would surely have led to cave-ins, causing her to look something like the *Titanic*'s stern, despite the stoutness of the battleship's construction. Instead we found a hull that appears whole and relatively undamaged by the descent and impact. The *Bismarck* did not implode.

As Ludovic Kennedy so aptly sums it up, "That she would have foundered eventually there can be little doubt; but the scuttling ensured that it was sooner rather than later."

From the evidence on the ocean floor it is possible to reconstruct the *Bismarck*'s final plunge and the geological events that followed its impact. We know from numerous eyewitness accounts that the *Bismarck* sank stern first after turning upside down at the surface. It seems likely that the four big turrets, held in place only by gravity, simply fell off the ship and sank straight down. Once the main hull was fully submerged, it would have quickly righted itself because of its low center of gravity and hydrodynamic shape and plunged quickly, keel first, to the ocean floor, probably landing soon after the turrets hit.

Although no eyewitnesses saw the missing piece of the stern break off at the surface, there is strong evidence to suggest that this is where it happened. First of all, the missing section is not near the main wreck, which is what one would expect had the damage happened on impact with the bottom (photographs developed after the expedition revealed one hull plate from the missing stern in the main debris field hundreds of meters northwest of the ship). Second, we know that the stern area, which proved to be the *Bismarck*'s Achilles heel because of the hit that crippled the rudders, was the weakest structural point in the entire ship. During the battle there were a number of shell hits in the stern area, which had already been weakened by the Swordfish torpedo. Third, the ship began to sink at the stern. Fourth, there was no structural support to hold the end of the stern in place once the ship turned over. These facts suggest strongly that a structural failure occurred before the ship sank and that the stern broke off at the surface. This hypothesis is supported by what had happened to the pocket battleship *Lützow* during the invasion of Norway and by the subsequent career of the *Prinz Eugen*, which were both similarly weak near the stern. In 1940 the *Lützow* took a torpedo hit aft and suffered a stern collapse, although separation did not occur. In February 1942 off Norway the *Prinz Eugen* was similarly hit and damaged, and her stern collapsed at approximately the same spot as the *Bismarck*'s broke off. (Like the *Bismarck*, her rudders jammed to port, but her propellers were undamaged.) Naval architects now know that the *Bismarck*'s stern was the only structural weakness on the ship, and its fatigue failure represents the largest such event we know that has ever affected a warship—but if anyone on board knew what had happened he did not live to talk about it. Only after the damage suffered by the *Prinz Eugen* were German warships of heavy cruiser size and larger modified to

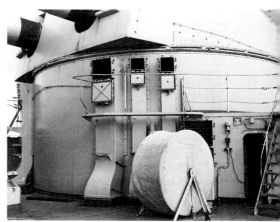

The *Bismarck*'s large gun turrets were wrenched from their barbettes and fell to the ocean bottom when the ship overturned.

strengthen their stern structures.

It is almost certain that the hull did not plane away as it descended, as did the bow of the *Titanic*. The one turret we found is approximately 200 meters (550 feet) from the main wreck. Presumably the turrets hit just before the hull and were carried along by the landslide. Of course, it is possible that this one turret did not leave the ship at the surface—perhaps shell damage welded it temporarily to the barbette—but was jarred loose on impact. If all four turrets turn up in the region of the wreck, that will confirm the theory that the ship fell almost straight down.

Even more puzzling is where the wreck actually hit. My first choice remains the area I investigated on June 6, confident I would find the ship there. This is about three-quarters of the way up the landslide near the point of intersection of the debris field axis and the landslide axis. A number of large pieces of wreckage remain in that area. However, the presence of this heavy wreckage may be coincidental. If the main hull was carried down the slide, why weren't these heavy pieces? The obvious conclusion is that they reached the bottom after the landslide had occurred.

Wherever the hull hit, it did so with such force that it triggered a landslide 2 kilometers (1.25 miles) long—an event that disturbed a large area of sediment and underlying volcanic rubble (this is why the landslide looked like rock and mud mixed up by a blender). Bottom failure—the sediment breaking loose and sliding downhill—would have occurred both upslope and downslope from the point of impact. In other words, the landslide could have started almost anywhere in the middle of its 2-kilometer length. If my point of impact—roughly two-thirds of the way up the slide—is correct, the main hull and presumably the one turret we found were carried 1 kilometer downhill with the slide.

The avalanche was over in one to three minutes. Only the heaviest pieces of the ship that fell as fast or faster than the hull hit bottom in time to be carried along by the landslide. As the avalanche slowed, something as heavy as the main hull would quickly have come to rest while less heavy pieces, such as turrets, may have been carried farther. For the next several hours, lighter debris rained down, spread out by a near-surface current flowing from roughly north to south to form the debris field. Given the fact that the sailing ship we found in 1988 left a debris trail pointing in the opposite direction from the *Bismark*'s, it seems probable that a variety of local currents are found in this area.

Much debris was dumped off when the ship turned over before sinking, falling much more slowly than the main body of the wreck, the turrets and the heavy pieces of superstructure. Everything except the wreck and this heaviest debris settled on the ocean floor after the landslide had occurred. This explains why the debris field pattern is superimposed on the landslide, and means that small debris has not been buried. It was this strange combination of debris and disturbed sediment that initially had us so confused in 1989. The fact the wreck wasn't where the debris trail led—to my predicted point of impact—made our search more lengthy and more frustrating.

We did not have time to survey the debris field properly. Even so, very few identifiable pieces of the ship were found. These included the

(Above) Crewmen from the *Prinz Eugen* attempt to steer the ship by hand after a torpedo has caused her stern to collapse near Trondheim, Norway in 1942.

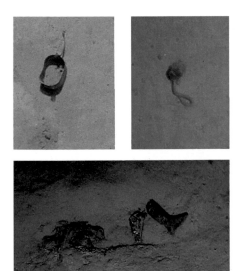

A Dixie can mess tin (middle left), gas mask, (middle right) and one of many boots (above), were among the personal objects found near the wreck.

louvers to the boiler intakes, some pieces of deck railing, and the one major piece of the stern hull with portholes and a section of ladder still attached which we found in the main debris field area about 700 meters northwest of the ship. Recognizable small debris was quite rare: a lantern, a bottle, a gas mask, a boxlike object that could have been a strongbox or safe. We found many pieces of pipe, and what looked like metal cable. And most haunting of all, we found boots.

Of the puzzles that remain, the location of the missing three turrets and origin of the small triangle of debris we found sitting at the eastern edge of the landslide are the most tantalizing. This smaller debris field is, as far as we can tell, unrelated to the main debris trail. What caused it? A major piece of wreckage we didn't find? Another wreck entirely? Who

(Below left) A ventilator similar to the one shown in the inset photograph lies near the severed stern.

knows what poignant fragments of the *Bismarck* story remain to be discovered?

The wreck we found will undoubtedly look much the same fifty years from now. There was some rusting of the hull, and along the corner belt we saw "rusticles" similar to the stalactites of rust that we found on the *Titanic*. And the warship was built much more sturdily than the famous ocean liner with her large open interior spaces (such as the area around the grand staircase where the ship actually broke in two). The *Bismarck* was also built with more modern technology—the hull was more than 90 percent welded rather than riveted. The wreck will be on the ocean floor a very long time—long after the last survivor has passed away. Eventually the spectral swastikas on the bow and stern will fade as seawater finishes its work.

Our discovery of the wreck of the *Bismarck* was greeted positively by many of the remaining survivors, even some who had initially opposed

(Above) A drum for one of the water hoses and (inset) how it once looked on deck.

How the *Bismarck* Sank

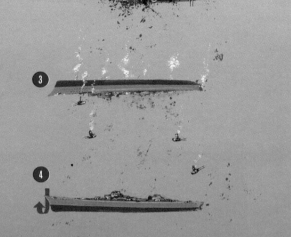

1) As the battle wanes the ship slowly sinks at the stern.

2) Just before sinking the ship rolls over and the bow points into the air. The four turrets and much other debris from the battle begin their descent. When the ship turns over, the weakened stern, with nothing to support it, breaks off.

3) Now fully flooded, the *Bismarck* starts its descent.

4) With all the air gone from the ship, it quickly rights itself and picks up speed as the plunge continues.

5) Perhaps ten or twenty minutes after leaving the surface the hull hits midway up the side of a submarine seamount and sets off a massive landslide. The turrets, which have hit just before the hull, are carried along with the slide.

6) The ship, and other heavy pieces of wreckage that have landed in the vicinity are carried down the slope with the avalanche, coming to rest about two-thirds of the way down the slide. (For the next several hours lighter debris rains down to form the debris field.)

THE WRECK SITE

1) Probable point of impact
2) Smaller debris field
3) Field of boots
4) Major piece of stern hull
5) Turret
6) Ventilator

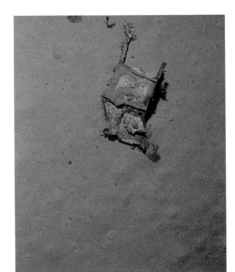

(Left) A rectangular metal locker from the deck (above) now lies in the debris field.

(Left) Piles of grating from around the gun emplacements and the open bridge (above) are scattered near the wreck.

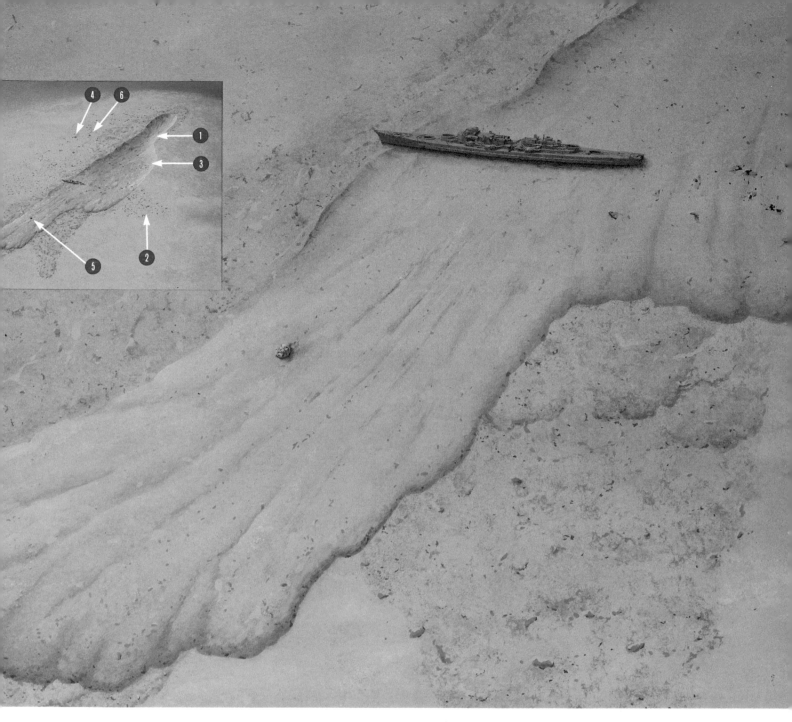

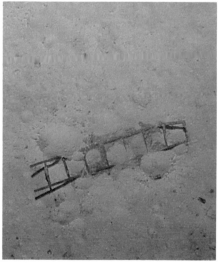

(Left) One of the many metal ladders from the ship (above).

(Left) A vertical stanchion (lower right) from the deck railing matches those in the photograph (above).

our expeditions. Although the reappearance of this ghost from their past can't have been easy for many of them, they seemed fascinated and moved by our accomplishment. When a group was shown the first footage of the wreck, some broke down in tears. Baron von Müllenheim-Rechberg, who'd been so skeptical when I first met him, has continued to applaud our accomplishment. He and a number of other survivors willingly cooperated in the making of the National Geographic documentary about our expedition and in the research for this book.

But some voices of discord continue to be raised. Ted Briggs, one of the three survivors from the *Hood*, commented: "She put up a bloody good fight, took on half the ruddy Navy and went down with honors. She should have been left alone and revered as a war grave." A number of *Bismarck* survivors agree.

I am not surprised by this minority response, and I don't discount it.

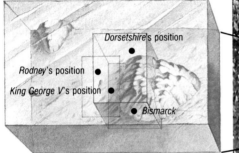

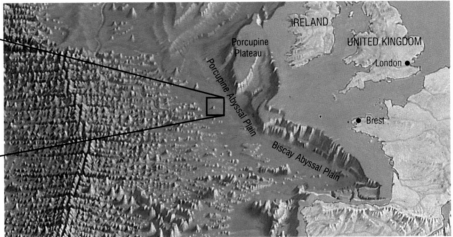

The overlapping 1988 and 1989 *Bismarck* search areas showing where we finally found the wreck on the side of an underwater mountain. The topography in the area of the Porcupine Abyssal Plain is fairly flat, but punctuated by isolated seamounts rising sharply from the seafloor.

Whenever you uncover a piece of history you run the risk of stirring up emotions. The more recent the history, the more powerful those emotions are likely to be. But to me the risk of rattling old skeletons is worth it. The deep ocean is a vast unexplored repository of the past. It is like a museum that was built but has never been opened to the public. With the discovery of the *Titanic* and now the *Bismarck*, we have opened up two rooms in this museum, turned on the lights and invited in visitors. And this is only the beginning. In the coming years undersea explorers will find other ships and open up other historical exhibits to public view. With the sophisticated technology we are developing, we will be able to explore these exhibits in living color on live television and share the excitement of our discoveries while they are happening.

I will look for more lost ships, other hidden treasures of the deep. I would like to gaze at the Japanese battleship *Yamato* that went down during the closing stages of the battle of the Pacific. I would like to find more ancient shipwrecks in the Mediterranean or perhaps one of the submerged cities archeologists believe lie off the coast of Sicily. I have already made plans to investigate Great Lakes wrecks from the War of 1812. Who knows what unimagined wonders lie locked in the underwater museum?

And I would like to go back to the *Bismarck* with JASON, once its cable is long enough. This robot would be able to investigate many places we couldn't see in 1989. It could search for evidence of shell damage along the hull, or see inside the after gunnery control station and the conning tower, and it could provide us with beautiful color video of the wreck. But I will only go back with the blessing of the German people and will abide by the expressed wishes of the West German government that we do not attempt to go inside the ship. According to international law, a warship remains the property of its country of origin. It is a war grave, and during any future visit I would treat it with the respect due to such a site.

The wreck of the *Bismarck* sits at a depth of 4,790 meters (15,700 feet) halfway down the southern slope of an extinct underwater volcano. This volcano rises about 1,000 meters (3,300 feet) above the surrounding Porcupine Abyssal Plain and dominates the area we searched in 1989. The ship's bow is pointed southwest away from France, the safe haven she came so close to reaching. She is less than 2 miles (3.2 kilometers) from the sinking position recorded by the navigator of the *King George V*, but I plan to keep the precise coordinates a secret. I don't want treasure seekers and souvenir hunters turning this war memorial into a scavenger's carnival.

Gulls swarm around the newly commissioned *Bismarck*.

The *Bismarck* lived and died as a ship of war, a floating gun platform dedicated to destruction. But her story is much more a tale of men than of machines. When I think about those eight days in May 1941, I will remember the acts of courage and endurance by the countless young men who played out the war games of the superpowers. I will think of Signalman Ted Briggs on the bridge of the *Hood* as she went into battle, of Lieutenant Percy Gick dodging shells and wavetops in his Swordfish biplane, of Ensign Tuck Smith in his Catalina flying boat suddenly spotting a lone ship in the gray Atlantic, of Lieutenant Herbert Wohlfarth in *U-556* cursing the wasting of his last torpedo on a convoy, of Seaman Heinz Jucknat leading his friends from the after computer room up the cable shaft to safety, of Midshipman Joe Brooks on *Dorsetshire* risking his life to save an armless German sailor and being censured for his trouble. Their experiences form the real story of the *Bismarck*. And they tell a tale of the arbitrariness of life and the futility of war.

CHAPTER TWELVE

Epilogue

Falmouth, Massachusetts—July 28, 1989

Only a few days ago I had been on top of the world. At a crowded press conference at National Geographic Headquarters in Washington, D.C., I had told the assembled media about our *Bismarck* discovery, shown the first videotape of the wreck and some beautiful color still pictures. My latest dream—the JASON Foundation for Education, a non-profit foundation designed to bring ocean exploration into the classroom—was about to become a reality. I was booked on the *Tonight Show* with Johnny Carson. Life was good.

Now I sat in speechless grief at the funeral of my son Todd, fighting back tears as Hagen Schempf delivered his eulogy. Todd, with his friend Chad Dalton, had been driving our Thunderbird late one evening. He had been driving too fast, they had missed a turn and driven into some trees. Both boys were killed instantly. It was a sudden senseless tragedy. Todd had been just four weeks shy of his twenty-first birthday. From being on top of the world, I had hit rock bottom. As Hagen spoke I sat with my arms around Todd's mother, Marjorie, and his brother, Douglas.

Hagen had known Todd a total of eight weeks, all of them at sea during our two *Bismarck* expeditions. He had seen the changes in my son. Now he was able to pay tribute to the maturing process he had observed. I listened as he talked about Todd's newfound sense of responsibility in 1989, his curiosity and keenness, his willingness to stand by his convictions. He had seen Todd, he said, "step over the line that separates the men from the boys.

"All boys pass that line sometime and only become fully aware of it in retrospect. Todd's fight to get there must have been tougher than most. Measuring up to peers, parents and siblings is no easy feat. But he had jumped out from behind these shadows and was beginning to cast his own. He was able to fight his way to the surface and chart a new course of his own, while retaining all those attributes that endeared him to us all."

The young men who died on the *Bismarck* and the *Hood*, on all the Axis and Allied ships in World War II, on all the bloody battlefields in Europe, Africa, the Far East, had passed over that line from childhood to adulthood. And they, too, left parents to grieve for them, whose pain was no less than mine, whose loss no greater. Perhaps some of them could rationalize their grief with the belief that their child had died in a just cause, fighting for his country. But when all is said and done, death is death, loss is loss.

The few who survived the sinking of the *Hood* and the *Bismarck* were the lucky ones. Most of them endured the indignity and hardship of interrogation, of imprisonment, of forced labor, of long separation from friends and family, then returned to their ravaged homeland to try to start their lives over. But they survived. Many of them still have nightmares, but they have led full and productive lives. None of them fail to mark May 27 in some way, to raise a glass in memory of their lost comrades or reserve a few moments for reflection, for thanks. One of them said to me, "I consider it to be my second birthday."

I raise my glass to the young men who died on the *Bismarck*. It seems fitting that their ship still sits upright on the ocean floor with many of her guns still poised and ready to fire. May the noble and defiant wreck we found stand as a monument to them and to all who have died before their time.

(Opposite) Todd on board the *Star Hercules* in June, 1989.

A German sailor blows a bosun's whistle aboard the *Bismarck* in 1941.

Appendix

Copyright Acknowledgements

Acknowledgements

Many people contributed to the making of *The Discovery of the Bismarck*. The wreck would never have been found without the highly skilled teams that participated in both the 1988 and 1989 expeditions and the support staff back home at the Deep Submergence Laboratory and the Center for Marine Exploration at the Woods Hole Oceanographic Institution. The Quest Group, the U.S. Navy, and the National Geographic Society provided the funding that made the *Bismarck* expeditions possible. I particularly wish to thank my sponsors, Don Koll and Marco Vitulli, for staying with me after our first year's search came up with a sailing ship, instead of a battleship.

In addition, the authors would particularly like to express their gratitude to the following:

Ludovic Kennedy and Burkard Baron von Müllenheim-Rechberg, who wrote the two best published accounts of the *Bismarck* story: *Pursuit* and *Battleship Bismarck*. Ludovic Kennedy also directed us to much of his original research, now housed in the Imperial War Museum, and read and commented on the final text. Baron von Müllenheim-Rechberg provided photographs from his collection and kindly consented to allow us to look at the text of the revised and expanded version of *Battleship Bismarck*, which will be published in North America in October 1990. This new version recounts for the first time the escape of Josef Statz, the only person to survive from the forward part of the ship, and describes in fascinating detail the baron's experiences as a prisoner of war;

Adolf Eich, Alois Haberditz, Franz Halke, Otto Höntzsch, Heinz Jucknat, Heinrich Kuhnt, Burkard Baron von Müllenheim-Rechberg, and Hans Zimmermann, survivors of the *Bismarck* who agreed to be interviewed and most of whom lent us some of their precious personal photographs;

Ted Briggs, Joe Brooks, Percy Gick, and Peter Meadway, the British participants in the *Bismarck* story whose interviews we drew on;

Tony Chiu, Tom Dettweiler, Graham Hurley, Bill Lange, Jack Maurer, Cathy Offinger, Hagen Schempf, Peter Schnall, Frank Smith, Chris Weber, the 1988 and 1989 expedition members who agreed to be interviewed;

William H. Garzke, Jr., and Robert O. Dulin, Jr., co-authors of *Axis and Neutral Battleships in World War II*, for acting as historical consultants and for vetting the manuscript for accuracy;

My assistant, Gretchen McManamin, who kept me on the right planes and in the right hotels and who fielded a thousand phone calls during our *Bismarck* adventure;

Also: Tom Crook, Steve Gegg, Bill Lange, Shelly Lauzon, Dan Martin, Gretchen McManamin, Hagen Schempf, and Dr. Elazar Uchupi of the Woods Hole Oceanographic Institution; Cathy Offinger of the Marquest Group; Bruce Norfleet, Peter Schnall and Chris Weber of National Geographic Television; Professor Jack Sweetman of the U.S. Naval Academy, translator of *Battleship Bismarck*, for their invaluable adminstrative and technical support;

Ken Marschall, who painted the magnificent images of the wreck as we found it, with the assistance of Michael Hughes;

Manfred Frenkel, for acting as translator and transatlantic intermediary; also Hanj-William Tersteegen;

The staff at Madison Press whose skill, tenacity and long hours made this book possible.

We would also like to thank the following: Sharon Gignac, for transcribing taped interviews; John B. Hattendorf of the Naval War College in Newport, Rhode Island, for information about Commander Joseph H. Wellings.

Madison Press Books would like to thank Katherine Bright-Holmes, of Hodder and Stoughton, and Sabine Oppenlander, for their great help in finding many of the historical photographs used in this book; Lisa Manning, of National Geographic Television, for providing the names of many excellent picture sources, as well as Lisa Page and Bill Allen, of *National Geographic* magazine, for the photographs by Joseph Bailey, Bates Littlehales and George Mobley; Brigitte Barkley and Ruth Eichhorn, of *Geo* magazine, for lending us countless valuable historical pictures; Paul Kemp and Nigel Steel of the Imperial War Museum; Steven Walton of the Public Records Office in Kew and Ron Clark of William Collins and Sons, for their help in finding historical material relating to the *Bismarck*; Marie Tharp (1 Washington Avenue, South Nyack, NY 10960), for her underwater map; John Siswick, for his translations from and into German and Jeremy Nightingale, for his *Titanic* photograph.

Photograph and Illustration Credits

Every effort has been made to correctly attribute all material reproduced in this book. If any errors have unwittingly occurred we will be happy to correct them in future editions.

Front Cover: Painting by Ken Marschall
Back Cover: (Top left) George Mobley © National Geographic Society
(Top right) Quest Group
(Bottom) *Sinking of the Bismarck* by Charles Turner, National Maritime Museum
Front Cover Flap: Hans Zimmermann
Back Cover Flap: George Mobley © National Geographic Society
Half-Title Page: Franz Halke
Title Page: Joseph H. Bailey © National Geographic Society
Title Page (Inset): Ferdinand Urbahns
Dedication Page: Bates Littlehales © National Geographic Society
Table of Contents: Bilderdienst Süddeutseutcher Verlag

Introduction
8 Ludovic Kennedy

Chapter One
10 George Mobley © National Geographic Society
12 Joseph H. Bailey © National Geographic Society
13 (Top) Baron Burkard von Müllenheim-Rechberg
(Bottom) Joseph H. Bailey © National Geographic Society

Chapter Two
14 Bibliothek fur Zeitgeschichte
15 (Top) Bundesarchiv
(Bottom) Zimmermann/Lindemann
16 (Top Left) Bettmann Archive
(Bottom) Joseph H. Bailey © National Geographic Society
(Right) Bettmann Archive
17 (Top) Joseph H. Bailey © National Geographic Society
(Bottom) Hans Zimmermann – Otto Höntzsch
18 (Top Left) Adolf Eich
(Bottom) Alois Haberditz
(Right) Franz Halke
19 (Top) Bundesarchiv
(Bottom) Zimmermann/Lindemann

20 (Top Left) Ferdinand Urbahns
(Middle Left) Ferdinand Urbahns
(Bottom Left) Ferdinand Urbahns
(Top Right) Ferdinand Urbahns
(Middle Right) Ferdinand Urbahns
(Bottom Right) Ferdinand Urbahns
21 (Left) Bundesarchiv
(Top Right) Bundesarchiv
(Middle Right) Ferdinand Urbahns
(2nd Middle Right) Bundesarchiv
(Bottom Right) Ferdinand Urbahns
22 Ferdinand Urbahns
23 (Top) Bettmann Archive
(Bottom) Herbert Wohlfarth, taken from *Pursuit* by Ludovic Kennedy
24–26 Profile diagram by Ian Lawrence
24 (Top row, left) Bundesarchiv
(Top row, middle) Bundesarchiv
(Top row, right) Bundesarchiv
(Bottom row, left) Bundesarchiv
(Bottom row, middle) Bundesarchiv
(Bottom row, right) Bundesarchiv
26 Colored schematic by Falcom Design Inc.
27–29 Overhead diagram by Ian Lawrence
27 Bundesarchiv
28 (Left) Bundesarchiv
(Right) Bundesarchiv
29 (Left) Bundesarchiv
(Center) Bundesarchiv
(Right) Bundesarchiv
30 (Top) Bundesarchiv
(Bottom) Bundesarchiv
31 Bundesarchiv
32 German Archives
33 Ferdinand Urbahns
34 Zimmermann/Lindemann
35 (Top) Zimmermann/Lindemann
(Left) Zimmermann/Lindemann
(Bottom) Zimmermann/Lindemann
36 (Top) *St. John's Harbour* by Harold Beament, National War Museum of Canada/Dill Nell
(Bottom) Bettmann Archive
(Top Inset) Robert Hunt Library
(Bottom Inset) Robert Hunt Library
37 (Top Left) Diagram by Jack McMaster
(Top Right) Bettmann Archive
(Bottom) *Sinking of the Rawalpindi* by Norman Wilkinson, Peninsular and Orient Steam Navigation Company

Chapter Three
38 Bates Littlehales © National Geographic Society
39 Bates Littlehales © National Geographic Society

40 Bates Littlehales © National Geographic Society
41 (Left) Diagram by Jack McMaster
(Top) Bates Littlehales © National Geographic Society
42 Bates Littlehales © National Geographic Society
43 (Top) Bates Littlehales © National Geographic Society
(Bottom) Bates Littlehales © National Geographic Society
44 (Left) Bates Littlehales © National Geographic Society
(Right) Bates Littlehales © National Geographic Society
45 (Left) George Mobley © National Geographic Society
(Right) Bates Littlehales © National Geographic Society
46 (Top) Bates Littlehales © National Geographic Society
(Bottom) Bates Littlehales © National Geographic Society
47 (Left) Woods Hole Oceanographic Institution
(Right) Joseph H. Bailey © National Geographic Society
48 George Mobley © National Geographic Society
49 George Mobley © National Geographic Society
50 Bates Littlehales © National Geographic Society
51 (Top) Bates Littlehales © National Geographic Society
(Bottom) Bates Littlehales © National Geographic Society
52 (Left) Diagram by Jack McMaster
(Right) Marie Tharp, Oceanographic Cartographer
53 (Top) Bates Littlehales © National Geographic Society
(Bottom) Bates Littlehales © National Geographic Society
54 Bates Littlehales © National Geographic Society
55 Woods Hole Oceanographic Institution
56 (Left) *Albert F. Paul 1917*, The Mariner's Museum, Newport News, Virginia
(Top Inset) Quest Group
(Bottom Inset) Quest Group

156 Joseph H. Bailey © National
   Geographic Society
157 Joseph H. Bailey © National
   Geographic Society

Chapter Nine
158 Quest Group
160 Joseph H. Bailey © National
   Geographic Society
161 Bates Littlehales © National
   Geographic Society
162 (Top) Joseph H. Bailey © National
   Geographic Society
   (Bottom) Quest Group
163 Diagram by Jack McMaster
164 Joseph H. Bailey © National
   Geographic Society
165 (Top) Quest Group
   (Top Inset) Bundesarchiv
   (Bottom Inset) Bundesarchiv
   (Bottom) Bundesarchiv
166 Joseph H. Bailey © National
   Geographic Society
167 Joseph H. Bailey © National
   Geographic Society
168 Joseph H. Bailey © National
   Geographic Society
169 (Top) Joseph H. Bailey © National
   Geographic Society
   (Bottom) Joseph H. Bailey
   © National Geographic Society

Chapter Ten
170 Painting by Ken Marschall
171 (Top) Bates Littlehales © National
   Geographic Society
   (Middle) Bates Littlehales © National
   Geographic Society
   (Bottom) Bates Littlehales © National
   Geographic Society
172 Joseph H. Bailey © National
   Geographic Society
173 (Top) Joseph H. Bailey © National
   Geographic Society
   (Bottom) Quest Group
174 Quest Group
175 (Top) Quest Group
   (Bottom) Landesbibliothek, Stuttgart
176 (Top) Joseph H. Bailey © National
   Geographic Society
   (Bottom) Quest Group
177 (Top) Painting by Ken Marschall
   (Bottom) Quest Group
178 (Left) Joseph H. Bailey © National
   Geographic Society
   (Right) Joseph H. Bailey © National
   Geographic Society
179 (Top) Joseph H. Bailey © National
   Geographic Society
180 Quest Group
181 (Top) Joseph H. Bailey © National
   Geographic Society
   (Bottom) Joseph H. Bailey
   © National Geographic Society
182 Joseph H. Bailey © National
   Geographic Society
183 Joseph H. Bailey © National
   Geographic Society
184 Quest Group
185 Joseph H. Bailey © National
   Geographic Society

Bismarck: **Then and Now**
186 Painting by Ken Marschall
187 (Inset) Bundesarchiv/Bettmann
188 (Inset) Painting by Ken Marschall
   Painting by Ken Marschall
191 Painting by Ken Marschall
   (Far Left) Quest Group
   (Left) Bundesarchiv
   (Right) Quest Group
   (Far Right) Bundesarchiv
192 (Far Left) Bundesarchiv
   (Left) Quest Group
   (Right) Quest Group
   (Far Right) Bundesarchiv
193 (Top Left) Quest Group
   (Top Right) Bundesarchiv
   (Middle Left) Quest Group
   (Middle Right) Bundesarchiv
   (First from Left) Quest Group
   (Second from Left) Bundesarchiv
   (Second Right) Quest Group
   (First from Right) Bundesarchiv
194 (Top) Quest Group
   (Bottom) Bundesarchiv
195 (Top) Quest Group
   (Bottom) Painting by Ken Marschall
196 Painting by Ken Marschall
197 (Top) Bundesarchiv
   (Middle) Quest Group
   (Bottom) Quest Group
198 (Top) Quest Group
   (Middle) Bundesarchiv
   (Bottom) Bundesarchiv
199 Painting by Ken Marschall
   (Left Inset) Quest Group
   (Right Inset) Quest Group
200 (Top) Bundesarchiv
   (Middle) Painting by Ken Marschall
   (Bottom) Bundesarchiv
201 Quest Group

202 (Top) Zimmermann/Lindemann
   (Middle) Quest Group
   (Bottom) Quest Group
203 Painting by Ken Marschall
204 (Top) Bundesarchiv
   (Bottom) Painting by Ken Marschall
205 Quest Group
206 (Top Right) Painting by Ken
   Marschall
   (Middle) Bundesarchiv
   (Bottom) Quest Group
207 Quest Group
208 Painting by Ken Marschall
   (Inset) Zimmermann/Lindemann
209 (Top) Quest Group
   (Middle) Bundesarchiv
   (Bottom Left) Quest Group
   (Bottom Right) Quest Group

Chapter Eleven
210 Joseph H. Bailey © National
   Geographic Society
212 Diagram by Jack McMaster
   (Inset) Jeremy Nightingale
213 Diagram by Jack McMaster
   (Inset) Bundesarchiv
215 (Top) Bundesarchiv
   (Bottom) Bundesarchiv
216 (Top) Imperial War Museum
   (Middle Left) Quest Group
   (Middle Right) Quest Group
   (Bottom) Quest Group
217 (Left) Quest Group
   (Right) Quest Group
   (Inset Left) Bundesarchiv
   (Inset Bottom) Bundesarchiv
218 Diagram by Wes Lowe
   (First from Left) Quest Group
   (Second from Left) Bundesarchiv
   (Second from Right) Quest Group
   (First from Right) Bundesarchiv
219 Painting by Ken Marschall
   (First from Left) Bundesarchiv
   (Second from Left) Quest Group
   (Third from Right) Bundesarchiv
   (Second from Right) Quest Group
   (First from Right) Bundesarchiv
220 (Left) Diagram by Jack McMaster
   (Right) Marie Tharp, Oceanographic
   Cartographer
221 Hans Zimmermann

Chapter Twelve
222 Joseph H. Bailey © National
   Geographic Society
223 Joseph H. Bailey © National
   Geographic Society

Index

Design and Art Direction:	Gordon Sibley Design Inc.
Editorial Director:	Hugh M. Brewster
Project Editor:	Ian R. Coutts
Editorial Assistant:	Shelley Tanaka
Production Director:	Susan Barrable
Production Assistant:	Sandra L. Hall
Original Paintings:	Wes Lowe
	Ken Marschall
Expedition Photographers:	Joseph H. Bailey
	Bates Littlehales
	George Mobley
Maps and Diagrams:	Ian Lawrence
	Jack McMaster
Typography:	On-line Graphics
Color Separation:	Colour Technologies
Printing and Binding:	Arnoldo Mondadori S.p.A.

The Discovery of the Bismarck
was produced by Madison Press Books
under the direction of Albert E. Cummings